ADVANCE PRAISE FOR *DEEP HANGING OUT*

"Armed with his legendary rolodex and even more legendary wit and keen perceptions, Malcolm Margolin has advocated vigorously to not only acknowledge Native Californians, but to provide the most prominent and honorable platform for us to advocate for ourselves and remind the modern world, 'We are still here, and we're not going anywhere.'"

—**GREGG CASTRO** (t'rowt'raahl Salinan/rumsien-ramaytush Ohlone), cultural activist and cofacilitator of the California Indian Conference

"This book implies the depth and sensitivity we immigrants must achieve if we ever hope to 'inhabit' a vital North America to the seventh generation. It will require centuries and an about-face of priorities to approach the intimacy chronicled in these pages. Every American should read this book, while there's still time."

—**PETER COYOTE**, author of *The Rainman's Third Cure*, Zen Buddhist priest

"Not only is *Deep Hanging Out* a wonderful celebration of the diverse, living Indigenous cultures of California, it's expressed with such easy eloquence that it's a pleasure to read. With modesty and self-effacing humor, Malcolm never places himself at the center of the narrative. Instead, he displays that rarest of attitudes among non-Natives writing about our lives—the ability to listen and truly hear what's being said."

—**JOSEPH BRUCHAC**, author of *Two Roads*

"Malcolm's lifelong curiosity, his abundant and sustained generosity, and his gift of deep friendship as revealed in this compendium— a memory palace of sorts—are invaluable."

—**GRETEL EHRLICH**, author of *Facing the Wave* and *Unsolaced*

"This collection, covering decades of Malcolm's transcendent writings about the Native California cultures that inspired him, provides welcome insight into his capacious mind and generous heart."

—**ELAINE ELINSON**, coauthor of *Wherever There's a Fight*

"*Deep Hanging Out* is an opportunity to not just wade, but to take a deep dive into the voracious curiosity of Malcolm Margolin. Malcolm's magic lies in how he connects us to what was and could be again by respectfully learning from, not just about, the Native people of California."

—**ANNE BOWN-CRAWFORD**, executive director of the
California Arts Council

"Malcolm Margolin has spent decades in deep, respectful listening to the Indigenous occupants of California. He gives us a vital window into a special, largely forgotten world that can teach us wonders, if we will only take the time to listen."

—**BRUCE HAMILTON**, national policy director of the Sierra Club

"This glorious collection of essays invites us to jump into Malcolm's old Volvo and travel alongside him for a deeply insightful, beautiful, and intimate exchange with Native California activists, leaders, and culture bearers. Margolin's gift offers an enduring and engaging record of the powerful forces of cultural renewal alive in Native California today— forces that inspire respect, cultivate appreciation, and stir emotion."

—**AMY V. KITCHENER**, executive director and cofounder of the
Alliance for California Traditional Arts

"This milestone monograph sheds light on one of the least understood and most fascinating corners of the Native American world."

—**DANIEL SHEEHY**, director and curator of
Smithsonian Folkways Recordings

"This book is for California's Indigenous Peoples, and for all the rest of us too. It is from an ally who views the beauty and wonder of life as an essential element in fixing the world."

—**JANEEN ANTOINE** (Sicangu Lakota), executive director of
American Indian Contemporary Arts

"Malcolm has always worked diligently to ensure that our Native world-view, culture, and traditions are presented through our own voice. This book is an extension of his commitment to our people with the utmost integrity and respect."

—**SUSAN MASTEN**, former chair of the Yurok Tribe,
former president of the National Congress of American Indians

"Malcolm Margolin brings to life the beauty, wisdom, compassion, and diversity of California's first people with wit, sensitivity, and style. This book should be required reading for any Californian interested in learning about our Indigenous people and their ongoing efforts to revitalize their languages, material culture and crafts, ceremonies, culinary arts, and lands."

—**KENT G. LIGHTFOOT**, professor of anthropology at the University of California, Berkeley

"This compelling, wise, and profoundly moving book is a must read for anyone with an interest in the contemporary peoples of Native California. The fruit of a half-century of intimate involvement, it has much to teach us about living among the First Peoples of this ancient slice of the world."

—**IRA JACKNIS**, research anthropologist at the Phoebe A. Hearst Museum of Anthropology, University of California, Berkeley

"With elegance, passion, and humanity, Malcolm Margolin takes his readers on a celebratory and profoundly hopeful excursion into the little known, diverse, vibrant, complicated, and deeply humane worlds of Native California past, present, and future."

—**BEVERLY R. ORTIZ**, chair of Native California Research Institute

"With his elfin nature and wry humor, Malcolm Margolin has modeled the most pure-hearted and humble allyship. Now he offers readers this deeply human, accessible, and wide-ranging storytelling, sharing what he has learned in order to benefit Mother Earth and all people who are Indigenous to her mysterious and complex interrelated systems."

—**NINA SIMONS**, cofounder and chief relationship strategist of Bioneers

"Malcolm Margolin is not only a California hero, he is a national treasure; in this personal anthology-memoir he has brought us even closer to the still-beating heart of our foundational and astonishingly surviving Native California world."

—**PETER NABOKOV**, author of *Where the Lightning Strikes*, editor of *Native American Testimony*

"Malcolm recognizes that simply recording stories is not enough, it's in the telling. His work, personality, energy, uniqueness, creativity, and interactions with California Native people seem to have emerged from a place deep within his spirit and soul."

—ANNETTE L. REED (Tolowa Dee-ni'), professor in
Native American studies and ethnic studies at
California State University, Sacramento

"Throughout his book, Malcolm provides a glimpse into the California Indian world without the burden of top-down anthropological jargon or theorizing. It is a beautiful collection of stories about a journey of friendships that span decades. Malcolm embodies in print and in practice what it means to be an ally, an accomplice, and—most importantly—a friend."

—PETER NELSON (Coast Miwok and tribal citizen of the Federated
Indians of Graton Rancheria), assistant professor of ethnic studies and
environmental science, policy, and management at the
University of California, Berkeley

"For every piece of insight or knowledge he has gleaned from our cultures, Malcolm gives back in savvy, tangible, imaginative support that empowers our cultures and our lives. It was a lucky day for us when this Boston Jew wandered into our homelands and hung out so deeply he's never left."

—DEBORAH A. MIRANDA (Ohlone-Costanoan Esselen Nation),
author of *Bad Indians*

"Malcolm has always been on the cutting edge of Native America, especially here in California. His work is his legacy; it will be a legacy unsurpassed but an inspiration to the countless others who will attempt to follow in his footsteps."

—HON. RON W. GOODE, tribal chairman of the
North Fork Mono Tribe

DEEP *Hanging* OUT

DEEP
Hanging
OUT

Wanderings and Wonderment
in Native California

Malcolm Margolin

Heyday, Berkeley, California

Cover Design: Ashley Ingram
Interior Design/Typesetting: Ashley Ingram

Cover photo by Ashley Ingram. Table by Reuben Margolin. Tabletop design inspired by a circa 1895 basket by an unknown Native maker, collected in the northern Mojave Desert (see *The Fine Art of California Indian Basketry* by Brian Bibby, Heyday, 1996).

Published by Heyday
P.O. Box 9145, Berkeley, California 94709
(510) 549-3564
heydaybooks.com

Printed in East Peoria, Illinois, by Versa Press, Inc.

10 9 8 7 6 5 4 3 2 1

CONTENTS

INTRODUCTION

Several years ago, I was invited by members of the Kashaya Pomo tribe of Sonoma County to be a guest at their annual acorn harvest celebration. I was honored and grateful to be there. So when Lanny Pinola, one of the ceremony leaders, asked if I would help by serving the acorns to the elders, I of course accepted. The acorns had been shelled, pounded into flour, leached, boiled into a kind of porridge, and spooned into little paper cups like the ones used for fast-food ketchup. I put some of these cups onto a tray and walked over to a group of elders sitting on lawn chairs. As I served them, a small wave of uneasiness and puzzlement spread throughout the group, then laughter. I noticed a mischievous smile on Lanny's face. I learned later that this ritual serving of the first acorns of the season was a job traditionally reserved for a young girl.

Although I should have been embarrassed, in truth I felt honored by their laughter and laughed along with everyone else. I recognized that one part of my function within the Indian community was to be laughed at. The laughter held much affection and gave me a role to play. (It was not my only role, however, as I did all kinds of other things.) Outsiders generally have specific functions that pretty much define and limit their relationship to the Indian community. Anthropologists study culture, linguists study language, lawyers advise tribal governments. As for me, I participated in the community as a writer and a publisher of a magazine that covered many aspects of Indian culture and history, and this gave me a chance to look at people's personal albums, ask deeper questions about their lives, learn about their histories, and get involved in all kinds of tribal activities. I felt very often that I was simply there as a friend.

I've often described my time spent with California Indians as "deep hanging out." The phrase has a connotation of hippie casualness, but it was coined by the anthropologist Clifford Geertz in 1998 to describe anthropological research done via an informal immersion in a culture, as opposed to research done by conducting formal interviews and distanced observations. Such an approach has been criticized as not being objective enough. And indeed the book before you is not an objective study of California Indian life, it's a personal view. It's seen through my eyes, it follows my passions, and it also exhibits my limitations. I've included things that were of special interest to me, and I did not cover equally important topics that were outside my interests at the time.

As a practice, deep hanging out very much corresponds to Indian ways of gaining knowledge. It is an older way in which you don't pursue knowledge as much as you put yourself out there with the hope that knowledge will come to you. I learned much from sitting on people's porches, playing checkers with them, listening to their stories, telling stories of my own. My academic reflections come from hours spent in libraries reviewing anthropological treatises, linguistic reports, and field notes. I'm proud of the research I've been able to do and very grateful for the trust and the access to their lives that Native people have given me. The book you are holding is the result of fifty years of such hanging out, often being useful as a publisher, yes, but often just being there as a participant, accepted to a degree I could never have anticipated. So how did a balding, bearded, Jewish guy from the other side of the country end up serving acorn mush to a cluster of Indian elders? Let me try to explain.

I was born in 1940 and brought up in a Jewish section of Boston. Milk was still being delivered by a horse-drawn wagon. The iceman came every two or three days with a block of ice for the ice chest. The older generation had been born in Europe. They spoke Yiddish—my grandparents on my mother's side had lived in the United States for fifty years without having learned a word of English—and they maintained the practices and beliefs of an older world. My parents spoke Yiddish to my grandparents and often to each other, and English to my brother and me. In public, my parents seemed mainstream American. They spoke English without an accent, read fashionable books, worked in the world at large, and were adept in modern ways. At the same time, they kept their families' food traditions, observed major Jewish holidays, and socialized almost exclusively with other Jews. (I can recall only one time when a non-Jew came by to visit and also how uneasy everyone was.) I grew up between two cultures. As an American teenager of the 1950s I was exposed to early rock and roll, could hardly wait to get an automobile, and read some of our culture's great books. Though the world of my grandparents seemed arcane, rigid, and not much fun, on the other hand the America of suburban houses, country clubs, careers, and high expectations didn't call to me either. In crucial ways I grew up an outsider, a step away from the dominant culture. Although Indians were not part of my world then and we belong to cultures that are completely different, nevertheless there was something parallel in that the older generations spoke a different language and adhered to traditions of another age. There were actually many underlying similarities in how

I was raised that prepared me to understand Indian culture. Among them, of course, is that I grew up in a neighborhood isolated from the rest of the city, with rules, customs, traditions, and practices outside the dominant way of life. I could sympathize with the older generation while at the same time identifying with many of the younger ones wanting to get away from it all. And Jews, like Indians, have a long history of being rejected and oppressed, and both groups have experienced genocide.

Also, Jews, like Indians, are a persistent people, sheltering a small flame against the fierce winds of oppression, maintaining their traditions, practicing a spirituality and using a language not readily available to others. Food and other traditions bound us together; a sense of tribalism prevailed. But I grew up with an odd ambivalence toward these traditions. On the one hand, traditions were compelling and meaningful; on the other, they were bound by so many rules and seemed to be owned by an older generation. The weight of their archaic rules rankled me from a young age. A wider world beckoned.

A large dose of the modern world's dominant culture was administered by Harvard University, where I received a degree in English literature, and where I met my future wife, Rina. My wanderlust ultimately led to our purchasing a VW bus for three hundred bucks in 1968 and heading out West. For the next two years, we lived in that curtained bus, camping out in Mexico, building a shelter on a beach in Canada, taking odd jobs like planting trees. The nature that I'd just read about in college was one I was now immersed in. We'd stop in various places and I'd pull a manual typewriter from the back of the bus and write articles and occasional stories. I was convinced that everywhere I was going I would find great truths to put into words.

In 1970, Rina and I settled in Berkeley, California. Ah, Berkeley, a place of bookstores, libraries, coffeehouses, and surrounded by large amounts of open space. With the birth of our first child, I found a job with the East Bay Regional Park District as a grounds person. My time there gave me my first taste of getting to know a place in depth, connecting emotionally with the land and its history. In 1972, I received a grant from Stewart Brand of the *Whole Earth Catalog* to write a book on my experiences at Oakland's Redwood Regional Park; that book became *The Earth Manual: How To Work on Wild Land Without Taming It* and it was published by Houghton Mifflin. *The East Bay Out: A Personal Guide to the East Bay Regional Parks* followed soon after; I ended up publishing it myself in 1974, and with it starting Heyday, the publishing house I was to run for over forty years.

Living in Berkeley also prepared me to better understand Indian country. For one thing, Berkeley had a tolerance for alternative institutions—things like natural foods, communal living, "back to the earth" philosophy, ecology, and similar concerns. It was an era of upheaval and uncertainty. The unpopular Vietnam War was covered every night on the evening news, people were becoming more aware of racial injustice and environmental degradation, the women's movement was gaining strength, and in Berkeley, as in so many other college towns, young people were questioning American values and behavior.

Native Americans also played a large role in Berkeley's sense of itself. The two-year occupation of Alcatraz Island by Indians of All Tribes beginning in 1969 had been covered daily by Berkeley's local radio station KPFA, and it seemed as if half of the city was glued to those broadcasts. In the early 1970s, books such as *Custer Died for Your Sins* and *Bury My Heart at Wounded Knee* filled the shelves of bookstores across town. The American Indian Movement (AIM) was part of the political culture of Berkeley, and the Native American Studies Department was being established at UC Berkeley. But while the presence of Native American politics and culture was all around, it was largely coming from a mix of tribal cultures from outside of the state. Indians were seemingly everywhere, yet I began to wonder about the Indians who were originally from Northern California. I decided to write about Indian life in the Bay Area, an effort that ultimately became the book *The Ohlone Way: Indian Life in the San Francisco–Monterey Bay Area.*

In the 1970s, Berkeley was a place rich in Indian historical resources, and it even had a burgeoning awareness of California Indian culture. Near us was the Phoebe A. Hearst Museum of Anthropology, with its superb collection of Indian artifacts and photographs and scholarship. The linguistic department at UC Berkeley was assembling archives of Californian Indian languages. The home of the Hearst Museum's researcher Vera Mae Fredrickson and her husband David, an archaeologist at Sonoma State University, attracted a steady stream of archaeologists, anthropologists, folk singers, and poets. At the Fredrickson home, as in many others in Berkeley at the time, there was an openness to other ways of living and thinking that fueled a seeming wildfire of exploration, innovation, experimentation, and creativity. But it wasn't until I was well along in my absorption of academic books and journals that Vera Mae asked if I would like to meet somebody named Philip Galvan. Philip was an Ohlone elder associated with Mission San Jose and a caretaker of a nearby convent. I spent many hours sitting on his porch in the South Bay community of Fremont. I had never met anyone like him. He was thoroughly Catholic—in fact one of his sons was a priest—and yet he'd grown up in Alisal, a re-established Ohlone village site near Sunol where the Ohlone language was still spoken and many of the old ways were kept.

I discovered, remarkably, that there were still California Indians living in the area, who, like Philip, had been born near the end of the previous century. They in turn had been raised by people who had known California before the gold rush. Many of them grew up speaking their Native language as their first language; the pacing and tone of their lives were of another time. These were people the world will never see again. Whenever I encountered one of them, I would enter another world. Listening to their stories, hearing their humor and ferocity, sharing their defeats and victories was an unexpected and great privilege. The experience moved and shaped me. I realized I'd found something of tremendous value. I couldn't keep it to myself.

I published *The Ohlone Way* in 1978. It was widely read and revelatory, since the presence and history of Bay Area Indians had barely been acknowledged. In subsequent years, I wrote more books about California Indians, including *The Way We Lived: California Indian Reminiscences, Stories, and Songs*. Under the Heyday imprint, I began to publish other people's books about California Indians too, many by Native authors. To sell these books, I would set up tables at various California Indian functions around the state, including conferences, art shows, and tribal events. As it turned out, sitting at a table selling books is a great way to meet people, and my address book swelled.

After then publishing other books on California's natural and cultural history for a decade, a change came in 1987 when my friend Vera Mae was let go by the Hearst Museum. I suggested we create a calendar of California Indian events. It seemed almost every day someone was telling me about a cultural exhibition or ceremony or some other important event I had missed. I felt such a calendar would prove incredibly useful. We met in a Chinese restaurant over Kung Pao chicken. I envisioned a calendar that would be about four pages. There might be some space left over, so maybe Frank LaPena could write an art column; Logan Slagle, a political action column; Victoria Patterson, an education column. Vera Mae was definitely on board, and we were soon joined by David Peri, a Coast Miwok and among the most brilliant people I've ever met. His mother had been the last speaker of the Coast Miwok language. When I worked with him in his living room in Sebastopol, he'd pull out an endless supply of objects, photographs, transcripts, and recordings. He kept me enthralled with his stories, and the ones he told about iconic elders like Elsie Allen, Essie Parrish, and Laura Somersal formed the basis of my understanding of California Indians. I have long since lost the founding napkin on which we sketched out our ideas, but this is how *News from Native California* began.

And now, as the publisher of a magazine that quickly became an important community resource, I had entry into people's homes, into art shows, into roundhouses and ceremonies, into tribal meetings. *News from Native California* was only a newsletter, but, in a time before computers, when people lived isolated in their communities, especially in rural California, it became the equivalent of a social media site, connecting remote peoples across California long before the Internet.

Another benefit of building a magazine around a calendar of events was that we got to know the cultural leaders of Native California, many of whom volunteered to write articles for us. Other magazines rarely featured material from California Indians, and when they did it was for a largely non-Indian audience. Little benefit accrued to Indians from the articles written about them. With *News*, a large number of readers were Native, and the information we carried, by promoting events and nourishing Native organizations, strengthened the community. We found ourselves widely welcomed.

As a publisher looking for articles and for inspiration, my job was to go into a community and find out what was meaningful and interesting there. Often, I'd write an article about someone and be heartened at how much it meant to them. It was a wonderful way of not just getting to meet people but getting to learn more about them. I found out what people thought was best in their lives, what they were most proud of, and I would help them express it. I went to various Indian gatherings, and my table of books and the magazine would become a gathering place because I made sure to have chairs available. Often, I had a place in the shade. There was also for Native people the novelty of seeing themselves or their families or neighbors in a book or an article in *News*. I want to mention one book in particular that we published called *First Families: A Photographic History of California Indians*, which was funded by historian Kevin Starr at the California State Library. It was a photo album of California Indians, and its purpose was to understand Indian history through Native eyes. To do so, we sent a couple of researchers around to Indian reservations and centers to collect photos from people's albums, and to listen to and collect stories. Each photo was accompanied by a description—who was in the picture, what was happening, the circumstances of it all. For years afterward I would sit at a table with copies of this book, and people would come up to me and bring friends by to look and tell stories of the relatives and family members in it. Traveling around to different communities, I became like a bard bringing news of other places and making connections.

In my visits to Indian country, I would often bring my kids with me. I would travel to different communities with them, where we'd go around to different roundhouses and hear different languages. Many of these languages were dying, and I was moved by the thought that at some point Sadie and Jake might be among the last people alive to have heard a full range of these languages. I also invited people back to my house in Berkeley. Visitors were constantly coming over. My life was on display as well as theirs.

News provided me with an introduction to hundreds of people I would never otherwise have met. Not of Indian descent myself, I seem to have been generally accepted into various communities as some kind of odd, well-meaning, benign, and occasionally useful "friend of the family," a role I have embraced. I have sat in many kitchens drinking coffee; been present at the sidelines of many traditional ceremonies; and attended numerous baby namings, weddings, shamans' healings, tribal council meetings, conferences, art shows, picnics, all-night stick game tournaments, and a variety of other events, some traditional, some modern, some public, some private. I have developed a wide network of acquaintances, and within this network I have made more than a few dear and true friends. I have also engaged in what must now amount to thousands of hours of conversations in which I could often feel old certainties dissolve and new understandings grow. It was and is a strange and wonderful world. During my period of publishing *News* and the books about and for California Indians, I was constantly surprised. The variety of people was endless, and the stories unlike stories I'd come across anywhere else. It was a privilege to have entry into this world, and I enjoyed it immensely.

Since retiring from Heyday after more than forty years at its helm, I've maintained many of the friendships formed over decades and have brought yet more stories into the world. I've created the California Institute for Community, Art, and Nature (California I CAN), a five-year-old nonprofit located in Berkeley. In the words of the Ohlone language spoken in the East Bay, *tappe ta-k hinnan*—we learn with the heart—and it is such heart learning that I'm attempting to foster through California I CAN programs, community events, articles, films, and art that show what a world informed by Native wisdom might look like.

As rich as the material in this book is, it is nowhere near a complete picture of California Indians. Not all subjects are covered: I mostly wrote about celebratory events and distant history, not topics like health or tribal recognition, and not instances of violence or tragedy. Also, this is a collection of pieces that I wrote at particular times: things may have since ended differently than I anticipated when I wrote about them. And I didn't cover everyone: some of the most significant people in my life have been left out of this collection because I didn't have the opportunity to write about them. This collection is in many ways just the tip of an iceberg—and especially so for those unacquainted with Native California. I hope you'll subscribe to *News from Native California*, check out Heyday's related offerings, and explore California I CAN through our website (californiaican.org).

I have sought independence throughout my career by publishing my own books, creating my own institutions, and following my own interests. Yet this independence is an illusion. My going out into the world has been supported by the staff of the magazine and the publishing company I founded; by the numerous foundations and individuals that have contributed to our efforts; by the many Native and non-Native people who have helped me understand things, answered my questions, and encouraged me in multiple ways; and finally by my family—my wife Rina in particular, and my children, Reuben, Sadie, and Jake, who have all worked with me at various times. I got into publishing and writing in order to be independent, but looking back I realize how dependent I have actually been on others, how much a part of a community. And such a sense of community is at the core of indigenous peoples' values and traditions as well.

The fact that my quest for independence actually led to a deep dependence on the community around me suggests that my life has not been well planned out. So much of what I did derived from my deep hanging out. I did not get involved with the Indian community because I had an agenda or because when I first got into it I saw things that would change my life or that would be of greater value to the world. As I was an outsider in my childhood, and just as I was drawn to living for two years in a VW bus, to embracing Berkeley's alternative cultures, and to creating a publishing enterprise that was regional and personal, one of the things that attracted me to the Native community in California was that, just like the Jewish world of my childhood in Boston, it was a world unto itself. What I have found in this world are values, insights, sources of wisdom, and ways of being that are profoundly moving.

While I am not Indian, much of what I've seen has nevertheless shaped my life, and I feel that the Indian world has a great deal to teach the rest of us. California has so many different Native cultures, an examination of which can provide society with tools for creating a better world, especially now as more of us are again reconsidering our understanding of basic institutions and how best to live sustainably on this planet.

The specifics of our two worlds—that of the Boston Jew and the California Indian—may be different, but I've moved through the Indian universe with an understanding of its terrain. When Native people talk about how strange their food traditions are, about the various restrictions as to what can be eaten when, I understand, having grown up in a Kosher kitchen in which there were four sets of dishes that could never touch each other. When I began this introduction, musing on how a Jewish guy from Boston ended up serving acorn mush to Kashaya Pomo elders, it seemed an unlikely transformation, but it derives from who I've always been. I was an out-of-it, daydreamy sort of kid. "Malcolm lives in a world of his own," I remember my mother saying. "Nose in a book, head in the clouds, building castles in the air." People assured my parents that I'd grow out of it. It was only a matter of time before I accepted my responsibilities, got a good job, got a haircut, bought a house, mowed a lawn. Reality eventually did corral me, but it was not the reality they'd anticipated. The reality that seized me is the reality of a world more abundant and wise and beautiful than anything I deserved, its people more courageous and more generous. For decades I've been adding rooms, corridors, whole wings to my castle in the air. There are rooms devoted to social justice, to diversity, to cultural preservation, to beauty, to mystery, to humor. There are rooms where the first peoples of California gather to tell their stories and speak in not-forgotten languages. So make yourself at home, wander from room to room. Beauty and wisdom abound.

Malcolm Margolin
Berkeley, California

CENTER POST FOR KULE LOKLO (1987)

It was morning, a chill still in the air. I pulled off the dirt road onto a grassy shoulder and walked into a field to join a small group of men who were stamping the ground, complaining about the cold, and waiting. A flatbed truck was warming up nearby. On the ground beside it were peavies, a chainsaw, jacks, a drawknife, shovels, bars, and come-alongs.

As we talked quietly among ourselves about the tools and the hydraulic tailgate on the truck, we were secretly sizing each other up the way men do in such a situation: who knew the most about the tools, who had the most experience, who would eventually emerge as a leader. Anyone casually glancing our way would have assumed this was a typical work crew scene. But we were not gathered together for an ordinary logging or construction job. A mix of Indians and Anglos, we had been invited by Ester and Lanny Pinola and Bun Lucas of the Kule Loklo village to help remove an old center post from a dance house and put in a new one. Despite the modern tools, the purring of the truck motor, and the requisite "macho" noises we were making at each other, we were all aware of a religious spirit to the undertaking. The dance house was a couple of hundred yards away. Bun, Ester, Lanny, and other members of the Coast Miwok and Kashaya Pomo people had been dancing and singing in the house for the last four nights, holding a wake for the old center post that was dying, preparing a welcome for the new post that would be installed.

I had known the dance house and its old center post for about ten years, and I had long admired it. But when I first saw it, I would never have predicted the deep spiritual activity that now suffused our enterprise. Kule Loklo was not, at least in its beginnings, an authentic Indian village. More like a museum, it had been set up by a group of Anglo schoolteachers to replicate a village of the "extinct" Miwok people who once lived here on the Point Reyes National Seashore in Marin County. The schoolteachers learned about Indians mostly through books, studying the ethnographies carefully, poring over the archaeological records. Then, using students and volunteers, they set about to reconstruct the village using only the old methods. The wood was shaped with obsidian tools. The ground was chipped at with wooden digging sticks, and bits of dislodged earth were scooped up with abalone shells and loaded into baskets to be carried off. It was a long and painstaking process; it took over a year just to dig out the dance house pit. Surely no California village had been built this way for well over a century. Nevertheless, bit by bit, a village grew: a dance house, a sweathouse, acorn granaries, a scattering of dwellings and shade houses. The teachers and the rangers of the National Seashore held their interpretive programs here. Busloads of schoolchildren, and on weekends family groups, descended on the village; they were taught ancient skills and ancient ways, generally by people who themselves had learned them from books only a few years before.

As the village gained prominence, however, an event occurred that the rangers and schoolteachers had never prepared themselves for. The Coast Miwok turned out not to be very "extinct" at all. Many of them still lived around Point Arena, others had married into the Pomo and were living on the Kashaya Reservation at Stewarts Point. Among them were people who still spoke the old language and who not only remembered the old ways but in many respects still lived by them. They came to Kule Loklo to investigate what these schoolteachers and rangers were saying about them.

The initial confrontations between the teachers and the Natives were at times ill-tempered, at times (at least to an outsider) quite comic. The situation had all the makings of a bitter fight, a long-term grudge, a power struggle, even—at times—a fiasco. But that is not what happened. Gradually, the Indian community felt itself more and more drawn toward the village. Perhaps, they admitted, they had something to learn from these people who had studied the literature and researched their past so devotedly. The teachers and rangers, for their part, came to realize that perhaps they were not well equipped emotionally and spiritually to interpret Indian culture.

Over a few years the Indians became integrated into the programs, until finally they took them over entirely. Under the direction of Ester and Lanny Pinola and with the help of Bun Lucas, Lorraine Laiwa, Gladys Gonzalez, and others, they began to run the interpretive programs and make the decisions. As time passed and the Indian presence grew stronger, they began to use the village for feasts and dances, infusing the buildings with spirit and belief. The schoolteachers had created a stage setting; the drama was now in the hands of the Indians. Kule Loklo was no longer just a museum. It had come alive.

The old center post had seen all these changes. Thousands of schoolchildren and visitors had passed around it, and the center post had heard the respectful voices of those whose hearts were open, as well as the nervous snickerings of those who did not yet understand.

It had witnessed—and lent strength to—the prayers and ceremonies of recent years. A month or so before our gathering, vandals had broken into the dance house and set fire to its base, scarring and weakening it. In the previous four nights it had been thanked with dances and songs, and perhaps its spirit was put to rest.

We entered the dance house through a low, northeast-facing entranceway. We had to stoop low, and during the rest of the day I would repeatedly whack my head—a useful, if painful, lesson about humility that was literally drummed into me again and again. A narrow, sloping passageway led to the interior. Within, it was dark and comfortable, about thirty-two feet in diameter, and dug about four feet into the ground. The walls below ground level were banked with stone. The earth-covered roof, with a smoke hole near the center, was held up by the center post, by four other posts around it, and by twelve shorter posts that stood closer to the edge. There were various interpretations about what the posts signified. Some Indian people, combining ancient beliefs with their conversion to Mormonism, felt that the center post was Jesus; the four middle posts were God, the Resurrection, Repentance, and the Witness; and the twelve posts around the edge represented the twelve apostles. Others, holding more traditional views, referred to the spiritual significance of the number four and the four directions. Interpretations varied, but one thing was obvious: These posts were not randomly or carelessly placed. They were here for a sacred reason. And as we pulled the shovels and digging bars into the dance house, we knew that we had entered sacred space.

The old center post was interlocked with the roof above us. To get it out, we first dug a deep trench from the entranceway toward the center post, so that we could slide its base along the trench and eventually out the door. There were several hours of digging. Bars chipped away at the hard floor, shovels plunged into the earth. I was secretly glad that Indians were running the show this time, not schoolteachers; otherwise, we might have been using digging sticks.

As we worked, I had the curious sense of this event running on two channels. On one channel was the physical work: a crew of men sweating, grunting, giving orders, "spelling" each other, even swearing. Then we would pause and switch to the other channel, the spiritual, as Bun Lucas said a variety of prayers, thanked the crew, and talked to the old center post. "The spirit is here among us," said Bun, and, deeply quiet, we could all feel it—not just in the prayers but in the air, in the wood, in the ground. We then returned for a while to the grunting, sweating, and giving or taking of orders as we deepened the trench and tried to detach the top of the post from the roof. We were finally ready to pull the center post entirely loose and carry it outside to where a funeral pyre had been prepared. We stopped for a final prayer. Spoken by Bun in Pomo, it was filled with deep ritual sighs and real tears that spread among all of us. At the end of the prayer, Bun gave forth with four prolonged howls. In all my life I do not think that I have ever heard a more unearthly, beautiful, moving sound. I call them "howls" for lack of a better word, but they were really something else—the sound a mountain might make, or a large tree, or the earth itself. This, Bun explained later, was the cry Earth-maker had made at the creation of the world. With this cry, the sense that I had had of two separate channels ended. As we bid the old center post farewell, pulled it down, and marched it to the funeral pyre, the physical and spiritual worlds merged. Like the warp and woof of a textile, they were now inextricably woven together in our aching muscles, with those howls reverberating deep within us.

News from Native California, vol. 1, no. 1, 1987

INTRODUCTION TO *THE WAY WE LIVED* (1981)

The following collection of reminiscences, stories, and songs reflects the diversity of the people native to California. The magnitude of that diversity is obvious in any gathering of California Indians, with great differences quickly apparent not only between those from Northern and those from Southern California, but often between groups of people living only a few miles apart.

In the days before the coming of whites those differences were even greater. Picture, for example, a typical spring afternoon in California two hundred years ago. On the prairies of the northeastern part of the state a man, hiding behind a clump of sagebrush, waves a scrap of deer skin in the air, trying to rouse the curiosity of a herd of grazing antelope and draw them within range of his bow and arrow. Along the Klamath River a boy crawls through the circular doorway of a large plank house and walks downstream to watch his father and uncles fish for salmon beneath the redwoods. In the Central Valley a group of women, strings of wildflowers in their hair, wade out into the deep sea of rippling grass to gather roots. As they push forward, herds of elk scatter before them. In San Francisco Bay two men paddle a rush boat through the quiet channels of a saltwater marsh. East of the Sierra, families—eager for change and weighed down with burden baskets—leave their winter homes in the desert and trek through pine forests toward thawing mountain lakes and the promise of good fishing. At the edge of the Mohave Desert men and women plant corn, bean, and pumpkin seeds in the warm, fertile mud of the Colorado River.

People first started appearing in California more than twelve thousand years ago. Perhaps they were placed here by the Creator, as many traditional people still insist, each group rooted in its own territory by divine ordinance. Or perhaps, as archaeologists tell the story, they were bands of bold explorers or maybe desperate refugees who had been ousted from homelands elsewhere, who came into California from many places and over the course of many thousands of years.

Their languages are many and varied. Some California groups speak languages of the Algonkin family of eastern North America. Others speak an Athapascan language related to languages of Canada. There are also speakers of languages from the Uto-Aztecan or Shoshonean language family; speakers of the Hokan languages more commonly found in the southwest; speakers of Penutian languages whose linguistic relatives may include the Tsimshian of British Columbia and perhaps even the Mayans of Central America; and at least two groups of Yukian speakers whose language can be linked convincingly to no other surviving languages in the world.

As group after group appeared in California, they gradually dispersed along the ocean beaches, settled into secluded mountain valleys, moved out into the open desert, and established villages in the oak savannahs of the Sierra foothills. They built wooden houses in the redwood and pine forests, underground earthen houses in the grasslands of the Central Valley, rush and willow houses along the fringes of marshlands. Centuries, sometimes thousands of years passed, and people of the same language family lost contact with each other. Some became almost totally isolated within their narrow valleys, some merged with neighboring groups of different linguistic stock. As a result, when white explorers first set foot in California, they found as many as one hundred languages being spoken, 70 percent of them as mutually unintelligible as English and Chinese. Stephen Powers, a nineteenth-century ethnologist, complained of traveling for "months in regions where a new language has to be looked to every ten miles sometimes."

The great variety of languages was matched by a great variety of customs, technologies, beliefs, and physical characteristics. The Yuman people of southernmost California and the Modoc of the northern border were among the most warlike people in North America, while residents of the central part of the state were among the most peaceful. The Mohave who lived along the Colorado River were the tallest of all Native Americans, the Yuki of Mendocino County the shortest. Dances, religious practices, foods eaten and shunned—indeed, almost every aspect of culture varied widely throughout the state.

As one example of California's extraordinary diversity, consider the matter of boats. The Yurok at the mouth of the Klamath River made dugout canoes out of redwood logs—crafts of "wonderful symmetry and elegance," according to an early visitor, "the sides as smooth as if they had been sandpapered." These Yurok boats were blunt and sturdy, made to withstand the battering of rocks and the scraping of river bottoms. The Modoc, by comparison, made extremely delicate dugouts hollowed out to an amazingly thin shell—boats well suited to the calm waters of Tule and Lower Klamath Lakes.

The Chumash of the Santa Barbara Channel had a totally different concept of boat building. They fashioned boats, sometimes over thirty feet long, out of thin planks. Lacking nails they drilled holes in the planks and sewed them together with thongs of deer sinew. Then they caulked the seams with asphaltum, painted the sides red with hematite, and decorated the bows with white seashells. These were ocean-going vessels in which the maritime Chumash voyaged to the Channel Islands, Santa Catalina, and even to remote San Nicolas Island sixty-five miles from shore.

The Choinumni, a Yokuts group of the San Joaquin Valley, bound tule (bulrush) together with willow withes to make barges fifty feet long. They outfitted these immense barges with bedding, baskets of acorns and dried meat, even clay-lined fireplaces. Firewood was taken aboard, and one or more families embarked onto the sloughs, waterways, and lakes of the Central Valley, for a combined fishing expedition and vacation that often lasted weeks.

Even this does not come close to exhausting the types of boats used in California. Dugouts were made in a variety of designs out of locally available wood: redwood, fir, cottonwood, juniper, and pine. Tule craft ranged from tiny floating platforms from which Tubatulabal fishermen hurled harpoons to thirty-foot boats that once plied Clear Lake carrying several persons or over a ton of freight. Some groups lashed logs together to make rafts. Others used large baskets or even clay pots—towed by strong swimmers—to ferry children and goods across a river.

The variety of watercraft in California suggests the remarkable variety of people and culture. The people we call "Native Californians" actually belonged to over five hundred independent tribal groups. Such diversity boggles the modern mind, overtaxing our systems of categorization and nomenclature. Consequently we moderns have tended toward generalization. We refer, for example, to the "Pomo" as if there had once been a Pomo tribe or a Pomo culture.

Before the coming of whites, however, the Pomo were several dozen independent tribal groups—small nations, as it were—each with its own territory and chief. Pomo groups who lived in the interior valleys differed widely in customs, beliefs, and languages from those who lived along the coast. The major justification for grouping such diverse people under a single name is that the languages they spoke—seven different, mutually incomprehensible languages—are linguistically related and of common origin.

Pomo, in short—like Miwok, Maidu, Yokuts, etc.—is largely a concept of our own invention. Nevertheless, for over a hundred years stories and songs, accounts of daily life, baskets and other artifacts have been collected from people described simply as "Pomo." Also, as generations have passed, the unique identities, characteristics, territories, and sometimes even the names of the many independent tribal groups have become obscured. Thus this book has no choice but to follow the conventional nomenclature and refer to people as Pomo, Maidu, or Miwok, however misleading. In fact this book does something much worse. In the following pages mention is often made of "Native Californians," "California Indians," or of a "California" way of thinking or acting. California, of course, is our own way of defining the world; the area it describes holds together as a unit only in the modern mind. In terms of Native culture, "California" is utterly meaningless. So be forewarned. References to California, even more than references to Pomo, are concessions to modern perspective and definition, rather than adequate descriptions of the incalculable human richness and multiformity that existed here two hundred years ago.

California is thought to have had the densest pre-Columbian population anywhere north of Mexico. In 1769, when the first Spanish colonists arrived, an estimated 310,000 Native people were living within the borders of the present state. Then came the missions and the ranchos; the goldminers, loggers, and farmers; the silting of streams, clearing of forests, draining of marshes, fencing of grasslands, and elimination of game; the diseases, the hatred, and the violence; the unspeakable tragedy. By the beginning of the twentieth century fewer than 20,000 Native people were left in the state.

After 1900 California's Indian population began to increase, but many of the survivors were children of mixed marriages and broken traditions. Those who spoke Native languages and who remembered and valued Native culture continued to decline. The twentieth century saw a steady, inexorable shrinking of witness to the old ways of life. Anthropologists and other scholars scurried among the survivors, trying to salvage what they could from those who still remembered. Carobeth Laird, wife of the linguist-anthropologist John P. Harrington, described the mood: "The vessel of the old culture had broken, and its precious contents were spilling out and evaporating before our very eyes. Harrington, like a man dying of thirst, lapped at every random trickle."

Harrington was not alone. Although it is dreadful how much has been lost—whole tribal groups have disappeared with scarcely a word recorded—it is nevertheless astounding how many Native Californian songs, stories, speeches, and reminiscences have been preserved: literally thousands of dictaphone cylinders, disks, records, and tapes; folders, boxes, and filing cabinets filled with field notes; and thousands upon thousands of pages of material published as monographs, books, or in scholarly journals; and (amazingly) innumerable songs, stories, and reminiscences still part of the ongoing cultures of California Indians.

It has been several years since I took my first plunge into this vast sea of linguistic and ethnographic material. I originally had, if

I remember correctly, a rather lofty ambition. I planned a comprehensive survey of Native California literature—one which would be, if not complete, at least representative. As time went on the impossibility of the task gradually dawned on me. Not only was I overwhelmed by the mass and variety of material available, but much of that material was in itself simply bewildering.

How could I deal, for example, with the large number of "autobiographies" that gave no details about birth, marriage, or occupation, but instead consisted of meticulous recountings of dreams and contacts with the spirit world? Such autobiographies made perfect sense in a cultural context. Native Californians traditionally lived in small tribal groups in which the external details of each person's life were intimately known. It would never occur to a woman, for instance, to talk about how she made baskets, how she pounded acorns, or who her children were, for such things were known by everyone. To mention them would have been too obvious—like mentioning the fact that she had two legs and a nose. The subject of autobiographies is what other people do not know—in this case the world of one's dreams and the nature of one's spirit-world contacts, which for most Californians were the most important and most individual aspects of their lives. Yet while I recognized that such dream and spirit autobiographies were typical and thoroughly indicative of the Native thought process, I found the bulk of them so foreign to the modern experience as to be inaccessible to all but the most dedicated student. Thus in preparing this collection I tended to pass over most of such material in favor of those autobiographies that were less typical but were structured more in line with our own conventions.

Similarly, many Indian stories and myths seem rambling and plotless by modern standards. Originally there was no real need for plot. After all, the entire audience—except for the very young children—had heard each story and myth many times. Since everyone knew the plot, the storyteller was free to concentrate instead on voice, cadence, and performance. Especially performance! Imagine, for example, a rainy winter night. People have crowded into the assembly house or large dwelling. A fire is lit—it crackles and smokes from the moisture in the wood—and the storyteller launches forth, voice rising and falling; now talking, now singing; adopting the tone of one character, then another; shouting, whispering, grunting, wheedling, laughing—and all in a language molded to the story by centuries of previous performances; all in an energized setting in which family and friends are crowded together.

Anthropologists, linguists, and folklorists have painstakingly recorded and transcribed many stories. Yet when such stories are stripped of the richness of human voice and the presence of living audience, cut off from cultural knowledge and tradition, translated into a distant language and set into type, they are often so diminished that many of them seem formless, empty, and incomprehensible to us.

Songs in particular suffer in translation. The tune, the rhythm, the nonsense syllables, the very life is often pressed out of a song as it passes into written English. How can one even begin to translate a Maidu shaman's recital, described by a listener as a "tangle of breathing and blowing sounds, bilabial trilling, nonsense syllables, and esoteric utterances?" How can one capture songs in Lower Lake Pomo, a language full of hissing sounds and sharp clicks such as one finds in certain African languages? Indeed, how can one convey any song except to sing it? Once again a huge body of very typical material had to be passed over in my final selection.

Thus my plan to present a comprehensive, or at least representative, survey of Native Californian literature quickly ran into trouble. In fact as time went on I strayed further and further from the goal, so that the reminiscences and stories, songs and speeches that follow—while thoroughly authentic and (as nearly as possible) true to tone—are basically a personal selection. Here, then, is what seemed to jump out of the mass of collected material, suddenly illuminating some aspect of Native life, or presenting me with something that I found beautiful, tragic, terribly interesting, or simply funny. Here are the selections that transported me, for a few minutes at least, into another world—that made me feel what it must have been like to have been a shaman dancing for power, a young boy awaiting initiation, an old man gazing at a pine tree he could no longer climb, a young girl hearing for the first time the mourning cries of her mother, a member of an audience listening to Coyote tales in an atmosphere of shared laughter. Here are the selections that have filled me with wonderment and have given me a deeper understanding not only of Native Californians but of all humanity.

The Way We Lived, Heyday, 1981

PREFACE TO *THE OHLONE WAY* (2014)

I began research for The Ohlone Way forty years ago, in 1974, and published it four years later, in 1978. I've revisited it now and then, perhaps as an older person will on occasion return to the streets of his youth. The Ohlone Way hasn't changed, but I have, and each time I return to it I realize something new.

What struck me this last trip through the book was how intimate and emotional it is. I had researched it as thoroughly as I could for three years in those pre-computer times, visiting libraries and archives, following trails that led me to county histories and old newspaper accounts, reading every shred of scholarly and popular work I could lay my hands on, talking to anyone I thought might have even a scrap of knowledge. Taking a sentence from here, an image from there, and a suggestion from somewhere else, I stitched together what I felt to be a richly textured quilt. Indeed, the book before you is loaded with facts and information that had never before been assembled in one place—technical details about how the Native people of the San Francisco and Monterey Bay areas fished, hunted, made baskets, cooked food, raised their young, structured their societies, worshipped their gods, and buried their dead.

Had I been an old-time anthropologist, strategizing for a tenured position at a good college, expected to submit my publications to peer review, trained in the restraints of a discipline that once aimed to keep the scholar aloof from the subject so he or she can be more objective, I would have stopped at the assemblage of facts, footnoted each of them, and in the end I would have had a good, safe, peer-reviewed book that would certainly have had value. It would have contributed to knowledge, and indeed I would have been proud of it.

But I was not just an assembler of data, an arranger of facts, a shuffler of index cards. I was a young man hungry for engagement and eager for experience. While I valued research and strove for accuracy, what I really ached for were those jolts of insight and imagination that would make this world I was studying come alive. The Indians of the past, when presented in the anthropological literature, seemed more like figures in a diorama than real, flesh-and-blood people. I increasingly found myself wondering not just what these people did, but, more importantly, who they were, how they thought and felt. When I pictured a woman weaving a basket, I knew from visits to museums and from studying academic papers what material she was most likely using, what style of weave, how the basket was used. But I wanted something more. I wanted to know what she was thinking, what she was feeling, and maybe even the big question—I wanted to know whether she was happy. If we met, would I like her? Would she like me? These are questions that a properly objective scholar shouldn't ask, but I did. And in pursuit of the answers, I took the facts at hand and created out of them villages in my imagination. Then I walked around in those villages, put myself inside the men and women who were there, and described what they were thinking, what they were feeling. On one hand, I fully recognize that this is suspect, and rightly so. But I wanted more than manikins upon whom to affix Post-its of facts. I wanted to imagine fully formed persons.

In truth, there was more to this quest than idle curiosity. There was a keen, deeply felt desire to know, something bordering on urgency. I did not just want to learn about the Native people of the area; I wanted to learn from them. The questions I was asking were certainly about their lives, but more fundamentally they were shaped by questions I was asking about my own life.

The mid-seventies, especially in Berkeley, were a creative, turbulent, troubling time. The Vietnam War, along with so many other cultural upheavals, had shaken a generation's belief in the tenets we were brought up with. Foundational values such as individualism, the nuclear family, capitalism, the promise of technology, and the inevitability of progress were up for reconsideration.

Berkeley responded to this breakdown in belief and inherited value by becoming a laboratory for reinvention. Communes experimented with family and how we organized ourselves; worker co-ops and consumer co-ops sprang up to redo the economic model; men grew their hair long and women cut their hair short; graduates of prestigious universities became house painters and handymen; and even those of us who tended not to join movements were having our babies at home, feeding them organic tofu, sending them to alternative schools, and bestowing on them names like Rainbow and Pippin. We were restructuring society, we were reshaping the world, and we were recreating ourselves. When showing our parents how enlightened we were, we exuded the brash confidence of youth. But I think we were also scared. We were looking for guidance and not sure where to find it.

Could it be that the past offered answers? Could it be that

the old paradigms that portrayed indigenous people as lesser beings were wrong? Could it be that when America crushed and marginalized the cultures native to this land it destroyed something of great beauty and value—a way of life that had sustained itself for millennia, a people of widespread artistic accomplishment, of spiritual depth and accumulated wisdom, replacing it and them with something barren, ugly, and destructive? Previous generations had treated Indians as people deficient in technological attainments, political organization, and religious development. They were "primitive," and for the most part those who didn't want simply to annihilate them wanted to "educate" and convert them so that they would be better able to assimilate into our "advanced" culture. Even in the seemingly dispassionate writings of many scholars, I could sense the whiff of superiority and condescension: the scholar was the person in the know, the Indians and their ways objects to be studied and analyzed.

The gestalt of the time, the Berkeley of the mid-1970s, gave me the orientation to see things differently. I was not alone in this line of thought. If you were to walk into almost any household in Berkeley during those years and look at the art on the wall or the books on the shelf, you would have found what served as doorways into the Indian world: sepia portraits, inspirational quotes, images of weavings and of pots. Maybe we had more to learn from them than they had to learn from us. If so, I wanted to present Indian life not as a scholar might, with an accumulation of facts, but through a fullness of being that went beyond our limited certainties. And I was willing to accept the possibility that I might be wrong now and then, I might be projecting my own thoughts, I might make mistakes. I took responsibility for that, but I felt that I had avoided the greater mistake that others before me had made: the mistake of shallow portrayal, the mistake of presenting people as unemotional and robotic, the embedded lies one tells when afraid to embrace humanity in its totality. I needed full human beings if I was going to learn anything from them, and I did learn much—about the Ohlones but also about humanity and, in the end, about myself.

Several years ago, in a totally different context, I was discussing with my friend Jim Quay what constituted a healthy society. I made a list that included the following criteria:

- Sustainable relationship with the environment. In a healthy society, the present generation doesn't strip-mine the soil, water, forest, minerals, etc., leaving the future impoverished and the beauty of the world degraded.
- Few outcasts. A healthy society will have relatively few outcasts—prisoners, homeless, unemployed, insane.
- Relative egalitarianism. The gap between those with the most wealth and power and those with the least should be moderate, and those with the least should feel protected, cared for, or rewarded in some other way.
- Widespread participation in the arts.
- Moderation or control of individual power.
- Economic security attained through networks of family, friendship, and social reciprocity, rather than through the individual hoarding of goods.
- Love of place. The feeling that one lives with emotional attachment to an area that is uniquely beautiful, abundant in natural recourses, and rich in personal meaning.
- Knowing one's place in the world. A sense, perhaps embodied in spiritual practice, that the individual is an insignificant part of a larger, more abiding universe.

- Work is done willingly, or at least with a minimum of resentment.
- Lots of laughter.

When I finished writing it all down, I looked it over and was taken aback to discover that what I was listing reflected not only the way of life of the Ohlone for millennia, but also values and practices still embedded in Native people today. An image comes to mind: On those early Spanish expeditions into California, explorers reported how their rations were down to a few moldy tortillas a day. While they were close to starving, they were passing through villages where people were feasting, but they refused to try the Native foods. The foods that nourished the Native populations weren't what these Europeans were used to eating. Not much has changed. European-based cultures are clearly in trouble, starving for fresh ideas and deeper truths, in need of profound reform. When will we learn to reach out to those ideas, philosophical concepts, and social practices that were at the core of the healthy cultures of Native California?

As I reread this book some forty years after I began writing it, I can see more clearly the struggles of a young writer stretching his mind and his heart to understand a different culture in as full and emotional a way as possible. The people that he was writing about were far from perfect, of course, as was the young writer. The book you are about to read does not offer you perfection. But I hope it offers you engagement, and through that engagement the opportunity to ask questions of your own and the chance to learn with the heart as well as with the mind.

A final word about bringing the past alive. In 2003, I wrote an afterword for the twenty-fifth anniversary of the publication of *The Ohlone Way*. In it I mention the heroic accomplishments of Ohlone individuals, families, and communities as they continue to shape their culture, mastering previously neglected skills and reinstituting traditional practices, blending them with the realities and challenges of modern life. This cultural renaissance has not only persisted, it has grown.

I am writing this Preface in Heyday's offices on University Avenue in Berkeley. As I enter the building, affixed to the front door are the words "Horse Tuuxi," "Good Day" in the Chochenyo Ohlone language native to this area. When I flick on the hallway light, I see the word "Ewwep." This is the work of a young Ohlone man, Vincent Medina, a friend and colleague, who, along with other family and tribal members, has been bringing his native language back to life. This allows me to do something I would never have thought possible some forty years ago—urge you to "learn with the heart" in the language of our area: "Tappe ta-k hinnan."

The Ohlone Way, Heyday, 1978, preface to 2014 edition

EXCERPT FROM *THE OHLONE WAY* (1978)

The hunt itself is a splendid sight. The hunter, often with a companion or two, his body painted, his bow and arrows properly treated, lean, hungry, alert, connected with the dream-world, his mind secure that he has followed all the proper rituals, approaches a herd of grazing deer. He wears a deer-head mask, and perhaps an amulet hangs from his neck. He moves toward the grazing grounds slowly, almost diffidently—in many ways more like a suitor than a potential conqueror.

As soon as he sights a herd he crouches low and begins to move like a deer. ("He played the pantomime to such perfection," noted a French sea captain who witnessed one such hunt, "that all our own hunters would have fired at him at thirty paces had they not been prevented.") So convincing is the hunter's imitation that he must keep his eye out for mountain lions and grizzly bears, who sometimes mistake him for a real deer.

As the hunter closes in on the herd, he has three strategies to choose from. First, he can keep his distance and try to entice one or more of the deer toward him. Perhaps if he acts oddly, he can get a curious individual to wander over. During fawning season he blows through a folded leaf, making a bleating sound that often attracts an anxious doe. In rutting season he rubs his antlers against a bush, knocks two sticks together to suggest the clash of antlers, and repeatedly twists his head sideways—ploys calculated to enrage a buck and cause it to leave the herd to challenge him.

A second strategy, often used when many men are hunting together, is to spread out over a meadow and frighten the herd of deer. Disoriented and panicked, the deer run in circles. The hunters study the circles and, positioning themselves behind rocks and bushes, ambush the deer.

The third strategy is for the hunter to move closer to the herd, indeed to become part of the very herd he is hunting. The hunter crouches down and drags himself along the ground, little by little, with his left hand. In his right hand he carries a bow and a few arrows. He lowers and raises his head so as to imitate the motions of the deer. The herd catches sight of him. The deer perk up their ears and strain their necks to get a better view. Suddenly, they toss their heads, and with wide-eyed terror they bound away. The hunter, too, tosses his head and bounds after them. They stop and he stops. They run and he runs. The hunter seems almost to be dancing with the herd. Gradually the deer feel soothed and—if the hunter has properly prepared himself—the herd accepts him. They push their noses into the cool, green grass and the hunter easily moves in among them. When it comes time to release his arrow the hunter is often so close that (according to one description) he can nudge the deer into a better position with his bow. He shoots, and the arrow hits silently. A deer collapses. The others look about confused. Another arrow is released, a second deer falls, and the herd now bolts wildly up the hill.

What is the hunter thinking about as he moves closer to the herd of deer? There is an intriguing suggestion by J. Alden Mason, an anthropologist who studied the Salinans, just to the south of the Ohlones. Writes Mason: "The hunter always chewed tobacco assiduously while approaching the game, as this tended to make it drunk and less wary."

Chewing the strong native tobacco undoubtedly affected the hunter's mind; but why, by altering his own consciousness, should the hunter think he was making the deer "drunk and less wary"? To understand this—to understand the subtle ways in which the hunter felt that his mind was linked to the mind of a prey whose nature and intelligence were not very different from his own—is to glimpse some of the drama and spiritual complexity of deer hunting as it was practiced by the Indians of California.

The Ohlone Way, Heyday, 1978

COMING HOME: REVITALIZING NATIVE CALIFORNIA CULTURE IN THE EAST BAY (2018)

This piece originally appeared in *Flora Magazine*. These are the editor's notes. *We are pleased and honored to share a conversation with two native Californians, Vincent Medina and Louis Trevino. These dynamic partners are leading an effort to bring the foods, languages, and practices of their Ohlone ancestors back to their families and community. Their vision is a modern one—a vibrant blend of traditional and urban culture. And not surprisingly, native plants are part of this important story. This month* [October 2018]*, they open the new Cafe Ohlone in Berkeley, featuring modern interpretations of Native California foods.*

We're grateful to Malcolm Margolin, one of the Bay Area's most influential authors and publishers, who interviewed his friends Vincent and Louis for this issue of Flora. *Malcolm founded Heyday Books and co-created two uniquely Californian publications,* News from Native California *and* Bay Nature Magazine. *More recently he has launched the California Institute for Community, Art, and Nature (California I CAN) to continue and expand upon his work.*

Malcolm: My name is Malcolm Margolin, and I'm speaking with Louis Trevino and Vincent Medina. I'm a member of the hippie tribe of Berkeley. I came in a VW bus in 1967, and I'm the real thing.

Vincent: [Laughing] Legit.

Malcolm: Very legit. So, who are you guys?

Vincent: My name is Vincent Medina. I'm a member of the Muwekma Tribe and represent my lineage on the tribal council. I come from an old family that's been living in the East Bay since the start and never left, never will. It makes us proud to know that we wake up and live every day in a place that every generation of our family has always been. It's a good feeling.

Louis: My name is Louis Trevino. I'm Rumsen Ohlone from the Carmel Valley and Monterey area. I live in San Lorenzo with Vince, my partner, and together we work on the revitalization of our languages, our foods, our songs, our arts—all of the things that make us people. We're bringing these things to our family. It's a collective, multigenerational effort, and we're grateful for the ability to live this way.

Malcolm: How did you grow up?

Vincent: I was born and grew up in the East Bay, in San Leandro and San Lorenzo, the Halkin area (sometimes spelled as Jalquin), where my family has always been. There are central, sacred waterways in our family's area: San Leandro Creek, which connects the tribal areas of Saklan and Halkin, and San Lorenzo Creek, which connects Halkin and Yrgin villages. They all drain into the bay. My mom's water broke right along San Lorenzo Creek, but in a Lucky's, a supermarket where she was grocery shopping next to this significant waterway.

When I was growing up, the Muwekma Tribe sponsored cultural programs that preserved and revived a lot of our traditional identity; that work was guided by an older generation of my family.

I'm grateful I grew up seeing and being around many of our elders, especially my great-grandmother Mary Archuleta. It fills me with pride to know the strength that we come from. These elders were central figures for our community; they had a solid identity and nothing to prove to anyone. As a young person I was raised to be proud of my identity, and I knew it was a special thing to be Ohlone. I saw how rooted my family is, and I grew up knowing we've been here in the East Bay since the start.

Malcolm: Can you talk about the cultural loss?

Vincent: Right now, it's hard to talk about cultural loss, because it feels like there is so much abundance. And while that's such a beautiful thing, abundance wasn't always our reality for the last century. I never grew up hearing my language as a kid, eating my traditional foods, knowing those old stories beyond maybe one from my grandfather. Those things were connected to the suppression of our culture by colonization, by people coming in and taking things that weren't theirs. But whenever my family could continue [our way of life], they did. They found ways. When I was growing up, I would always see the strength of those older people, just how proud and undefeated they were. They stood with their heads high, and that was passed down to me, and I know to Louis too.

Malcolm: When I first started meeting your people back in the early seventies, I was saddened by how much of the old ways had been lost. But when I looked deeper, I was impressed by how much had been retained: a sense of family, of relationship with the land and other living beings, attitudes, values, an understanding of life. While the visible structures had been destroyed, the foundation was amazingly intact, and it's provided a solid basis for cultural revival.

Vincent: Thank you. And I think so too, because what we're doing would be impossible unless we had people to learn it from.

Malcolm: Do you want to talk about Alisal?

Vincent: Mission San Jose was secularized in 1834. While the Mexican government freed the Indians from slavery, the people had nowhere to go. The places where they had lived for thousands of years were now part of big land grants and ranchos, controlled by white folks who didn't want Indians on what they thought was their land. A Californio [Spanish Californian], I believe it was Bernal, allowed my family and other Indians to continue to live on the rancho he managed in Sunol, which was stolen from Ohlone people in the first place. However, that place was called Alisal [sycamore grove], and there things began to flourish once again. A roundhouse was constructed, and powerful ceremonial dances returned. The structure of a male political leader and a female spiritual leader was resumed.

With the missions behind our people, life became vibrant and culture thrived. Although Alisal held together through the 1920s, the U.S. government took away our federal recognition, and people started slowing leaving the rancheria. My great-grandmother moved from the rancheria around our East Bay homeland to Niles, to West Oakland, and then to Halkin, our family's old tribal area along the San Leandro and San Lorenzo Creeks before the mission era, and we've been there ever since.

Malcolm: How about you, Louis?

Louis: Well, I grew up in Los Angeles, away from our Rumsen homeland. That history is tied to our displacement as a people. While some Rumsen families were able to stay in the Monterey area, my family wasn't. In the 1830s, they moved northward to Mission Santa Cruz and then to Mission San Jose, where we lived at Alisal. In the 1860s, we moved southward to Mission San Gabriel [in East Los Angeles.] My impression is that my family was always looking for someplace safe where they could live, be together, and find work.

Gloria Castro, my great-grandfather's cousin, remembers those old people who made that trek to Los Angeles. Gloria is of the generation that got to hear our language, got to know those people. She remembers her mother keeping her hair, disposing of it later in private, and burying her food. And she remembers how, when older relatives would come, the adults would go off and tell stories. They would cook together in earth ovens and pits. They would go into a house and close all the doors and stop up all the gaps. The kids weren't allowed to hear what was going on. It was probably that they were sharing old things they didn't want the kids to know, she says.

Those are the people that we come from in my family. People who had all these memories. I think there are a lot of different kinds of remembering: some of these things are sensory, some are emotional, some are spiritual. Some things are intellectual facts about our homeland, the geography, ways of being in that place. I think what we're doing by talking to our older family and by learning from the documentation is making those memories into living things again.

Vincent: That's such a beautiful and articulate way to express that. We have these elders in our families, Gloria and my Aunt Dottie, who are just about the same age. They can remember these powerful, traditional ways. But outsiders imposed shame on our communities for no reason. It can sometimes feel isolating when you're the only person walking down the street wearing abalone or clam shells, or you're the only person gathering your food, but we still see the value of these ways. People have tried to make us feel bad for doing these things. They gave us derogatory names and insulted us. Whites called California Indians "diggers" for digging our bulbs and roots up, these things that shouldn't be insulted. I feel when we do these things again and keep traditional ways alive, we bring pride to them, to our families. It's something I feel grateful for.

Malcolm: So, what kinds of foods did you eat as kids? Greens collected from the fields, or "real" food like Twinkies?

Louis: Twinkies [laughing]. The occasional Twinkies. A lot of the foods in my family are Mexican foods—foods that our family acquired from people who married into our families. My great-grand-parents had a restaurant that was all Mexican foods that were my great-grandmother's recipes.

Vincent: For me it's similar. One of the things I've noticed is how our family has adopted things from the outside and made them our own. It makes me feel comfortable to know that there were things that were embraced, like coffee. We have stories in our docu-mentation about how much people like coffee, and we created a word in our language for coffee—"sii-sirkewiš," literally "black water."

Do you remember, Malcolm, years ago when you had Native people come together in the Heyday conference room to imagine what a Bay Area would look like with a stronger Native influence? A lot of people were talking about a very traditional, all pre-contact world, nothing of foreign influences or from the outside. I like that thought. But I imagined the Bay Area as it is but with a very heavy dose of everything that's Ohlone. So you'd hear, walking down these busy streets, people talking Chochenyo everywhere, and you'd see roundhouses in the hills instead of churches, you'd see freeway signs and BART stations with Chochenyo place names, and tule boats in the bay. Ohlone architecture and basketry aesthetics everywhere, and acorn soup in coffee shops. But it would still have that busy urbanity that is the East Bay I grew up in.

What would the Bay Area look like if our culture had been allowed to adopt things on our own terms without having them imposed on us? I like to think that what we're doing is what that would look like in the twenty-first century, like having hashtags in Chochenyo, having our food be slightly modern. Those are things that we do intentionally as well.

Malcolm: That's wonderful and utterly refreshing! Some people might insist that, to honor tradition, you should use only the plants that were here before contact. But adapting to different environments, borrowing from others, and creatively embracing change is not only a basic Indian tradition but, I think, is a fundamental necessity for any culture that wants to survive. Take language, for example. Vincent, you now speak Chochenyo, the language of the East Bay, fluently. But the language that was spoken in pre-contact times is not well suited for the modern world. You've had to create words for coffee, automobiles, the telephone, etc. I'm seeing some of the same issues with food. To use only traditional foods and cook them entirely by traditional methods seems like an academic exercise, something done in a museum as part of a cultural demonstration rather than in the kitchen as part of everyday life. The question with food is how to make it vital, how to make foods that are delicious, contemporary, and fun.

Vincent: One of the really beautiful things about this revival is seeing how connected the food is to every other aspect of our culture. My cousin Tina called me not too long ago. Louis and I were in the car, she was on speaker phone, and she said, "Suyya, suyya," which means "relative" in Chochenyo. "I need to come by your house and pick up acorn flour really fast. I'm in a hurry." There was something about that that was so cool. Language being used effortlessly and naturally. Also, somebody in our family craving acorn flour as a commonplace ingredient again and wanting to swing by casually to get it. When Louis and I do this work, it's exciting to see how quickly these things can change and come back to us. It's holistic, and it touches on a lot of big things at once.

One of the things that Louis and I see is how deeply connected each of these foods is to the cycle of the land that we come from. When we're gathering in the Oakland Hills in January or February looking for chanterelle mushrooms, we're there at a specific time when those mushrooms are available to us. We know what that area is called, the cultural connection that comes from those old village sites. We can't just get these things when we want them. It teaches us moderation, and patience.

Louis: There's a redwood grove in Carmel Valley, we call it "summentak" (redwood place), that is carpeted with yerba buena. The air is sweet with mint in that place. We think about these foods and all the practices that went into their being: those burnings, the cleaning away of brush, the prayers that were given for those seeds and foods. What we experience today is the result of all those things. So when we find chia in the hills, we know that was a seed that was prayed for, and we get to enjoy it today and be grateful for what those people did before so that those seeds could still be there.

Vincent: If we're walking by an area where yerba buena or some other valuable plant might be growing, we'll stop and gather, even if we're on our way elsewhere. If the plant is growing there, its purpose is for us to be gathering it to make it into medicine or tea. If we don't, one of the things we think about is that the plant must get lonely. Our way to show love is to go and gather it, giving it gratitude, and letting it serve its purpose. When we do those things, it's much more than simply gathering. A relationship is formed where you're interacting with your place; you're interacting with your home.

There is a responsibility not to over-gather. Do we want people outside of our community gathering in our villages? No, we don't. That's just the reality that's there too. While we're doing these things, there's a different relationship that's there than with people who might not have that same relationship and might not be as respectful.

Malcolm: Do you feel as Native people you have a right to these plants that other people might not have?

Vincent and Louis: Yes, in our places.

Malcolm: I agree. I would defend that right. I think part of the conquest was taking that right away from you guys, and I think it should be returned. It's a kind of sovereignty.

Vincent: That's what we're seeing come back. We're thinking big. Maybe one day we'll see controlled burns come back. Maybe one day we'll see these old native flowers come back. Maybe one day the eucalyptus will be here less. We want to be a part of that conversation and part of that dialog. As the first people of this place, we have connections and rootedness here in the East Bay that no one else does.

Louis: I think there's an idea people have that plants exist independently of people, and that parks or other conservancies have to protect plants from people, that people are just a harm, even Indian people. But those plants and us are an ecosystem. We exist because they exist, and they exist because of us. In our creation story, we're taught about all of the foods and how to get them in ways that encourage those plants to grow. By digging with a digging stick you aerate the soil, when you harvest certain roots or bulbs at the right time. When certain flowers are extracted for their seeds, some seeds are ejected from the flower and land in that loose soil and are able to take root.

Vincent: Because so much of what we have is seasonal, the menu is always changing. For example, we'll collect traditional greens for salad, like watercress and sorrel, and purslane in honor of my grandmother, and we'll dress that with elderberry and walnut oil and native gooseberry and native blackberries when possible, toasted hazelnuts and walnuts and popped amaranth seeds.

Malcolm: I'm drooling.

Vincent: Sometimes we'll have a side of sautéed fiddlehead ferns that are crunchy and sweet and tasty. We'll have that with some sea salt that we've gathered from San Francisco Bay, quail eggs, walnut oil, smoked venison wrapped in yerba buena and bay laurel, smoked for several hours until it becomes almost like a jerky, and dipped in blackberry and elderberry sauce, sweetened with honey, bay laurel, yerba buena, elderflowers . . . all really tasty things.

We want people to understand that these are foods to be enjoyed, but also that these foods have a deep history. We want people to understand our identity better, the ways that our identity has adapted and has always been able to survive.

What we're trying to do through this food is having it connected to every other aspect of our culture. We want to have it be a regular thing, not be something that is tokenized or a novelty. Acorn will be something that the next generation will grow up with, and it will be alongside our language and our stories.

Malcolm: I would love to continue this discussion, maybe at a future meeting of the California Native Plant Society, about the responsibility of recent arrivals in California toward Indians— toward their rights to gather native foods, medicines, material for basketry and dance regalia, whether everybody can gather or only a few. These are touchy, controversial questions, and I'd love to see them addressed—not necessarily for right or wrong but for increasing our awareness.

Vincent: What we're asking for is to be listened to. As the first people of this place, I feel that's the respect we should have. That's why we're sharing our story, telling about who we are, having people understand that the things we're asking for make sense.

Malcolm: I think that one of the worst things that has happened is the attempt to erase you guys. I think that if people want to preserve native plants, they have to preserve native people.

Vincent: That's right. We're an endangered species too. [Laughing] But we aren't going anywhere.

A few examples of contemporary Chochenyo words:

- sii-sirkewiš—coffee, lit. "black water"
- sii-sirkewištak—café, lit. "the place of the black water"
- 'irrite kool—super cool, using Chochenyo words for "very/super" and our orthography
- nonwentetak—phone, lit. "talking place"
- i-nonwentetak—iPhone

Flora Magazine, published by the California Native Plant Society, cnps.org/flora-magazine/coming-home-12801, October 8, 2018

CULTURAL REVIVAL SALONS AT HEYDAY BOOKS (2008)

When I launched *News from Native California* in the early spring of 1987 with co-editors David Peri (Coast Miwok) and Vera Mae Fredrickson, a large part of what we had in mind was to record the wisdom, knowledge, and fullness of being of what we (along with many others) perceived as cultures that were assimilating with appalling rapidity into the modern world. A generation of people, some born in the late nineteenth century—people who grew up speaking Native languages and practicing traditional ways, who in many cases were reared or instructed by grandparents who remembered California before the gold rush—were now reaching old age and passing away. It was common then to meet elders who hadn't learned English until they were five years old and who conveyed a sense of the old Indian world not just in their knowledge but in their laughter, their manners, in the earthy grace and elegance of their bearing. It was a generation that was passing, and it seemed as if their accumulated knowledge of dance, basketry, food processing, religious practice, language, story, and the beautiful complexity of the old ways was destined to be lost. Languages were not being passed onto a younger generation; dances and ceremonies were withering except in a handful of resistant areas; a rich heritage of cultural knowledge seemed to be evaporating before our very eyes. Those of us who had the privilege of having met culture bearers such as Mabel McKay, Essie Parrish, Rudolph Socktish, Flora Jones, Nelson Hopper, the Beecher sisters, and Laura Somersal felt that we had come in contact with truly remarkable people. When they passed, we knew we would never see their like again, and the world would be impoverished by their absence. We wanted to document what we could of the richness of that older world, so that once these cherished elders were gone, at least a record or memory of them would survive.

The sense of loss that we felt was shared by many within the Indian community. But whereas we were setting out to do what writers, scholars, and publishers could do—interview, write, and record— there were members of the Indian community who were then setting out to do something far more remarkable. They took it upon themselves to learn the fading languages, sing the songs, continue the dances and the ceremonies, weave stories and baskets, restore and revitalize, breathing new life into cultural activities that seemed on the verge of extinction or even then seemed to be lost forever. The result has been a statewide movement of enormous beauty, vitality, and significance—a full-fledged and widespread cultural renaissance.

Whereas it once seemed that basketweaving was dying, today there are hundreds of weavers, many young, who are practicing this intricate, highly evolved art. Ceremonies, some dormant for decades, have been everywhere revived. At one time the Southern California bird songs lived only as fragmented memories in the minds of a few elders; today they are part of the fabric of Southern California life, and bird song festivals attract an enthusiastic following of performing groups with audiences that number into the many hundreds.

Languages down to their last handful of speakers, and indeed some totally extinct, are once again being spoken, sung, used in prayer and in everyday life. Skills such as regalia making, Southern Californian pottery, food preparation, flute music, hand game and peon, religious practice, and more have all seen a flowering of interest and participation.

As publisher of Heyday Books and *News from Native California*, it has been my ongoing privilege and joy to be witness to this revival of California Indian culture. In more than thirty years of publishing poetry, literature, and art—in all these years of presiding over the river of beauty that moves through Heyday Books—I haven't witnessed anything that has touched me more deeply. It seems on the surface to be miraculous, and I thought it would be helpful to everyone if instead of just looking at it with open-mouthed amazement and admiration, we could examine more consciously what is taking place and perhaps make some observations as to what makes a good revival effort work. I hoped that by doing so we would not only celebrate this wonderful flowering but perhaps we could also provide some useful guidance to those who are engaged in the various cultural revival efforts. I guess what I originally had in mind was something like the Harvard Business School model of "case study." Just as business school students examine successful businesses to better learn how they work, I thought it would be worthwhile to examine successful revitalization efforts. To that end, *News from Native California* obtained a generous grant from the Walter and Elise Haas Fund to sponsor a series of talks by five active participants in the cultural revival movement. These talks were held in our Berkeley office between February and June of 2007. On the morning after each public event, the speaker would return to our offices for a private interview that would explore the various issues in greater depth.

QUIRINA LUNA

On February 15, 2007, Quirina Luna spoke about the revival of the Mutsun Ohlone language. Quirina is the founder and president of the Mutsun Language Foundation, an organization dedicated to preserving the Mutsun Ohlone culture and reviving the language for generations to come.

Growing up, Quirina struggled with language as an identity marker. The kids at school, knowing her mother was Mexican Indian, would ask, "You don't speak Spanish, so what are you?," to which she would reply, "I'm California Indian," because her father was Mutsun. Her classmates would bark back, "Then speak your language," but Quirina didn't know it. She knew that she was Mutsun Ohlone, but she thought that the language had been lost.

Later in life she found a book by a Spanish missionary that listed hundreds of Mutsun phrases, giving her the fuel she needed to go in search of more information on the Mutsun language. The last fluent speaker had died in 1930, but with the help of UC Berkeley and anthropological records, she was able to start piecing together her language. She gathered a small group interested in learning Mutsun, and together they compiled a dictionary with the help of a linguistics professor at UC Berkeley. Quirina even translated Dr. Seuss's *Green Eggs and Ham* as a way to get the younger generation interested in learning the language.

"There is something about language that really gives you an identity, who you are and where you come from."

ROBERTA CORDERO

On March 15, 2007, Roberta Cordero spoke about indigenous maritime culture revitalization. Growing up in Santa Barbara in the forties and fifties, Roberta was told of her Chumash ancestry, but as it was to most Chumash people at that time, the existence of Chumash culture seemed vague and very much relegated to the past. After moving to and living in Seattle for many years through university, marriage, and raising five children, Roberta got to know many of the Northwest indigenous nations, as well as Hawaiians, who were undergoing a great revitalization of their canoe cultures. In 1993, while attending a huge gathering of the canoes in Bella Bella, British Columbia, the people there encouraged and instructed her. "Why don't you have a canoe?" they asked. "You're a canoe people—tell your people to get busy." They gave her an eagle feather and said, "You go home and build a canoe."

Roberta returned home to Santa Barbara and in 1997, with a small group of local Chumash people, including her daughter, Julie Cordero-Lamb, she participated in building the traditional Chumash canoe *'Elye'wun* (swordfish). Shortly afterward, this small group formed the Chumash Maritime Association (CMA), a nonprofit group seeking to revitalize indigenous maritime heritage. Beginning in 2001, the association has sponsored or co-sponsored five crossings of the Santa Barbara Channel, each culminating in an encampment of about two hundred members of the Chumash community and supporters. The most recent crossing was in September 2007, from Ventura to Limuw (Santa Cruz Island). Now, Cordero says, a second generation of paddlers is seeking to learn the culture of the tomol. "It's a huge success to have children who grow up with the canoe as an ordinary part of their lives."

ERNEST SIVA

Ernest Siva spoke on April 12, 2007, about cultural revival in terms of music. Ernie received his bachelor's degree in music education and his master's in choral music at the University of Southern California. He has worked with tribal elders and singers from throughout Southern California, recording and learning traditional music.

In 2003, Ernie founded the Dorothy Ramon Learning Center, Inc. (and its publishing arm, Ushkana Press), a nonprofit 501(c)(3) public-benefit corporation. The Learning Center, serving Indians and non-Indians alike, saves and shares Southern California's American Indian cultures, languages, history, music, and other traditional arts. Dorothy Ramon, Ernie's aunt, was an elder knowledgeable in traditional ways and was recognized as the last pure speaker of the Serrano language. In the final years before her passing in 2002 she worked tirelessly with a linguist and helped save the region's own Serrano language and much cultural knowledge.

FRANK LAPENA

On May 10, 2007, Frank LaPena spoke about the Maidu Dancers and Traditionalists, the group he helped start in the early 1970s that is dedicated to the revival and preservation of Native arts. Frank explained that when you watch children at play there is a natural sense of movement that you will see—a natural sense of being alive. Children cannot resist movement, and this is one of the most important aspects to understanding dance—the presence of music everywhere and the ability (and necessity) to move to it.

Frank has worked with the elders of the Nomtipom Wintu, the Nomlaki Wintun of Northern California, and elders of neighboring tribes studying dance. He lectures widely on American Indian traditional and cultural issues, emphasizing California traditions, and he is a professor emeritus at California State University, Sacramento. His art has been exhibited since 1960 in twenty-two one-man and numerous group shows across the United States, Europe, Central and South America, Cuba, Australia, and New Zealand.

He says, "If you think it, if you do it, you give it reality, and if it's reality, it exists."

JULIA PARKER

Julia Parker hopped off the train from Yosemite Valley on June 7, 2007, with two bags filled with willow, sedge, basket starts, and a couple of beautiful baskets. We drove to the office, where she carefully laid out her materials and spoke about basketry as a form of cultural revival, using stories from her life. Most of her stories made the audience laugh, some made them cry, but all of her stories touched upon basketry as a way to preserve and enhance Indian culture.

Julia Parker is Kashaya Pomo and Coast Miwok, but she moved to Yosemite Valley as a young woman, and that is where she first learned how to make baskets. She learned from Lucy Telles, Mabel McKay, and Elsie Allen, some of the great basketweavers of the twentieth century. Because she learned many different styles of weaving, she has an interesting perspective on cultural revival—one that doesn't focus on one particular tribe but on basketweaving as a culture.

"When I look at the CIBA [California Indian Basketweavers Association] gathering and all the women coming together—that's what I dreamed of—all people coming together," she says. "Not just Pomo, not just Miwok, but also everybody together, because we do have something in common. We all use willows. We all take from the earth. We're still tied together by the roots and the plants because we use them in almost the same way."

❖ ❖ ❖

As might be imagined, there was tremendous variation in what each of these participants told us. Some, like Quirina Luna and Roberta Cordero, were working with material lost to current memory and preserved largely in archives, museums, and scholarly publications. Others had living practitioners from whom they learned. Just as there is no such thing as California Indian culture—each community differs significantly from its neighbors, and the variety from one end of the state to the other is enormous—it seems that there is no easily replicable model for what works and what doesn't.

There was nevertheless a wealth of observation, always the result of deeply felt and deeply lived experience, and in the end perhaps a couple of universal truths emerged that might be helpful.

FAMILY

Not surprisingly, family seems to play an important role in cultural revival. For some, family was the source of their knowledge. Ernie Siva, for one, talked of what he learned from his mother, his Aunt Dorothy, and other relatives when he was growing up. More commonly, however, a strong and passionate impetus to cultural revival seems to be the desire to work with one's children. Two of Frank LaPena's children, Craig and Sage, have long been active in dance; Julia Parker has passed the art of basketry to her daughter Lucy, her granddaughter Ursula, and even her great-granddaughter Naomi Jones. In reviving Chumash boat building, Roberta Cordero had the joy of working in partnership with her daughter Julie. "Learning a language," says Quirina Luna, "starts with my family and teaching my children." Many celebrated the fact that what for them was an awkward and self-conscious relearning was for their children something more natural, something they had grown up with rather than come to as adults. When speaking her language, Quirina Luna has to consciously think, "Okay, I have to put the adjective here." For her children, she hopes this will be a more natural and ingrained process.

COMMUNITY

One might expect that when someone begins to revitalize culture, the community would respond with applause and offers of help. While approval and support were not entirely absent, they were often in short supply, and some of those we talked to reported having to confront significant community criticism: accusations that they were on a power trip, they were in it for money, they weren't following rules or doing things the right way. Often the criticism was personal and at times even vicious.

More, in traditions where continuity had been broken, the knowledge of how to put on complex ceremonies has to be rediscovered. In the old days there was a division of labor within the community; each family had a responsibility. Some would make food, some would erect a dance house or arbor, some would fix the regalia, etc. When a ceremony is revived, that knowledge is hard to come by and even harder to implement, and often the work falls on the shoulders of one person. It takes one or two or even more repetitions before things once again fall into place.

How does one meet criticism from one's own community? Ernie Siva has this advice: "Ask what did your people do. What did the leaders and people sing about or dance about that you admire? What did they look up to? They all had beliefs. Speak true to yourself, and if you believe, then that's your guide to carry on in today's world, to survive and to prosper and to get stronger." Julia Parker likewise found herself looking inward to deal with criticism: "I had the best of teachers, and they gave to me their best. So I know in my heart that I'm doing something that is okay." Frank LaPena reminds us that the involvement of the entire community is not necessary: "Not everybody and not a whole lot will be able to preserve the tradition, because it doesn't take a whole lot of people; what it takes is a group of people sacrificing a whole lot of time to do something, whatever that is." For Quirina Luna, her advice in dealing with community criticism is "to have patience. Because, you know, we're all learning." And for Chumash canoe-building and paddling, says Roberta Cordero, it is simply not possible without community members working together, learning harmony as they go.

MONEY AND ORGANIZATIONAL STRUCTURE

There was a mixed response to the questions of whether outside funding was needed and how desirable was the forming of a nonprofit institute to carry on cultural revival. Quirina Luna's group did form a 501(c)(3) nonprofit to promote the revival of Mutsun language and culture, but for her the benefits were mixed: On one hand, the nonprofit institutional status enabled them to get grants, and it increased their visibility. On the other hand, she felt that the work that went into applying for grants, writing reports, and administering an organization took time and energy away from language learning itself. "The couple of grants that we got . . . the things we did with them we probably could have done without them. To really learn the language, it has to come from your heart, and you have to want to do it. If you want it badly enough, you'll find a way no matter what."

Roberta Cordero and the other co-founders of CMA had a somewhat different take on their reasons for forming a nonprofit, and they felt that it gave more than it took: "One reason is that it's not connected to a particular family; it's not a tribal entity, and we can keep it as inclusive as possible."

Ernie Siva, in the launching of the Dorothy Ramon Learning Center in Banning, is doing something at a scale that needs a responsible fiscal body to raise money, handle the financing, and accept tax-deductible contributions. Ernie, in fact, is comfortable with this corporate form of enterprise, quoting elder Francisco Morongo as saying that to be successful you have to learn to do new things. Frank LaPena, on the other hand, reported, "At one time we thought about doing a 501 kind of thing. And we looked at it and thought, 'To hell with it, we don't want to go through all this crap.' So we just threw it aside."

WHAT HAS BEEN LOST

One of the striking things about the series of interviews was the extent to which various people had confronted the painful truth of how much has been lost, had looked unflinchingly at the magnitude of the damage done to traditional culture. One might imagine that this acknowledgment of loss would be debilitating, but that seems not to be the case. Perhaps at work here is a psychological principle understood by twelve-step programs: that to rebuild the self one first must come to terms with and acknowledge the fullness of loss. Otherwise, what you are doing is building on a foundation of delusion.

Roberta Cordero was especially eloquent and passionate about what she calls "historic trauma": "I just saw how much had been lost in my own family, just in terms of knowing about ceremony, just seeing how that happened . . . . What I remember as a kid growing up is that I would have these bouts of what I call melancholy—I know that's an old-fashioned word, but it works for me—and this led me to look deeper . . . . Let me just say, for an overall picture, that the thrust in studying and understanding historic trauma is a thrust toward healing. It is understanding that people need to, first of all, have a lot of knowledge about what happened to their ancestors, about what that means to them today. They need to understand the oppression that they continue to suffer—that it is institutionalized, both overt and covert, personalized . . . . And also to understand that when people have not had a chance to grieve, that has physiological implications. You can become depressed, and depression can lead to high blood pressure and other diseases. Just the absence of joy is a huge deficit on health . . . . I was so in touch with the extreme rage that many men in my father's family were experiencing because they were not able to support their families in the way that they once did; not being able to go to the land to hunt, not being able to fish—all because of lack of access. It was then that I understood completely the way that people self-medicated with alcohol. That was to me the key, for the men—intense rage and helplessness . . . . I think the whole thing with historic trauma is just that: facing the loss, understanding it, knowing that you were victimized, knowing that you have iden-tified as a victim, moving out of that to some kind of healing, and really transcending that whole idea so that you're no longer identify-ing yourself by the trauma."

RESEARCH AND TRANSMISSION OF KNOWLEDGE

Clearly, the traditional and preferred way of learning is directly from a knowledgeable elder. Ernie Siva absorbed Serrano and Cahuilla songs, stories, and a complex of beliefs from his family and from oth-ers in the community. Julia Parker studied with her mother-in-law, Lucy Telles, and learned from master weavers such as Mabel McKay and Elsie Allen. Frank LaPena gained much of his knowledge from the teachings of Frank Day, Wallace Burroughs, Al Thomas, and others. But sometimes elders aren't available. Quirina Luna told of a friend of hers whose native language was down to one speaker. The friend was really down about it. "What I would give to have one speaker," said Quirina. "It would mean the world to us." Without a speaker, her language revitalization efforts have depended on archives and documents created by scholars and held in university libraries. But she has been able to draw out of them tremendous riches. "The only thing is to deal with what we have, and work with what we have. In my case, we have a lot to work with. I could probably work for the rest of my life on the materials we have."

Julia Parker, while learning directly from an older generation of master weavers, draws instruction and inspiration from museum collections: "I looked around in museums and saw different styles of baskets, so then I began to think maybe we should bring back some of this old basketry that was done a long time ago but is not being shown. We need to know the utility baskets, like berry baskets . . . . That's what we're missing. All the exhibits that I see always have these beautiful, fancy trade baskets . . . . What about the old, old baskets that were used every day? They were made very quickly, like the big, coarse woven willow baskets for acorns. Yet they still made them beautiful."

Roberta Cordero found that through scholarly archives she was able to sense the presence of ancestors. "When we look at [linguist J. P.] Harrington's notes . . . sometimes he's not looking for the use of the plants; he's interested in naming them. But once in a while, there is a comment from his informants about what they were used for . . . . When looking at *December's Child* [a 1975 collection of Chumash stories collected by Harrington and edited by Thomas Blackburn], where all these wonderful stories are recorded, . . . you have this feeling that the ancestors are talking to us. And they're using the ethnographers as a conduit. I see that happening a lot. When you go see artifacts in the museums, when you have a chance to talk to them and look at them, there is that sense that they are imbued with the spirit from the people that made them. So conversations happen because of that. It's also part of the recreating of material culture."

CORRECTNESS

In traditional times there were strict rules and a demand for correctness that sometimes are impossible to follow today. Ernie Siva recalls going to some of the older singers: "I would ask them about a certain part of a song, because I wasn't sure how it went . . . . They could never—or would never (I don't know that they couldn't)—sing that isolated part, that verse, or whatever specific section I was looking for. They had to sing the whole thing, and they wouldn't stop until it was over. You had better get it the first or second time through. So it just tells us that people were trained in that culture: to listen, to learn, to be very keen in the hearing and discerning, which we can do, we just need to practice, we need to be honed, to be in that mode if we're going to do it in the old way, the traditional way." But things change with time, as Ernie acknowledges. "Singing all night is a custom, but we don't do it anymore. Sometimes we make a point to sing all night, but many times we have a curfew in the building where we are because they have to clean it up and close the building."

Doing things correctly was a major concern of everyone, and at times a hindrance that had to be overcome, especially at the beginning of a cultural revival project. When asked about obstacles, Quirina Luna replied: "In the beginning it was not knowing if you're saying these words correctly—if you're reading it the way it should be read, or the way the linguist who wrote it down intended it. And you know, sometimes I would just do the best that I could. It was something that I wanted so badly, I was just going to do it, even if I was doing it badly."

Roberta Cordero reported similar feelings. "When I first learned about these old songs, I was very nervous about using them the wrong way . . . . Ceremonies were very important to me. We were singing these songs; we didn't know what the words meant; we didn't know what we were singing. We kind of had a general feeling. And I had this sense of the ancestors standing around saying, 'Listen, they're singing that song again! Isn't it great? They're so cute; they're singing it all wrong, they don't even know what they're talking about. But it's so wonderful.' In that way, you do have to be careful about how you use the songs and ceremonies. But there's also that element of intent that is so important in connecting back."

When asked about the issue of correctness and about how "doing it right" sometimes becomes an impediment, Frank LaPena offered this observation: "There's all kinds of talk about how we're going to do this and do that, but nobody does it. I've talked to some of the people on some of the reservations. 'Well, you know, we want to do language, but everybody talks and they're not doing it.' And I said, 'That's because we've set up this barrier that everybody has to be pure. Everybody has to know it all. But we don't. But with all ten of us around the table, if we each put our two bits' worth in, look how much more we would know.'"

SENSE OF PLACE

When asked what advice she would give to someone from any culture who wanted to learn his or her native language, Quirina Luna said without hesitation, "Go to the area in which it was spoken."

Roberta Cordero felt likewise. "There's a realization that I had that I think is very important, and it springs out of the idea that spirituality or religion is shaped by the place where you are. If that's true and we've missed the old ways being passed on directly to us, if the habitat is sufficiently intact, you can go back and learn that again because it's the land and all its inhabitants that talked to the people in the first place. The land and the animals are our ancestors as much as human ancestors are."

PASSION

Passion, needless to say, not technique or structure or anything else, seems to be the fuel that keeps cultural revival rich. Every person we talked with was deeply and emotionally connected to what they do, and throughout the cultural revival series tears flowed frequently, from participants and audience members alike.

Frank LaPena expresses his commitment this way: "Can you imagine anyone who is a creative person and an artist, or writer or thinker or painter, doing something they don't have a vested interest in and excitement about? They're not going to do it. They're going to do something that has meaning for them. They're going to do something that elevates them. They're going to do something that is important, and what is important? Well, in my case it's ceremony and song."

Julia Parker, for her part, exudes love for basketry and for the generations of artists that preceded and will follow her. "I always wanted to do the best I can . . . . The [old-time weavers] left a story in their baskets—so beautiful—and it's a whole world of high technology. They could put a straight line in a circle. They could weave these designs, which the person who looks at the basket doesn't realize what they're looking at. The technology of these ladies sitting flat on the ground and working these beautiful baskets, and the strength that you might say they had . . . . The drive is in me to do the best I can and maybe do things that no other people are trying to do. But then when I look at those women, it just makes tears come in my eyes to see how they just did all this."

These five presentations and interviews were more than informative and helpful in examining successful cultural revival efforts—they touched hearts and inspired listeners. Each presenter brought unique perspectives on individual cases, but they were brought together by not only their success and drive to revive but their kindness, humble attitudes, and genuinely sincere personalities. After five interviews in five months, we were five for five—not once had we left the room with dry eyes, and it is with that emotion and passion that these people have so gracefully succeeded in leading the way in cultural revival.

News from Native California, vol. 21, no. 3, 2008

THE RETURN OF THE HUNDRED-AND-ELEVENS TO NORTHWEST CALIFORNIA (1990)

On April 1, 1990, following instructions that Peter Nix had given me over the phone, I drove north alongside the Trinity River through Hoopa Valley, then turned east, following the Klamath River until I came to a sign for the Aikens Creek Campground. There was a flat, open area (Woxti) here, upon which Otsepor, the easternmost Yurok village along the Klamath River, once stood.

I was early, so I walked from the picnic area to the riverbank. The Klamath was icy and swollen from the snowmelt, the country-side through which it flowed just awakening to spring. Splashes of showy white dogwood flowers lined the roadsides; clusters of wild iris glowed softly in the woods; overhead the oaks, until recently bare-limbed, were putting forth showers of fresh green leaves and cascades of tiny pale oak flowers.

Before long a huge, white, slightly battered old Cadillac floated into the campground like an ocean liner. Bertha Peters Mitchell got out of the car, flipped open its cavernous trunk, and began to unload picnic supplies. Beverly Nix Walsh, the other guest of honor, pulled in shortly afterward. Dozens of additional guests arrived with salads, salmon, eel, breads, acorn, bean stew, pie, cake, and more.

Soon a fire was blazing, elders were seated comfortably in aluminum folding chairs, people were chatting, and kids were running about. It was, it seemed, nothing more than an ordinary gathering of family and friends—a happy, casual Sunday afternoon picnic. There were no speeches, no songs, no ceremonies. Yet it was very much on my mind, as it was surely on everyone else's mind, that this picnic had been called to celebrate a most extraordinary event. A few weeks before, Bertha and Beverly became the first California Indian women in over a century to have their chins tattooed with the traditional three vertical bars—the hundred-and-elevens, as these tattoo marks are generally called. And this gathering was, as in the old days, a feast held to honor the women and allow them to show their tattoos to family and friends.

Beverly, Bertha, and many of the guests are often identified as Yurok Indians. But many of those who were present at the picnic prefer to call themselves Pohlik-lah. Yurok, they explain, is an outsider's term, originally a Karuk work that means "Downstream People." "Pohlik-lah" is the word by which they describe themselves in their own language.

Pohlik-lah towns and ceremonial centers still extend along the Klamath River from above the juncture with the Trinity River to the coast, and north and south along the coast north of Humboldt Bay. From ancient times the women of these towns had chin tattoos. They were so common at the turn of the century, so taken for granted, that one visitor noted: "It is not long before a younger woman or half-breed who has escaped the tattoo strikes one with a sense of shock, as if something necessary is missing."

Those who grew up in northwestern California during the 1940s, '50s, and '60s still remember the older generation of women who bore these distinctive hundred-and-elevens, and their names are still mentioned: Nellie Griffith, Susie Little, Maggie Pilgrim, and others. "They were common," recalls Bertha Mitchell. "They were simply the people you saw when you were growing up. That was the way it was, no fuss about it."

"You just accepted it as normal," affirms Beverly Walsh.

Although no one is quite certain, it seems that Jessie Hancorne, who died about fifteen years ago [in 1975], when she was in her nineties, may have been the last of the older generation with hundred-and-elevens. Peter Nix, a tribal scholar and a leader among the Pohlik-lah, remembers her well. "You'd see her driving everywhere. She had a big, four-door Chevy, and as she grew older she grew smaller, so after a while you couldn't see her anymore. You'd just see the car zipping down the freeway with a couple of hands on the steering wheel, nothing else."

Beverly Walsh and Bertha Mitchell were both born at home on the sites of ancient villages—Beverly at Witspus (Weitchpec), Bertha at Murek. Beverly went to school at Eureka and Arcata in the late '40s and early '50s. She lived in Anchorage, Alaska, for some eight years, where her husband was a heavy-equipment operator. After returning to California for a vacation in 1974, she refused to go back to Alaska. She now lives in Hoopa Valley, where she weaves, practices other traditional arts, and spends time with some of her eight children and seventeen grandchildren.

Bertha also lives in Hoopa Valley. One of twelve children born to Daraxa Peters and the late James Peters, her family moved here in 1953 to be closer to the high school. She shares a house with a daughter and grandchild, and she has been employed as a social worker for the Hoopa Health Association since 1976.

For both Bertha and Beverly, the decision to have their chins tattooed was far from a spur-of-the-moment impulse. The desire had come to each of them independently some ten or fifteen years before, and as time passed they became increasingly firm in their resolve.

What was it, I kept asking them, that made them do such a seemingly bold and irrevocable thing? Each time I asked, I kept hoping for some kind of grand or important statement—perhaps something about how they were militantly snubbing the beauty standards and fashion dictates of the Anglo world; or about how they were advertising to all the depth of their Indian identity. Yet try as I might, I could never move them into any kind of grandiose statement. It was as if the idea of getting their chins tattooed was perfectly ordinary, an idea that found a place in their minds, settled in for a while, and finally made itself quite comfortable. With disarming matter-of-factness, they insisted that they were simply doing something that they had long thought about and that now seemed right.

It took a while, of course, for such certainty to grow. Ten or so years ago, when they first brought up the idea to other people, they were showered with contradictory advice. "Oh, the tattoos mean this." "Oh, they mean that." "You should get it done this way." "No, that way." "This time of year." "That time of year."

As years passed, an informal Pohlik-lah study group began to form around Peter Nix, and it was Peter who undertook to do some research on chin tattoos, consulting both elders and the written record. As Peter explained to me one evening at his Hoopa Valley house, the tattooing was traditionally done with soot gathered from the sweathouse, and it was cut into the skin with a white obsidian blade. A surehanded person was needed for this—a specialist who would have to be well-paid. He cut the soot in with straight lines down the chin. Then he covered the tattoos with bear grease and put pitch over them while they healed.

As to why the tattoos were done, there does not seem to be a clear and simple reason. They were considered to be beauty marks, completing the face, as it were. They were also, according to Peter, a sign of strength and power for both the woman and her family. They showed that the family had the wealth necessary to hire the tattooist, and they signified that the woman was strong enough to withstand the pain. A woman with such tattoos, said Peter, had more control over her life than one without. She had the right, for example, to refuse a groom that her family was urging upon her, and when it came to the marriage negotiations, she would be considered more desirable (and thus able to fetch a greater "bride price") than those without tattoos.

Particularly important to Bertha and Beverly was the fact that the research uncovered no religious significance to the tattooing. Had that been the case, there would have been special rules, special considerations, and certain dangers—especially since there was no one alive who knew quite how to do it in a proper ceremonial manner. Along with the older generation who bore hundred-and-elevens, the generation of specialists had long since died. Calvin Rube, a religious leader of the Yurok, offered to do it for Bertha, but he died some four or five years ago. Randy Thompson had offered to do Beverly's tattoos, but he too died in the mid-1980s.

Of particular concern to Beverly and Bertha was the fact that by the late 1980s there was a whole generation of children who were growing up without ever having seen a hundred-and-eleven. "A lot of kids know about it but have never seen it," notes Beverly. "When I was growing up," explains Bertha, "it was common enough not to question. Kids nowadays see it only in a book."

So it was that on February 9, 1990, a small group of people gathered together in a storefront tattoo parlor on San Pablo Avenue in Berkeley. Present were Bertha, Beverly, Peter, three of Bertha's sisters, Julian Lang (a family friend who was in Berkeley at the time), Lee Davis of the California Indian Project, and me. The walls of the tattoo parlor were, as one might expect, decorated with the customary design samples: dragons, skulls-and-crossbones, roses, battleships, Christ with a crown of thorns, motorcycle trademarks, hearts, etc. Untypically, there was a fascinating collection of photos and prints showing the worldwide history of tattooing. Charles Eldridge, proprietor of the Tattoo Archive, is not only a tattoo artist of some renown but also a tattoo historian.

I had expected that the occasion would be a solemn, almost religious experience. Instead, when I entered the Tattoo Archive, I found a scene so funny and wonderful it seemed for a while that I must have stepped into some kind of zany TV comedy special.

Bertha was lying down on a low, narrow table, something like a massage table. Charles Eldridge, his own arms so covered with tattoos that they reminded me of the branch of a tree covered with vines, was bent over her head. His drill was whining away, and the scene reminded me more of a dentist's office than anything else.

This was the first time in his long career that Eldridge had ever tattooed anyone on the chin, and he was struggling to work out a new set of problems. The tattoos had to go over the lip toward the inside of the mouth, and there was considerable bleeding in one tender area. To stop the bleeding, he had to stuff tissue behind the lip. "You look like a Ubangi," commented one of the sisters, and everyone laughed. Another problem had to do with putting the line on a reclining chin in such a way that when Bertha stood up and the chin sagged slightly, the line would be straight.

"You look beautiful," said Twee, one of the sisters, as the tattoo slowly took shape. "It matches your hair and your eyes."

Bertha got up to look in the mirror: "It looks like I fell in the dirt, she replied. She then walked over to me. "When are you going to get tattooed?" she asked.

"With a beard like this, no one would ever know whether I did or didn't," I responded.

"No, no," she said, patting me on my bald head. "I meant up here."

Charles Eldridge went back to work. "You're not changing your mind, are you, Bert?" someone asked when the tattoos were nearly finished. "I think he's running out of ink," said someone else. The jokes continued. Only the burning of angelica root in a corner and an occasional song that Julian sang made one feel that beneath the raucous joking there was something serious happening.

Peter Nix put another piece of angelica root in a dish to burn. "Don't start a forest fire," someone said. Yet more laughter, and it occurred to me that this was surely one of the funniest scenes I had ever witnessed in my entire life. Yet beneath the laughter, almost sheltered by the nonstop joking, as we watched out of the corners of our eyes a transformation took place.

Three strong bars were outlined and filled in, growing gradually into three columns under the lip, giving strength and weight to the chin, giving the face completion, fullness, dignity, and power. When at last Bertha stood up, the effect was stunning.

I had seen pictures of the hundred-and-elevens, but these were of old women and generally in photos taken long ago, so that the tattoos looked worn and faded. These tattoos, fresh and new, were remarkably bold. Everyone stopped for a moment and stared, awestruck and silent. The silence lasted no more than a few seconds. "Okay," said Twee, pointing at her sister. "It's time to get her back to the mental institution before it closes." Everyone laughed, and as Beverly lay down, a new round of joking began.

"What kind of reaction have you been getting from people?" I asked Bertha and Beverly the night after the picnic. The response of people in Hoopa Valley had so far ranged from some who said, "How pretty you are," to others who wanted to know, "Why did you disfigure yourself for life?" Men seem to like it, reported Beverly, while women react more ambivalently. But the most common reaction as time passes has been for people to take it for granted.

"We did this to make time stand still for a little while," said Peter Nix.

So much has changed along the Klamath River since the invasion of miners and European settlers nearly a century and a half ago. Yet here and there one still finds something of the pacing, the tone, the movements, and the thoughts of the old ways. People still make baskets, trade materials, fish for salmon, gig for eels, argue over lapses in ceremony, make regalia, prepare for dances, sing songs, and some still speak the fine old languages of the Klamath River area. Whether going to a traditional feast or walking through the supermarket, Bertha and Beverly move with something of the older rhythm.

Several months after the tattooing, people no longer stare quite as much. Their presence has become normal, ordinary—just the way they want it.

"My cousin said, 'You can't bring back the old ways,'" Bertha recalled. "I answered: 'I'm not bringing back the old ways. I'm continuing them.'"

News from Native California, vol. 4, no. 4, 1990

GREEN FURNITURE WORKSHOP FINDS
A HOME AT HOOPA (2006)

Under a grove of young oaks on a flat above the Trinity River is an outdoor "furniture workshop." Shave-horses and pole lathes, rugged and handmade, are lined up, ready for use. Basic hand tools—augurs, drawknives, chisels, mallets, and saws—lie on a table, ready for use. Benches and chairs, the products of this furniture workshop, are in various stages of manufacture. The scene before me looks European and medieval. If the old English poet Chaucer were to walk out of the woods and into this clearing, he would feel right at home.

Strange things have a way of happening on the Hoopa Reservation, but to find a bit of merry olde England here is among the strangest. Stranger yet is how appropriate this furniture workshop feels: it seems to fit right in, and its influence and values are beginning to spread to the Indian community around it.

Breathing life, energy, and boundless creativity into this unusual enterprise is Hupa artist George Blake. George produces art the way an oak tree produces acorns—naturally and abundantly. He is a master at whatever he undertakes, traditional and experimental alike. Blake is a highly skilled and highly regarded regalia maker, working in leather, shell, feather, and other natural materials to make exquisite dance regalia for Hupa ceremonials. He builds dugout canoes, having learned the art from master builder Dewey George. He makes sinew-backed bows, elk-horn purses, and acorn mush paddles—all done with great style and adherence to traditional aesthetic values. He also is a master of a number of modern artistic media, including ceramics and, his latest passion, print and monotype. In 1991, the National Endowment for the Arts awarded him the prestigious designation as a National Heritage Fellow; he is acknowledged locally, nationally, and even internationally as a major artist, and he travels frequently abroad.

In a creative collaboration with British-born artist Bella Peralta, Blake visited England's Ruskin Mills in 2001. Ruskin Mills is a former fabric mill that fell into disrepair and has been reconstructed as a center devoted to traditional English crafts. Essential to its mission is instilling knowledge and love of place. Its spiritual forefathers include artist William Morris and writer John Ruskin. Another important figure is green woodworker and furniture maker Philip Clissett and his latter-day disciples, furniture makers Gudrun Leitz and Ben Orford.

Green woodworking advocates for the use of hand or hand-powered tools and the use of green, untreated wood, often "waste" wood—wood left behind in traditional logging and lumbering operations. Hardly new, green woodworking dates back to the activities of traditional British foresters and land stewards, called "blodgers," who trimmed, coppiced, and tended forests for maximum use. In a formulation familiar to those versed in Native American attitudes, the blodgers made sure that nothing went to waste, that once a tree was felled every part of it was used.

Blake had gone to Ruskin Mills not only to learn and observe but also to teach, especially the art of bow making. In 2001 he was in turn visited in Hoopa by furniture maker Gudrun Leitz and English cultural activist Cloe Darling. As the guests looked at Blake's large metal shed—empty except for a dugout canoe—and at the surrounding woodlands and clearings, inspiration struck. They suggested that George establish a green woodworking furniture workshop right there in Hoopa.

On the surface, traditional northwestern California Indian values, developed in a millennia-old relationship with the redwoods, firs, oaks, rivers, and divinities of the Trinity/Klamath River area, have little to do with ancient British forestry. But looking for a moment below the surface, one finds striking resonances: care for the land, a deep reverence for and knowledge of wood, a highly evolved respect for the art and skills of woodworkers, a strong sense of place, and an equally strong sense of community.

As everyone who knows George Blake is well aware, he is if nothing else an enthusiast. Once an idea seizes him, it seems to seize not just his mind but his whole body. His excitement over a new idea is physical, volcanic, and contagious. The thought of opening a furniture workshop in Hoopa grabbed hold of him and wouldn't let go.

Raising money and support for any cultural endeavor is difficult, and one would think that raising money to put a European-style traditional furniture workshop onto the Hoopa Reservation would be passed off as quixotic, romantic, even delusional. It wasn't. To this day, George nods his head in wonder and gratitude for the two local funders who saw the potential, realized the vision, and had the courage to take the risk. As we looked over rocking chairs, benches, tables, and "priests" that were being made, he often paused and pointedly acknowledged the organizations who made it possible: the Northern California Indian Development Council, whose director, Terry Coltra, was an early and dynamic supporter; and likewise the

Seventh Generation Fund and its director, Chris Peters. Further funding came from England—from the Chairs Symposium Committee, Woodland Heritage, and members of the Pole Lathe Association—and from individual donors such as Adrian Rozey.

Still in its infancy, the furniture workshop has attracted local involvement. It was moved downstream to Weitchpec for a short period last summer, and it has had a healthy and beneficial effect on everyone who has been involved with it. George and Bella, both artists, have been documenting it with photos, and when I visited them they flicked through hundreds of photographs, stopping now and then to linger over one or another with a pride reminiscent of a grandparent showing off pictures of the grandkids. These photos document the victories and successes that come from engaging people with their landscape and with each other, connecting people to the skill that lies (often unknown and unused) in their hands. An early photo shows a woman scarcely able to hold a tool; a later one shows her full of confidence as she displays a lovely bench she has made. Youngsters display their neatly turned "priests." (A priest is the club that dispatches a fish caught in a net, giving it the so-called last rites.) In one series of photos, George's eight-year-old grandson sits on a shave-horse next to eighty-six-year-old Glen Moore, the two of them conversing collegially as each works on his own project.

I was genuinely moved by what I saw at Hoopa. Something of beauty is being created here as wood is pulled out of the forest, sawn, sliced, turned, fitted, and polished to bring out the grace of form and the strong swirls of grain. Objects of value are being created, skillfulness and artistry encouraged, and social bonds tightened. So much of what Europe has brought to this continent has been destructive; what a joy to see something like the green furniture workshop, which fits well into Native values and adds so much.

As for George, he is of course an artist in his own right, but one of his greatest gifts is a generosity of spirit that allows him to create a space in which others can be artists as well. We all have good cause to thank George for his generosity, and to thank the Northern California Indian Development Council and the Seventh Generation Fund for their generosity and vision as well. What an unexpected, joyous enterprise this is, full of artistry, beauty, meaning, and surprise.

News from Native California, vol. 19, no. 4, 2006

BASEBALL AND BIRD SONGS:
REMEMBERING JOHN ANDREAS (2002)

A few months back I got a call from Anthony Andreas. Tony—or Biff, as he is generally called—is an elder of the Agua Caliente Band of Cahuilla Indians from Palm Springs. A bird singer and culture bearer, he is a man of great kindness, humor, warmth, and deep knowledge. I seldom hear from him, but when I do I rejoice. Not this time, however. He called to tell me that his brother, John, had died, killed along with John's son Joshua in a dreadful shooting incident at the Morongo Reservation. There would be a commemoration for John at a powwow in Sacramento on August 9; would I come?

I did, of course. Tony, for the last few years confined to a wheelchair, had brought with him a large group of singers. We talked for a while—about people we knew in common, about bird songs, about life in general, about his last days with John. When their turn came, the Cahuilla singers assembled, singing the beautiful songs of the California desert, a tribute to John Andreas.

John Damen Andreas was born in Indio, California, on January 3, 1941. A descendant of Juan Andreas, the last hereditary leader of the Painiktum clan, he was raised, along with Tony, his older brother, and two sisters (Shirley Joyce and Deanna Marie), at the Andreas Ranch near Andreas Canyon, named after their ancestor, Captain Juan Andreas. Instructed in traditional knowledge, Tony and John both began singing the bird songs in the early 1960s, studying with Joe Patencio, the last traditionally trained singer of the Agua Caliente Band.

Throughout his life, John actively participated in cultural activities. Upon Joe Patencio's death, John and Tony, joined by their uncles Matt and Eugene Pablo from the Morongo Reservation, kept the bird songs alive. They formed the Cahuilla Bird Singers and Dancers group in 1978, drawing members of the younger generation into it, including John's son Joshua. John was married to Mary Ann Andreas, for many years chair of the Morongo Reservation, where he lived most of his adult life. He was active with the Malki Museum and every year helped prepare the grounds for the annual fiesta.

But it was his participation in baseball that most dramatically marked his life and for which he will long be remembered. Baseball, too, is a Cahuilla tradition. His grandfather, John Joseph Andreas, after whom he was named, played in the Indian leagues in the early 1900s. His father, Anthony (also called Biff), was remembered as a first-rate pitcher, shortstop, and first baseman, and played for the Morongo All-Indian baseball team.

When John was ten he was playing in a summer boys' softball league for the Agua Caliente–sponsored team. At twelve he was playing fast pitch in a Palm Springs men's league. The Seattle Rainiers wanted to take him north to train him further, but his grandparents felt that twelve was too young an age for him to travel. By fifteen he was being scouted by the Chicago White Sox and the Los Angeles Dodgers. By nineteen he was playing semi-pro ball.

John continued to play baseball into his mid-forties, playing just about anytime and with anyone, for the love of the sport. In later years he became a coach, mentoring the Little League team in Banning. "What I liked best was trying to get the kids to think about playing ball. It's a lot of fun, but it's also something serious. You can't just fool around and expect to be good. I would get them to listen. Get them to play ball and maybe they would really make something out of it. I would try to play all the players whether we were winning or losing because I felt that including everyone on the team was important. I didn't want any kid to sit on the bench."

John did more than play and coach. He sponsored countless players on many teams, underwriting with his own money uniforms, equipment, travel, or whatever the teams needed. As tribute to his long involvement, superb athletic abilities, and immense but quiet generosity, John Andreas was inducted into the Southern California Latino/Native American Hall of Fame in 2000.

A man of modest bearing, John rarely boasted or made much of his accomplishments. When asked, he would say simply: "My grandfather and my dad played baseball, and I followed in their footsteps." Tradition. Like bird songs, like other forms of cultural preservation, one simply does what one is intended to do. And John Andreas did it very well.

News from Native California, vol. 16, no. 2, 2002/3

PRESTON ARROWWEED, PLAYWRIGHT (1990)

I visited Preston Arrowweed in early October 1990, the day after his fiftieth birthday. We were sitting in the living room of his small Sacramento apartment. As we talked, my gaze kept straying to the photographs of family and ancestors that decorated his wall, to an open closet in which the uniforms of a security guard were neatly hung, and to a small desk between the kitchen table and the stove on which stood an old-style manual typewriter and a sheaf of paper.

There was something in his voice—not so much an accent as a precise way of putting words together, a pacing, an intonation, per- haps—that suggested that English was not his first language. I asked, and found out that he grew up speaking only the Quechan (some- times called Yuma) and Kumeyaay languages of Southern California. He is a traditional singer as well, sought by his Quechan tribe and neighboring tribes for various ceremonies, especially funerals.

"The funeral singer is a mediator," he explained in a matter- of-fact way. "Songs help the deceased find their way and prevent their souls from wandering endlessly."

Preston has about him—I don't know how else to say this—the

mannerisms and bearing of an old-time Indian: the good humor, the dignity, the cultural self-confidence, the tolerance, the patience . . . While he is in many ways traditional, there is another side to him as well. He earns his living as a security guard, and he takes his occupation seriously. He studied it at school, and his bookcase has several texts on various aspects of security. He is also a playwright. Writing, producing, directing, and acting in plays are what Preston loves to do most.

"How did you get into such a nontraditional art form as theater?" I asked him.

The answer surprised me. He leaned forward in his chair and began to talk about the annual mourning ceremony of Southern California that is in some areas called the *keruk*. It was held in houses that had been constructed like the houses from the time of the creation of the world. Songs and dances re-enacted the creation story. During the *keruk*, people made images of the dead, and they danced with the images. They had mock battles in which warriors rushed in and shot at shields with arrows. Women, too, ran back and forth as if in battle.

"These events were never rehearsed," explained Preston. "No one belonged to Actors' Equity. But it was drama. It was pageant. It was theater, great theater."

Preston Arrowweed was born in 1940 at the Fort Yuma Indian Reservation along the banks of the Colorado River. He grew up with his grandmother and aunt in an old-style house made of willow withes packed with mud. They lived without electricity, using kerosene for lighting, pumping water by hand, and cooking in an old washtub that was kept outside. On cold nights they dragged the washtub indoors to draw whatever warmth they could from its ashes.

Once a month they set out through the forest of mesquite,

tamarack, willow, and cottonwood for the Fort Yuma Store. In front of the store sat the older men of the tribe, including his uncle, Red Bean, an orator and storyteller, who was generally the center of a crowd. When he saw Preston he would interrupt the flow of the story, greet him as ".Nephew," and buy him a soda. Other than that, however, the family lived a relatively isolated life, and Preston grew up speaking Quechan with the neighboring kids. From his grandmother he learned Kumeyaay as well.

When he was six, the law came to get him, and, against his grandmother's wishes, he was taken to the Fort Yuma Indian School. He could speak neither English nor Spanish. He did not know how (or why) to raise his hand, he did not know how to ask to go to the bathroom. During his first days at school he learned a song by rote, without knowing the meaning of the words. "The rains begin to fall, the rains begin to fall," he sang, extending his arms and wiggling his fingers. The other members of the class gathered around him and fell gently to the ground, like raindrops. Preston hadn't the vaguest idea what it all meant, but he knew that he just loved it. He loved the food, too. School for him was a wonderful adventure, and within two weeks he was speaking English.

He continued to acquire traditional knowledge as well. He was especially fortunate in having been singled out by an old Kumeyaay man named Takai. Takai, who died in the 1960s, had been born near Pilot Knob along the Colorado River. Pancho Villa wanted members of the Pilot Knob Kumeyaay community to join his rebellion, and in the ensuing confusion many members of the community got killed, while others fled. Takai eventually settled on the Fort Yuma (Quechan) Indian Reservation.

"He had one leg," recalled Preston, "with a board strapped to the stump. He was always barefoot, and the skin on his foot was thick and scaly.

"Takai was an orator, a healer, and a singer. He had a little, iddy-biddy house. I followed him around, and he was always teaching me. I listened and I watched. I knew that in the cremations and other ceremonies there were songs I couldn't sing until I was older, until I had training. But when I followed him around the house he allowed me to sing with him—to sing for fun, not for ceremony—and that's how I learned. I listened. I watched. He was an example."

When he was about fifteen years old, Preston decided to leave the reservation and live with a sister in Los Angeles.

"I'm leaving," he told Takai.

"You're not ready to leave," Takai answered.

"I'm going."

"Don't go!"

"I made up my mind."

"If you go, I'll kill you," said the old man.

Preston thought for a while. He knew that the old man had the power to kill him without even touching him.

"Kill me, then," he said at last.

Takai smiled. "You're ready to go. You have the courage you need. You can't have fear. When the time comes to do something, don't be afraid. Do it! Do it!"

These were the most important words that Preston was to hear in his life, and they would come to him in later years to guide him through difficult times. The first time he was asked to help at a cremation, for example, he was deeply afraid of the nightmares and bad thoughts that might come to him as a result. But he was ready for the role, and he recalled the words of his teacher: "When the time comes to do something, don't be afraid. Do it! Do it!"

He became a singer, and once when the lead singer failed to show up for a ceremony, he was asked to take the lead. Fear hit him, as he wondered whether he could take on this difficult role. But the time had obviously come, Takai's words provided him with the necessary strength, and he rose to the occasion.

There were many other times when these words gave him courage. They helped him learn to sing the Lightning Songs, despite a threat that these songs would bring him death. They helped him find the courage to research the sacred and the dangerous, to present figures such as Satan (the Hoofman) in his plays, and to overcome alcohol. "I have been sober five years this January," he said in a tone of voice that suggested his sobriety was an important and hard-won victory, a battle that must constantly be fought.

After high school in Los Angeles, where Preston played varsity football, he joined the Marine Corps, and when his time was up he served an additional two years in the Marine Corps Reserves. There he met a fellow reservist who was working as a bit actor in Hollywood and who urged Preston to try his hand at it. Preston's big break came when he gained access to an assistant director for Universal Pictures.

"Can you act?" asked the director.

"Yes."

"Can you throw a tomahawk?"

Preston gulped. "Of course."

"We got a part for you."

Preston was immediately taken to the make-up room, and when he emerged he was handed a tomahawk and told to throw it into a black preacher's back. First they allowed him to practice, and they set up a blanket as a target. Preston threw the tomahawk. He missed. "Fortunately, the tomahawk was made of rubber, so it just kind of bounced around on the ground." After a bit of practice, though, he got the hang of it. The cameras rolled. A savage Preston Arrowweed, with a cruel glint in his eye, threw the tomahawk, burying it in the back of the actor. The scene, however, ended up on the cutting room floor; the studio censors would not allow a preacher to be killed on the screen.

"Too bad," said Preston. "It was the best part I ever had."

It was not, however, the only part. For the next few years, Preston continued working as an actor. "I rode horses, shot soldiers, attacked wagon trains, strolled in and out of scenes." He was in a scene with John Wayne in the film *El Dorado*. His career, however, was dealt a severe blow when he got injured on the set. He was expected to ride a wild horse, and for the part he was dressed in buckskins so tight that he had to be picked up and put onto the horse. The horse fell, and Preston was seriously hurt.

While recovering, he continued to study acting. He attended the Indian Actors Workshop in Los Angeles, run by Jay Silverheels, who played Tonto in *The Lone Ranger*. This led to Preston's working as a member of Actors' Equity at the Inner City Cultural Center of Los Angeles. He later attended Arizona Western College to continue the study of drama.

Meanwhile, at the Fort Yuma Indian Reservation where he was born, Preston was elected to the tribal council and became embroiled in a dramatic land dispute. A private corporation was trying to acquire land from the Imperial Irrigation District upon which to build a resort. The Quechan Tribal Council felt that this was Indian land, and they had documentation to prove it. But when they demanded a title search, the demand was ignored. They went to the Zoning and Planning Commission of Imperial County, who refused to listen. They tried to get a restraining order through the courts, but they were quickly dismissed.

A division now appeared in the tribe. Many of the political

leaders wanted to continue legal maneuverings, although time was running out and it seemed that they had reached a dead end. One of the spiritual leaders, however, wanted stronger action, and under his advice and guidance Preston supplied himself with firearms and moved onto the land to occupy it and defend it if necessary. He was accompanied by one other tribal councilmember and by several recovering alcoholics from a nearby halfway house. Although the defenders were ceremonially supported by the spiritual leader, and although other tribal members joined them on the land for an afternoon pot-luck meal, they were fundamentally left alone for six days to stand guard and await an invasion. Preston was prepared to die—indeed, he felt that this was the end. He also came to understand that if he did die, it would not be as a hero in the eyes of others. If he got killed and lost the battle for the land, he would be considered a misguided victim. If he won, others, ashamed of their cowardice, would in the end either forget or downgrade his actions. Whatever the outcome, he slowly came to realize, he would never be rewarded, never thanked. Yet he held his ground, as much against inner despair as against the possibility of violent death. His time had come. "When the time comes to do something, don't be afraid. Do it! Do it!" Once again, Takai's words came to give him courage when he needed it most.

The awaited invasion never came, and the land was eventually saved. Preston put down his firearms, puzzled—in fact, disoriented—because he had thoroughly expected to die, and now he found himself alive. Trying to come to terms with the paradoxes and ambiguities of what had happened, he wrote his first play, *Whirlwind Warrior*, in 1973.

The play takes place at a time before the coming of whites. The cast of characters includes a young man (the warrior), his pregnant wife, a war chief, and a spiritual warrior. The young man, left for dead after a battle, rouses himself and heads home to his wife. In seven scenes, the various characters mix and intermingle, speaking of their fears and doubts, reflecting on war and on life.

War Chief: There is no victory in battle.

Spiritual Warrior: You have always known this, the first time you led a war party.

War Chief: No. I cried after the first battle, and no one knew. I led other war parties again and again. It is my destiny, what I was meant to do, I thought.

Spiritual Warrior *(walking closer to the War Chief)***:** You are the greatest warrior that I have ever seen. You are a born killer, sent to defend your people.

War Chief: I kill to defend my people. You are a spiritual warrior who speaks of peace. You cannot see that we have failed.

Spiritual Warrior: We are just mortal men, doing what must be done.

War Chief *(close to anger)***:** Before the battle, my young warriors said, they had the powers of the cat and cannot fail. They are fierce, they said. What has become of this great creation?

Spiritual Warrior: War Chief, listen to me. Man will always weaken to evil, and you and I will always carry the guilt.

For the next several years, Preston wrote more plays, while also doing archaeological work and serving as a member of the tribal council. Then, about five years ago, his brother who worked in the Bay Area invited him to sing at an Intertribal Friendship House event in Oakland. The next year he came again, and also stopped by at D-Q University in Davis for a powwow. This led to his offering to produce plays at D-Q, where he came to teach Quechan and Native American culture as well as drama.

Between 1987 and the present, Preston has performed, produced, and directed many of his plays in places such as D-Q University; the Oak Park Community Center in Sacramento; the California State Indian Museum; California State University, Sacramento; the University of California, Davis; and before Indian communities in the Owens Valley.

Being a playwright is, perhaps, the most difficult and frustrating of all artistic enterprises in modern American culture. A writer needs only a pen, a pad of paper, and a photocopy machine; a painter needs a canvas, a few brushes, a couple of tubes of paint, and a wall. A playwright, however, needs a troupe of actors, as well as lighting, costuming, a stage, and an audience. This is difficult for anyone, and it has been particularly difficult for Preston. The theater community tends to be fairly tight, with its own (often highly academic) standards, and in their eyes Preston is uncredentialed, an outsider. His plays are not, in truth, written for sophisticated theatergoers, and consequently Preston has found himself cut off from the grants sometimes available to more mainstream playwrights.

Nevertheless, he perseveres with a good heart and a noble spirit. "I like what I do," he says. "I'm an actor, I'm a singer—a tribal singer—and I'm trained as a security officer."

As we talked, he put a videotape into the VCR unit and introduced me to one of his most recent plays, *The Hoofman*. The first scene takes place in a hotel lobby and bar. An Indian lawman, played by Preston himself, has rescued a sixties folksinger who had been stranded in her car and fallen into unpleasant circumstances. The second act takes place outside a prison and features among others a black woman jailer, a white desk sergeant, an old Yaqui Indian man, and Night Hawk, an Indian who has recovered from alcoholism and "wanders the streets trying to help his fellow man." Then enters the figure of the Hoofman. It is clear from the moment he enters that this is no one other than Satan, and as the plot unfolds I realize that despite the modern setting of the play, I am watching an old-fashioned morality play in which the forces of good and evil engage in a tug-of-war over a man's soul. "The power of dope and alcohol is strong," acknowledges Night Hawk as the finale draws closer, "but not as strong as the Indian way or the ways of good."

In his efforts to get his plays performed, Preston has found a friend and sponsor in the Inter-Tribal Council of California in Sacramento, and its director, Toni Candelaria. Toni has been helping Preston apply for funding that, if it should come through, would allow him to train a troupe of actors, get the lighting and costuming he needs, and put on performances with the Intertribal Theater, as he calls his group. It's such a delight to see the vehicle of Elizabethan consciousness taken over by someone such as Preston Arrowweed. I keep wondering what Shakespeare would have thought.

News from Native California, vol. 5, no. 1, 1990/1

THE QUECHAN LANDSCAPE (1992)

Preston Arrowweed, a playwright, has been living in Berkeley for almost a year now, writing plays and struggling to get them produced. Often, however, he gets a call from someone of his Quechan tribe, letting him know that there has been a death, at which point Preston drops everything he is doing and drives the long roads that lead back to the Fort Yuma Indian Reservation where he was born. Preston grew up the traditional way, in a Native-style home, speaking the Quechan and Kumeyaay languages in his early youth, and despite the fact that he has only recently turned fifty, he finds himself in the role of lead singer, traditionalist, and (to his amazement) elder.

The traditional Quechan funeral rites involved cremation. Singers were expected to sing for four night in a row, dusk to dawn, to help the soul of the departed find the right path to honor the deceased, to give comfort to the living. Preston remembers once attending an Anglo burial at which the family and friends gathered, said a few prayers and words, shed a few tears, and quickly lowered the casket into the ground. "Is that all there is to an Anglo life?" Preston wondered—these few embarrassed words, this hasty disposal of the remains, this flight from the cemetery even before the casket was covered? There is at least much more to a Quechan life, and Preston answers the call to return to the reservation to ensure a proper service, a full honoring.

The reservation has many cremation sites. Everyone knows, of course, where cremations have been held, and the ground is rendered sacred by that act. No one would ever build a house or collect plants on a place where there had been a cremation. But what about the people who lived and died long ago? Quechan land has seen thousands of years of human habitation; people have lived here since the beginning of time in villages long deserted, in places long forgotten. Their ashes lie buried everywhere. "Wherever we live," says Preston, "we are aware that people lived here before, and that we may be living over the remains of another person. Wherever we walk, someone may have been cremated on that very spot." This awareness invests the entire landscape with a sense of the sacred, with a sense that one needs to act carefully. It lends mystery, power, and depth to the land. "Once you know that," says Preston, "you have no choice but to live differently on the land."

While there are many possible songs that a singer might sing at a funeral service, Preston generally prefers the Lightning Songs. In stanza after stanza, hour after hour, the song recounts the spiritual journey of a dreamer. Although the song and the incidents in it seem ancient, the dreamer was nevertheless a relatively modern man who lived in the 1890s. In his dream vision he finds himself at the sacred mountain of the Quechan, Ave-Kwami, near present-day Laughlin, Nevada. Here he encounters World Creator, who comes to him in the guise of a young boy, called variously Lightning Boy or Wonder Boy. Lightning Boy offers to take the dreamer on a great journey through the world, but first he wants to bring along a friend. The friend turns out to be First Man, the first human ever created, now sick and frail. As they set out, they are joined by Coyote.

All night Preston sings of the great journey of the magical foursome: the dreamer, Lightning Boy, First Man, and Coyote. The songs take them step by step from one named place to the next, through the land of the Quechan and through neighboring lands as well. Sacred places are revisited, acts that happened at the time of creation are reviewed, re-echoed, sometimes re-enacted. When they reach the ocean, they watch as the waves sweep up the beach, then retreat to leave behind a certain bug. It is the very bug who was present at the funeral of World Creator at the time of the beginnings, and who with its buzzing taught people how to cry.

As the journey progresses, First Man weakens; in his hallucinations he sees the House of Darkness, and then he dies. At his cremation, Coyote leaps into the funeral pyre, steals First Man's heart, and runs away with it into the mountains, thus duplicating the horrendous crime he committed at the dawn of the world, when he stole World Creator's heart from the original funeral pyre. Now watching Coyote's dreadful act, Lightning Boy—the manifestation of World Creator himself—is deeply saddened; he not only misses First Man, his friend, but he finds that he misses Coyote as well.

Within this profoundly mysterious and wonderful journey, there was one incident in particular that always puzzled Preston. The four travelers are heading along the Colorado River when without explanation they suddenly turn west. Why did they take this apparent detour, so carefully described with place after place named and dwelled upon, through a land that is now desert? Preston found the answer to this question when he was doing research with archaeologists who pointed out to him the location of "Lake Cahuilla," an ancient lake that dried up centuries ago. The song, Preston realized, was leading the magical beings alongside the shores of an ancient lake, past places where people had once lived, where acts of creation had once taken place.

As I listened to Preston recount this and other incidents from the Lightning Song, I tried my best to follow, to understand. But it was difficult. In particular, I could never seem to get straight in my mind the time sequences. Was the act that Preston was describing taking place at the time of creation? Was it part of the dreamer's journey? Was it part of Preston's explanation to me? Did it take place some other time entirely? Ancient acts were being relived, re-echoed often in slightly altered form, redescribed, and they seemed to resonate through all time. There were stories within stories within stories within . . . I felt sometimes as if I were gazing at a pair of mirrors set opposite each other so that a single image could be reflected and re-reflected in a never-ending sequence that stretched from the present to the most distant past in an infinite progression—an infinite progression that invests the entire Quechan landscape with mystery and depth, with history and sacredness.

News from Native California, vol. 6, no. 2, 1992

THE MATTOLE PROJECT (1992)

Several years ago Julian Lang (Karuk) was doing linguistic research when he came upon a six-minute tape of the Mattole language. Six minutes and six seconds, to be exact. All that he then knew of the Mattole was that they were a name on the map, an Athabaskan-speaking people who once lived south of the Wiyot and north of the Sinkyone, along what is now known as the "lost coast" of California. Although widely traveled in the Indian community, Julian could not recall ever having met a person of Mattole descent. The culture, so close to his own geographically, was apparently lost, even the memory of it extinguished.

He listened to the tape again and again. It was clearly a "death-bed tape." At the end of his life, the last speaker of the Mattole language, a man by the name of Johnny Jackson, had spoked these few words into a tape recorder. Was that all that was left of the Mattole language? Was it all that remained of an entire way of seeing the world, of understanding life, of living? What this was it was reduced to—six minutes and six seconds of the sounds of a dying man?

The tape hounded and haunted Julian for years, not only as a scholar and linguist but as an artist as well, and it became the seed for a remarkable multimedia installation known as the Mattole Project that was displayed at the Capp Street Project in February and March of 1992. The Capp Street Project is an art gallery/performance space at the edge of San Francisco's Mission District. It is located about a block from Highway 101, in a rundown area that is partly industrial, partly residential, entirely urban.

The main part of the exhibit on the second floor of the building is entered literally through a hole in the wall, gallerygoers bending over the way people have bent over for centuries when entering the old-style Indian houses. The installation consists of sound, music, sculpture, light, photographs, artifacts, natural objects, paintings, documents, and maps. Walking around the space, one happens upon a rendition of a traditional Indian house. Sounds emerge, and one expects that people will be present, eating, talking, working, living. Peer inside, however, and the people are poignantly absent. Instead— amazing to see!—the floor is covered by abalone shells, glowing, mysterious, unspeakably beautiful, yet alone, sad, and at the same time utterly gorgeous. They are a tribute to the legend of Abalone Woman, whose presence is woven in many ways throughout the exhibit.

In some respects this is an exhibit of fragments: a six-minute tape, a legend, a photo from museum archives, paintings, an old newspaper clipping, a map, landscape photographs, a rumor, an image—as if to say that it is only through such fragments that we can understand the Mattole. We cannot see them directly; we can only see them reflected in a mirror that was broken long ago.

Yet somehow these fragments of sound and vision manage to create a coherent whole, a mood perhaps, a questioning, a sense of rightness. And since this is a multimedia installation, unlike a painting in a frame it has no clear bounds. The people walking around become as much a part of the artwork as the objects being viewed. As people talk, their knowledge and feelings seem to enlarge the installation. The sound of the tapes mixes almost conversationally with the sound of our language as we listen and view. Lectures by Julian and by Joe Babcock, the photographer with whom Julian collaborated, add history and depth to the installation. Surprising information accumulates. Despite his original assumption, Julian has learned that the Mattole are not extinct; their descendants are very much alive, surviving within other tribes or within the dominant culture.

That anyone has survived is something of a miracle. Before the gold rush, the Mattole numbered some fifteen hundred people. The remoteness of the area protected them from settlers until the mid-1850s. But once soldiers and settlers arrived, the remoteness became a severe liability. A federal Indian agent, Superintendent Thomas J. Henley, reported in 1858:

> I have to report the arrival of James Cunningham from the Mattole Station near [Cape] Mendocino with the intelligence that the settlers in that vicinity have attacked, killed or driven away all the Indians who have been collected at the station, and are now raging an indiscriminate war upon all who can be found either in the valley or in the mountains.
>
> He saw on the day he left for this place several Indians shot without any known provocation . . . . Those Indians are peaceable and well disposed, and this is a most outrageous and murderous expedition.

According to census figures, only ten Mattoles were left in 1910.

The broken mirror can never be repaired. But as we work these fragmented images into our lives, we get some sense of who the

Mattole might have been. There is such great sadness for what has been lost. A lost culture, a lost language, the Mattole will always be elusive and mysterious. Yet in dwelling on the loss and in dwelling on the fragments that remain, we pay homage. And by that act of homage, Julian has brought at least something of the Mattole back to life.

News from Native California, vol. 6, no. 3, 1992

BEAR DANCE (1992)

In the early 1940s a Wukchumni man from the San Joaquin Valley, Joe Pohot, described to anthropologist Anna Gayton a bear dance he had once witnessed. The arms and legs of one of the dancers had been painted black, and spectators kept calling to him, "If you are a bear, let's see your hair." All at once, the black portions of the dancer's body turned into hair; before their eyes the man had been transformed into a bear.

Joe Pohot then went on to explain that the bear dances done by the people of the San Joaquin Valley were re-enactments of dances that bears actually did. To illustrate this point, he told the following story:

> A man was out hunting once about sundown and saw a little bear dancing beside a small oak tree. He was standing on his hind legs and holding up his paws; he jumped at the tree three times. Then he clawed up some earth and threw it at the little tree. The tree was his singer, and the little bear was mad because the singer made a mistake.

To people who are distant from traditional California Indian culture, the idea that humans can turn into bears or that bears and humans do the same kinds of dances might seem strange. Those better acquainted, however, will hardly be surprised; after all, the line between bears and humans isn't that sharp, and it is a line that can be crossed in both directions.

On a midsummer day, July 26, 1992, I had reason to think about the closeness of bears and people. I was in the city of Orange, on the lawn of a Catholic church that had chosen to honor the local Indian community on this, the day of the annual church picnic. Everyone, it seemed, from Southern California had turned out: Cindy Alvitre, Jimi Castillo, L. Frank Manriquez, Tony Romero, David and Mingo Belardes, Cathy Wolf, Tony Andreas, Paul Apodaca, Carolyn Kuali'i, Sisquoc Cano, and so many more. Here on an expansive green lawn of almost golf course proportions, Anglo churchgoers in their Sunday best mingled easily with their Indian guests. Later that day there would be a service that would combine elements of Indian religious belief with elements of the Catholic. It was all refreshingly refined and genteel, a welcome (and one hopes permanent) truce in the long and tragic conflicts between the Catholic Church and the indigenous way of life. As the sun shone beneficently, the entire scene was reminding me of a French impressionist "Day in the Park" kind of painting, when suddenly the sound of raunchy laughter reached my ears. I looked around and noticed a small group of burly men who were joking, rough-housing, horse-playing, at times almost rolling over with laughter.

I knew that I had found the bear dancers.

It was Paul Apodaca who introduced me, and one of the dancers, Howie Maruffo, accepted the role of spokesperson and agreed to be interviewed. Howie was originally from the Stewarts Point Rancheria (Kashaya) in Sonoma County, but for the last four or five years he has been living on the Tule River Reservation in the southern San Joaquin Valley. "I am from Kashaya," he said, "although my mom's people were Wappo. But all my life was Kashaya. That's where Lorin Smith taught me about *weya* [spiritual power]."

The Wappo and Kashaya Pomo both have strong beliefs about bears, but they see them quite differently. Among the Wappo, Howie explained, bears are good. His great-uncle was a bear-man. People who could become bears by putting on bear skins had remarkable powers; they could, for example, travel through strange territory to the coast and back again at superhuman speeds.

In Kashaya, people could also turn into bears—it is occasionally rumored that there are those who still can—but it was generally to do harm. "The Kashayas fought bears. Bears did bad, and the people would have to fight them. There were those who could turn into bears, who were bear shamans. But it was a mystery who they were."

Then, after a long pause, Howie smiled and added: "Everything was a mystery at Kashaya."

When Howie moved to the Tule River Reservation, he found that this area too was steeped in bear lore.

> There is a village with a river running by it. A man could leave the village and walk through the river. On the other side he would be a bear, and could go about and do things as a bear. When he returned, he would walk back through the river and enter the village as a man again.

There was also a long tradition of bear dances among the Wukchumni, Tachi, and other people of the San Joaquin Valley (people often lumped together under the name "Yokuts"). Each group had its own practices. For some the bear dance was held in the fall, for others in the winter. Among some the dancers wore full bear skins;

among others they wore only claws strung as a necklace and perhaps bear-paw mittens, the rest of the regalia being a skirt of eagle down strands, an upright feather bunch on the head, and sometimes body paint that reproduced the markings of the bear. One thing that all people had in common, though, was that the dances were short and intense, and they were held to bring the beneficent aspects of bear power into the community.

It was after he moved to Tule River that Howie began to get involved in bear dance activities. Clarence Atwell, a shaman from Santa Rosa Reservation, gave him his first bear skin. And at Pala Reservation Clarence was present when the bear first came to Howie.

> I was dancing with the bear skin. Clarence saw the bear enter me. I felt it, too. The dancing changed, and I became a bear. It's a feeling you can't describe, can't put into words. After the bear entered me, I fasted for two days. I fasted for understanding and guidance, so I wouldn't do anything bad. There are two ways to go when you're a bear: bad and good. You walk a fine line. I went into the fast to ask for help.

Howie later fasted a second time, and again the bear came to him. This time the bear had a message, telling him that it was time for the bear people to stand up and do work, to dance for the Earth, to make others understand bear power.

"What does it sound like when a bear talks to you?" I asked.

Howie smiled slightly. "They talk simple. You've got to put the pieces together sometimes. It's like a child talks, simple and broken up."

As Howie describes the experience of being a bear dancer, it is clear that the bear skin is an essential piece of regalia, deriving its power from the spirit of the bear who once wore it. If the bear was big and strong, the skin will possess and transmit great strength and power.

In the old days, it is likely that dancers got their skins by buying them from hunters. There are reports of how when a hunter killed a bear, he would bring it to a member of the bear clan, who could not kill bears himself and who would be obliged to purchase the skin and claws, later using them for ceremonial purposes.

Today, of course, there are few bears wandering the San Joaquin Valley. Bear skins are gotten wherever they can be found, and they are in short supply. There are over twenty bear dancers, but only eight skins, said Howie. Howie's first skin, that of a grizzly bear, had once been a rug. Howie sweated with it and fasted with it, praying to Grandfather to put the spirit back into it. Eventually the skin wore out. "I had to put it to rest. I burned it after the last dance, returned it to Grandfather."

"Is this the replacement?" I asked, pointing to the fresh skin that Howie was now using.

"Not a replacement," he corrected gently. "Another brother that came to help."

Those who have witnessed the Southern California bear dances have noticed that in addition to the dancers and the singers, there are "wingmen." The wingmen, usually one to each dancer, are so called because as they circle the dance arena, they each carry a massive bird wing. Auggie, a wingman, now joined Howie and me on the lawn, and I asked him to describe what he did. He talked about how before the dance he would smudge the skin, himself, and the dancers. Then he helped paint the dancers and dress them in their skins. The wingmen would then lead their dancers out into the arena, following them around at the periphery, keeping an eye on them. When the dance was over, the wingmen would bring the bears out. This, said

Auggie, was the hardest part. The dancers had the spirit in them, they had become bears, and while being led out and waiting for the skins to be taken off, they were often wild. "They act just like bears, clawing and fighting," said Auggie.

As the time for the dance got closer, more and more of the bear dancers, wingmen, and singers joined us on the lawn. This was truly a boisterous, fun-loving, rowdy bunch of guys. "I'm going to need cattle prods to control you today," said a wingman to one of the dancers. "Yeah," agrees another. "Maybe we better get some hot wires and two-by-fours." There is more clowning, horse-playing, and good-natured teasing.

"We joke like this now," someone explained to me. "But when the dance begins, the joking stops. Really stops. When the bear power enters you, you hang on for dear life."

Later that afternoon, I stood among a huge crowd of people who ringed the dance area on the lawn, completely encircling the three bear dancers, the singers, and the wingmen. The first song was slow and stately, and the bear dancers, each dressed in a skin, moved to its rhythm. It was a slow, lumbering movement as they swayed back and forth, raising their heads to sniff the air, then dropping back on all fours. Their faces were painted white, and as they shuffled around the dance area, never looking directly at the audience, their grunting and low growling seemed to express, to themselves rather than to anyone else, their discontent at being confined by a ring of humans.

The second dance was faster paced, and on the third and fourth dances members of the audience were invited to join. Each bear now headed a long line of dancers. The lines snaked around each other, and the singers increased the intensity of their songs. The dancers were crouched over, shuffling and swaying. They had, it seemed, become true bears. Bears had entered human society and were leading the people! It felt satisfying, very right.

As I watched, I thought about what Howie had told me earlier when I'd asked him what the dance was all about. "It's a beautiful dance," he said thoughtfully. "It makes you feel good. When the spirit enters the dancers, they feel good; and when people see it happen, people feel good. It opens the heart."

As I watched the wingmen lead off the grunting, snuffling bears, I felt something of the openness Howie was talking about. People and bears had linked arms and danced together, reaffirming the ancient compact. Howie was right. It felt good, and it opened the heart.

News from Native California, vol. 6, no. 4, 1992

WEALTH AND SPIRIT (1993)

I doubt that the Hearst Museum of Anthropology in Berkeley had ever witnessed a scene quite like this one. On March 20, 1993, the museum hosted three regalia-making families from northwestern California. Crowded along the narrow aisles of the collection area were Loren and Lena Bommelyn, Frank and Cheryl Tuttle, Amos and Maria Tripp, the Tripps' daughter Paula and her fiancé Alme Allen, Ira Jacknis of the Hearst Museum, Lee Brumbaugh (a photographer with the museum), Jeannine Gendar and I from *News from Native California*, and occasional wandering souls who were working in or passing through the belly of the Hearst.

Moving slowly and methodically through the collections, Ira pulled out one tray after another of Tolowa, Yurok, Karuk, Hupa, and Wailaki regalia. Laid out before us was one of the world's most stunning and remarkable assemblages of Indian treasure. Woodpecker feather headdresses, obsidian blades of great size and rare color, white deer skins, civet-skin kilts, dentalia necklaces, magnificently ornamented dresses, and still other priceless items were passed around for admiration and examination.

Matching the wealth of the materials was a wealth of commentary from the regalia makers themselves. As they handled the objects, some of which are more than a century old, the regalia makers discussed the materials and skills that went into their manufacture, noted their uses, and described the social and spiritual contexts into which they fit. All the while a small tape recorder whirred on, keeping careful record (I assumed) of these wonderful proceedings.

When the time came to write about the visit of the regalia makers, I sat down to listen to the tapes. What disappointment! All I could hear were blurred and barely audible remarks interspersed with robust eruptions of "Oh, wow!" and "Look at that!" as Ira pulled out one piece of regalia after another.

That plus laughter. Every thirty seconds, it seemed, the tape bore witness to yet another wave of laughter. In some cases the particular joke or remark that set it off was lost, but the laughter remained: eddies of laughter, ripples of laughter, now and then grand cascades of laughter. I listened to the tapes with growing delight. Laughter and expressions of wonderment! Celebration and beauty! Joy and good feelings! In an odd way, the faulty tape recorder had managed to capture something of tremendous importance, something that I might never have understood if the tapes had been technically better.

It is difficult for outsiders to understand regalia and the role it plays in the lives of the Native people of northwestern California. The dominant culture does not have anything quite like it, and the language and thought structures by which outsiders attempt to describe regalia never quite fit.

Take, for example, the matter of wealth. Among the tribal groups of northwestern California, regalia means wealth, and individuals pursue that wealth with tremendous enthusiasm. As Julian Lang, Karuk tribal scholar and ceremonial leader, writes:

A most cursory survey of the mythology of the area instantly reveals *wealth acquisition* as a primary motivation within the culture. There are songs to beckon dentalia. There is hunting medicine which when spoken assures that the hunter will kill an albino or red deer. Dentalia charms are hung from a boy's baby basket or are tied like a bracelet to a boy's or girl's ankle so that money will come easily to the child. A common expression of gratitude to youngsters from elders is, "May you find an elk-horn purse [full of dentalia money] on the path as you walk along home."

In story after story, the central character is compulsively meditating, if not obsessing, about wealth. A good life, the stories seem to say, depends in large part on one's ability to own and publicly display one's regalia at the grand annual ceremonies to fix the world.

The age-old preoccupation with acquiring wealth is alive today. Regalia makers, dance makers, and dance owners talk about regalia. They bring it out of storage to touch it, to talk to it, to feel it, to admire it. *[This and subsequent comments by Julian Lang have been excerpted from extensive notes he made especially for this publication.]*

In European and Asian religions, the model of a holy person is generally not one who chases after wealth but rather one who voluntarily embraces material poverty in order to attain spiritual riches. One who pursues wealth too avidly is said to be greedy or driven; one who holds onto it too tightly is stingy and miserly.

Such judgments miss the mark when one is trying to understand regalia in northwestern California. For while clearly constituting wealth, regalia is not used for mundane purposes. It cannot, for example, be used to buy food, to put gas in the car, to make a down payment on a home, or to pay for a vacation in Hawai'i. As Julian Lang writes:

> Regalia means wealth, but not the Wall Street wealth of today. Instead we mean a wealth that is of the "other world," the spirit world. Regalia is not to be traded or sold like stocks and bonds, and shouldn't be regarded as just a valuable collectible.
>
> In contemporary society the idea of obsessing about wealth sparks certain negative connotations, especially greed. To transfer today's ambivalent feelings about wealth onto the cultural inclinations of indigenous peoples of northwestern California robs one of an opportunity to understand a distinctly indigenous and quite different role that wealth can play within one's life and one's community.
>
> For indigenous people, owning regalia is strongly associated with the spiritual and the natural worlds. The wealth system of northwestern California brings together the earth, nature, and spiritual enlightenment.

Regalia, in fact, is divine wealth, created near the beginning of time by Spirit Beings to give themselves and the people who would follow something of transcendent beauty. To wear the regalia in the great dances is to put on the dress of the gods themselves, to partake in their luminous beauty.

Merely to see such beauty is a transforming experience, not just for humans but for all creation. "Almost every night one can hear the mice laughing, and the frogs, because they are glad that they are traveling on the way to the dance," tells an old Yurok story. Even today one might hear an elder, nearing the end of life and with a weakened body, express a fervent desire to live to see the next dances, to lay eyes one last time upon the magnificent regalia.

This emotional, unabashed love for regalia does not sit easily with those who have been brought up within the religious traditions of Europe and Asia, where it is taken for granted that the world is divided into two realms, the spiritual and the material. Material things, in this view, are inferior, transitory, and profane—unless, of course, they happen to "symbolize" something spiritual. Thus, for example, a priest's robe is not valued for itself but only because, say, its whiteness might symbolize purity.

How different this attitude is from that of a Native person viewing the resplendent scarlet woodpecker-feather headdresses worn during the Jump Dance! This headdress is not merely a symbol, not merely an image of some power that lies invisibly beyond. Rather, it is, in and of itself, powerful and beautiful. It is a direct gift of the Spirit Beings. In fact, according to the Karuk people, it is a Spirit Being itself, a divine personage named Paathkir, who (as recounted in creation stories) transformed himself into the woodpecker headdress.

Regalia, in short, does not derive its powers from somewhere else but is itself full of power and history, possessed of a manifest ability to transform people and to infuse the world with goodness, balance, vitality, and beauty.

Each piece of regalia is a living being and, like all living beings, has needs and desires. Foremost among these is the need to be danced and displayed. When David Hostler, director of the Hupa Tribal Museum, visited the Hearst Museum in June 1993, he made this point quite emphatically:

Regalia needs to come out. It needs to be danced. Our belief is that when the regalia is being used, that is good. If you don't use it, you lose it. If it doesn't come out, something bad will happen.

Loren Bommelyn recalled how Tolowa elder Irene Natt used to ask him to come and sing to her regalia when it wasn't being used, "just to keep it happy." Keeping the regalia happy and healthy was part of humankind's obligation to the regalia. "If something breaks, you fix it. You keep it going. You don't just let it die."

Frank and Cheryl Tuttle reminisced about how just before coming to the Hearst Museum they took out a dress that Frank had made for his daughter, Ruby. When she recognized the sound, or song, of her dress being moved, she came from another part of the house "to touch it and to talk to it."

For the regalia-making families who came to the Hearst Museum, the sense that the regalia was alive and meant to be used was cause for some sadness. Looking at regalia in the collection that was in disrepair, Lena Bommelyn said, "That's why Indians have trouble with museums. If it's broken, fix it." Indeed, mixed with the wonderment, laughter, and joy of that visit, there was an undercurrent of sadness that the great beauties of the world were kept in dark drawers, were not being used and repaired, were not being danced. Julian Lang summed it up with a story about finding a stone knife in the Hearst's collections that had once belonged to a Karuk man, Little Ike:

It was like coming upon an old friend who had been thought dead, but who suddenly appears. There's a sense of happiness. But sadness, too, because the old friend has been so long out of contact and has been changed so drastically by the experience.

Regalia, of course, was never meant to be owned by a museum but rather by individuals within a cultural setting. Some individuals accumulated a tremendous store of it. As Julian recounts:

> David "Pop" Risling, Sr., acquired a vast treasure of regalia in modern times. He was a man intent upon acquiring Indian wealth. By the time of his death in 1982, he was one of the richest men. He inherited the lion's share of the regalia from his Karuk mother, but kept acquiring more and more throughout his life. He owned enough dance regalia, for example, to outfit forty to fifty Brush Dancers head to toe with the scarlet of the pileated and California woodpeckers. He owned vast sums of regalia used in every dance. He displayed the regalia at the various ceremonies—that is, he danced the regalia. The wealth he brought out was beautiful and unforgettable; it imbued the dances with "spiritual reality."

In the thinking of the dominant culture, people with great wealth are suspect. They often obtain wealth by aggressive means and then use their riches to indulge in excessive, even harmful behavior. The exact opposite tends to be the case within the traditional Indian culture of northwestern California. There is a firm belief that woodpecker scalps, dentalia, white or other unusually colored deerskins, huge obsidian blades, etc., come only to good people—to people who are steadfast, restrained in their personal behavior, and disciplined.

The manufacture of these raw materials into dance regalia likewise demands good character. As David Hostler recalls having learned from the late Hupa traditionalist Rudolph Socktish:

Whenever you're working on dance stuff, you have to be in the right mind, the right spirit. You need a song in the heart. You need the right spiritual feeling.

Ownership of the regalia is even more demanding. A wealthy man who has much regalia [regalia was traditionally kept and controlled by men, even when owned by women] is of necessity a person of almost impeccable behavior, for (especially in the old days) if he were to insult or offend anyone, the injured party might demand that the injury be compensated for and balanced by a transfer of regalia. Thus a person who is mean-spirited, who fails at social obligations, or who is immoderate or violent will never be able to maintain a great quantity of regalia. It is assumed, and with good reason, that a man with great wealth is by definition a man of great virtue.

One of the chief obligations of a wealthy man is to sponsor or "put on" dances, using his considerable store of regalia to outfit those who come to the dance. Amos Tripp explained some of the planning and strategy that goes into putting on a dance:

You might have a Brush Dance in which there are thirty guys dancing and fifteen girls. During the night you might have three or four rounds, changing the regalia each time, so that you would need 90 necklaces, 180 feathers, etc. Everything you bring has to get danced, so you have to figure out how many rounds you're going to put up, how much stuff you've got to bring, and make sure that everything gets danced. And as dance maker, you've also got the responsibility to make sure that there's enough regalia for everyone.

The distribution of regalia among the dancers is anything but casual. The first dances of a ceremony are performed by the youngest and least experienced dancers, who will be given the least valuable regalia. Over the course of the ceremony, things build to a climax, with the last dance featuring the best dancers, the strongest singers, and the most dazzling and exquisite regalia. The following observations made by anthropologist Alfred Kroeber over seventy years ago are still entirely valid today:

> The dances are conducted with a distinct attempt at climactic effect. In the first days they are brief and the property carried is inconsiderable. Gradually they grow in duration, intensity, and splendor. The famous treasures begin to appear only toward the last day: the most priceless of all are reserved for the final appearance of that day. The number of dancers, the vehemence of their motions, the loudness of the songs, the crowd of spectators increase similarly; even on each day of the series, an accumulation is noticeable. The performances are always conducted by competing parties. Each of these represents a village—the hometown and from one to five of those in the vicinity. These match and outdo one another, as the rich man of each village gradually hands over more and more of his own and his followers' and friends' valuables to the dancers to display.

The tremendous value of the regalia, while now inherent to the regalia itself, derives from the long-ago actions of a race of Spirit Beings who lived on Earth just before humans came into existence. This race of divinities is called *Ikxaréeyav* by the Karuk, *Woge* by the Yurok, and *Kixunai* by the Hupa. Knowledge of how each piece of regalia came into existence during the age of the Spirit Beings is preserved to this day in creation stories. And a true understanding of any particular regalia is not complete without one's knowing how it first came into being. As Julian Lang writes:

> They [the Spirit Beings] formulated the customs, the regalia, ceremonies, the schedules of all the dances, and all aspects of daily life. Their decrees determined what Indian wealth was to be both for our ancestors and for us today. The ceremonial displays of wealth occur because the *Ikxaréeyav* discovered that this act makes people happy, and helps to make the Earth fast and stable. Displaying wealth creates social balance and makes things right.

The rarity of regalia also influences its value. White deer skins, for example—those taken from albino deer—are not only of stunning beauty but they are also extraordinarily uncommon. At the turn of the century, probably no more than two dozen of them existed in all of northwestern California. Similarly, so few of the longest dentalia shells existed that to own a string of them was enough to make a man famous during his own lifetime and for some time thereafter.

The rarity of the materials that go into a piece of regalia is sometimes not immediately apparent. Loren Bommelyn examined a profusion of small, clam-like shells sewn onto a dress. These shells were carefully graded and arranged by size so as to present a marvelous pattern, and there were so many of them that the dress gave a rich and full musical sound when it was shaken. Fingering the shells, Loren noted: "If you spent all day searching the beach, on a good day you might find six. It might take twenty years or so to collect fifteen hundred shells for a dress like this." Other materials on the dress, he observed, were "imported." The pine nuts strung on the fringes, for example, had probably come by trade from as far away as Hoopa Valley.

They had been scorched so that they would be black and so that they would sound better when they tapped against each other. Also strung on the fringes were juniper berries that had probably come all the way from Mount Shasta. "People used to put them next to ant hills to let the ants eat out the sweet centers," noted Maria Tripp.

The woodpecker feather headdresses used in the Jump Dance provided yet another example of the huge amount of work and care that went into each piece of regalia. A quick calculation showed that a particular headdress had four rows of 42 feathers to a row—a total of 168 woodpecker crests, sewn tightly together to produce a solid rectangle of eye-dazzling scarlet.

Through the eyes of the regalia makers one becomes aware of the tremendous amount of time that goes into collecting feathers, gathering shells, harvesting bear grass, and procuring other raw materials. And this is merely the beginning. The raw materials need to be tanned, treated, or otherwise prepared; one must collect iris leaf fibers to make cordage for sewing; one must continually trade, accumulate, weave, braid, etc. And it all has to be done with great care and exactitude. Examining an old-style skirt in the Hearst collection, Amos Tripp noted how precisely and evenly the fringes had been cut, probably with an obsidian blade. "I could hardly do as well with my best pair of scissors," he said with admiration. The dress he was looking at had hundreds of such fringes.

Is old regalia more valuable than new regalia, one might wonder? Julian Lang answers this question with two stories:

> Howard Ames is a Yurok elder, a teacher of his culture and a mentor (i.e., medicine man) for the biannual Jump Dance held at Pekwan, a World Renewal village site located twenty-five miles upriver from the mouth of the Klamath River. He is descended directly from the Pekwan

ceremonial site people. He likes to tell stories about the Jump Dance ceremony, its regalia, and the regalia owners he personally knew or saw.

There was a dance owner, he tells us, named Wohkel Harry. During one Jump Dance, he was about ready to dress the dancers from his camp, the Pekwan dance camp. In total there were three separate families/villages who owned rights to give the Jump Dance, and they do so in turn, each trying to outdo the other by presenting the most beautiful dance. Some dance makers came to Wohkel Harry's camp to dance with him. It is expected that the leaders of each camp will "help out" (i.e., dance) the other camps periodically. The dance makers looked at the feathers Harry had stuck into the ground arranged in a circle.

They looked at the feathers and one of them said, "What kind of feathers are those? They look like buzzard feathers." "I'm not rich like you fellows," was all that Harry said. Howard says, "The feathers he had out there were tall and black, blacker than black. The fact is, those feath-ers were the old kind, they were condor feathers." This ceremony story occurred in the 1920s, and by then the ornamented tail feathers of the golden eagle had become the dance plumes in general use at the Jump Dance. The point of the Wohkel Harry story is that he was dancing ancient plumes.

On the other hand, there is a lovely Yurok story of a poor young man who is teased about his poverty. The young man completed the prescribed rigors necessary to make luck, the prerequisite condition to successfully acquire wealth. Being shamed by his peers, he focuses his life and in fact acquires enough regalia to put on two White Deerskin Dances, without borrowing regalia from other families who presumably had teased him. In his story (he is Weitchpec Young-Man), the people, his peers, are infatuated with the idea that in his dance everything will be new, never seen before. Hence, new regalia is of extreme value.

It seems, then, to matter little whether one insists that the regalia of greatest value is old regalia or new regalia. *Vaa vureeshpukach*: "It is money just the same."

When the three regalia-making families visited the Hearst Museum, they spread out on a table a magnificent collection of their own freshly made regalia, vivid in color, supple in texture, radiant, a delight to the eyes. It was inevitable that the regalia they brought would be compared to the material in the museum's collection, most of which dated back at least seventy-five years.

Clearly, there were changes. Perhaps most noticeable—and surely most expected—was the fact that some of the materials had changed. Red woodpecker scalp feathers, eagle feathers, wolf skins— materials such as these had become virtually unobtainable. Other materials that had once been rare had now, with the advent of the automobile and the breaking down of geographical barriers, become more abundant. A person might, for example, go to a bead or craft supply store and purchase obsidian or dentalia for a few dollars that in the old days might have taken a lifetime to collect. Likewise, thread that once would have taken days to make out of iris leaf fibers is now available for pennies in supermarkets and drugstores.

With the change of materials there has also come a change in the way materials are collected. The old stories suggest that the collection of the regalia material was perhaps even more important than its manufacture into finished dance regalia. To acquire red wood-pecker scalps in large number was proof of divine acceptance. The search for an albino deer might consume an entire lifetime.

But today people have jobs, and even in northwestern California life tends to get hectic. Although each regalia maker felt that the gathering of the material was important, it was clear that the emphasis had shifted from the collection of material to the skills needed to turn this material into finished regalia.

Also changing are the social contexts in which regalia is used. In the old days, regalia was constantly changing hands, essential to restore balances and correct injuries throughout the entire society. When a man was to marry, he would offer regalia to the family of the bride to compensate them for the loss of their daughter. A man who committed a crime (even murder) or caused an injury could achieve absolution only by paying regalia to the injured party to redress the wrong he had done. Thus regalia—divine wealth—flowed through the society, righting wrongs, bringing balance, restoring harmony. This use of regalia is today much diminished.

There have been, in short, changes in material, in the habits of collection, and in the social context. Change is, of course, to be expected: after all, Indian society is a dynamic culture, not a "living history" exhibit frozen in time. It continues, as it always has, to evolve and change, to adopt new customs and to drop old ones.

Far more remarkable than the changes, however, are the similarities between the regalia of today and that of previous times. The levels of craftsmanship are still extremely high, the regalia itself is stunningly beautiful, and the role that it plays in the religious and cultural life of northwestern California is still strong.

The regalia at the Hearst Museum is an extraordinary, world-class treasure. For non-Indians, it has much to offer. Acquired years ago by anthropologists who felt the need to preserve the knowledge and art of a people they saw as "vanishing," the regalia collection at the Hearst Museum undoubtedly has a multitude of academic uses. But it also holds forth something that the dominant culture needs far more than scholarship. It offers, to those who approach it with an open mind and an open heart, a glimpse into a worldview in which certain things of the world are neither dismissed as mere material objects nor degraded into symbols but rather are understood as divine gifts—valued and even loved for their extraordinary power, their transcendent beauty, and their inherent holiness—linking the human with the divine in an ongoing effort to bring joy, restore balance, and ultimately keep the world healthy.

For Indian people the Hearst collections are a "library," in which are preserved the craftsmanship and knowledge of a previous generation. The regalia is an inspiration and a benchmark against which to measure change. It is, in the words of Julian Lang, a reminder that "we are descended from a people who made beauty, and who used that beauty, to fix the world."

News from Native California, vol. 7, no. 4, 1993/4

AMONG KIN (1992)

At the heart of the California Indian understanding of the environment is the sense that everything—plants, animals, mountains, rocks, streams, everything—is alive. And everything is alive in much the same way that people are alive: with intelligence, power, and history.

In such a world, people did not stand out as separate from the things around them. When the people of the northern Sierra foothills were asked the name for themselves, they responded, "Maidu." It was long assumed that Maidu meant "people," which it does. But, as linguist William Shipley has pointed out, it means not only "people" but perhaps something like "being." Animals, birds, fish—these too are Maidu. In other words, when asked who they were, these people did not say, "We are human," but, with great inclusiveness, and I think great wisdom, they said, "We are beings."

The dominant culture in this country today puffs itself out and makes a big deal out of being human. "Man is the measure of all things," enthused the Greek philosopher Protagoras, and in countless ways the dominant culture extols the human over "brute" creation.

Yet are we really so different from other beings—from bears, for example? Anthropologist Anna Gayton, who worked among the Yokuts and Western Mono in the 1930s, gave the following wonderful anecdote, a story that suggests that bears not only shared the same landscape as humans, not only shared many of the same foods, but, on occasion at least, they even shared a joke.

> Palaha, who was a fine hunter, told of an experience. He set up a rude platform in an oak tree where he intended to hide just before dawn to drop acorns down a bear lure, then shoot the animal as it fed. He went out as planned— it was barely light. As he came under the tree something hit him on the head; acorns were falling from the platform. Looking up, he saw a small bear standing on the framework and nuzzling at the hoard of bait which rolled off the sides. This Palaha thought it excessively funny: that their positions should be reversed, and that the bear was doing to him what he had intended doing to the bear. But beyond this was the sense that the bear thought it funny too, that somehow it was intentional on the animal's part to engage in a humorous trick.

What did it feel like to grow old in a world in which the plants, animals, rocks, and mountains were seen as family members? A Wintu woman, Sadie Marsh, recalled hearing her grandfather pray to the World Maker, Olelbes—"He-Who-Is-Above." As part of the prayer he talks directly and intimately with the things around him— the deer and other animals whose "nature it is to be eaten," the rocks, trees, acorns, sugar pine, water, and wood. He talks to these other beings as one might talk to kin, sharing with them his sadness and regret, calling upon them to witness his approaching death and to mourn for him. As he addresses them, we hear the voice of a man who is about to depart from a world in which he is thoroughly at home.

Oh Olelbes, look down on me.
I wash my face in water, for you,
Seeking to remain in health.
I am advancing in old age; I am not capable of anything
    anymore.
You whose nature it is to be eaten,
You dwell high in the west, on the mountains, high in the
    east, high in the north, high in the south;
You, salmon, you go about in the water.
Yet I cannot kill you and bring you home.
When a man is so advanced in age, he is not in full vigor.
If you are rock, look at me; I am advancing in old age.
If you are tree, look at me; I am advancing in old age.
If you are water, look at me; I am advancing in old age.
Acorns, I can never climb up to you again.
You, water, I can never dip you up and fetch you home
    again.
My legs are advancing in weakness.
Sugar pine, you sit there; I can never climb you.
In my northward arm, in my southward arm, I am advanc-
    ing in weakness.
You who are wood, you wood, I cannot carry you home on
    my shoulder.
For I am falling back into my cradle.
This is what my ancestors told me yesterday, they who
    have gone, long ago.
May my children fare likewise!

The reference to "northward arm" and "southward arm" is provocative and informative. In English we would refer to the right arm and the left arm, and we might also describe a certain mountain as being to our right or left, in front of us or in back of us, depending upon which way we are facing at the moment. We use the body—the self—as the point of reference against which we describe the world. The Wintu would never do this, and indeed the Wintu language would not permit it. If a certain mountain was to the north, say, the arm nearest that mountain would be called the northward arm. If the person turned around, the arm that had previously been referred to as the northward arm would now be called the southward arm. In other words, the features of the world remained a constant reference, the sense of self was what changed—a self that continually accommodated and adjusted to a world in which the individual was not the center of all creation.

News from Native California, vol. 6, no. 2, 1992

FOREWORD TO
THE MORNING THE SUN WENT DOWN (2016)

Darryl Wilson was constantly on the move, driven from one city to another, sometimes in response to opportunity, sometimes pushed by need, sometimes seeking refuge from yet another of the personal disasters that so remorselessly pursued him throughout his life. When I first met him in the late 1980s, he was living in Davis. His wife, Danell Garcia, had died—tragically and ironically like his mother, in an automobile accident—and he had only recently pulled himself out of the depths of despair, enrolled at UC Davis, and was struggling to get a bachelor's degree while raising two infant sons, the twins Seterro and Theo (known throughout Indian country as Hoss and Boss). Then came the years he spent in Tucson, where he got a PhD at the University of Arizona; in San Jose, where he was cobbling together a livelihood as a lecturer at a number of colleges, traveling the state as a storyteller, and turning out a body of literature—at once lyrical, angry, and visionary—that would gain him friends and admirers everywhere; and in Gardnerville, Nevada, where he was teaching culture and language to young Washo tribal members. In 2000, while in Nevada, he suffered a nearly fatal stroke that left him severely disabled. He returned to San Jose, then moved to Santa Cruz, California, where he lived with his twin sons, now grown to adulthood, and a local Indian community that listened to his stories, cherished his wisdom, and cared for his needs until he passed on in May 2014.

Yet for all his wanderings, Darryl—in his imagination, his writings, his stories, and in the deepest part of his soul—never, even for a day, left Hamma'wi, Pit River Country, the land where he was born. Rich in intimate memories and emotional ties, Hamma'wi was also holy land: it was his Jerusalem, his Bethlehem, his Mecca. *The Morning the Sun Went Down* is thus more than a memoir of an individual life: it's an atlas of a spiritual landscape. Each chapter, whether recounting a personal experience, a historical incident, or a story from Dreamtime, is self-contained and always rooted in a defined and named place: It'Ajuma (Pit River), Bo'ma-Rhee (Fall River Valley), Haya'wa Atwam (Porcupine Valley), Goose Valley, et cetera.

Individuals so dominate our modern sense of being that we often name places after people, and Pit River is no exception. A modern map of the area bears names such as Clayton Canyon, Burney Falls, Pittville, McGee Peak, and a host of others. (I can't help but wonder: Did anyone ever ask the peak whether it wanted to be named McGee?) In the world into which Darryl was born, in contrast, place defined and named the person. "My native name, Sul'ma'ejote," Darryl once explained, "is an act of culture, referring to the landscape where I was born, on the north bank of Sul'ma'ejote (Fall River, at Fall River Mills)." In a 2007 interview with *Indian Times*, a publication from UC Riverside, he explained his name and his identity in this manner:

> My connection to my mother and to the Earth is in the Fall River Valley, there beside the Fall River. Therefore my

native name must show that connection. I am Sul'ma'ejote. There is only one Sul'ma'ejote (the river) recognized by the great universal powers. In the recent past all males were named for the landscape of their birth. In this manner anyone would know you, your birthplace, your genealogy, and your history, just by your name. Ramsey Bone Blake, at birth, was named Chuta'pu-ki ahew, jui ajijujui. So, instantly one should know who he is and who his people are, and where that mountain is that has seven springs and one of them called Jui ajijujujui ("where the water comes up and the moss and grass are always dancing"). In this manner, the male person becomes an identifiable part of the landscape. So, like my Aunt Gladys said, sweeping her arm around the mountainous landscape, "Our spirits shall endure long after these mountains turn to dust." That gives us tenure unlimited. She also said, "You must have a 'real' name or the Great Powers won't know who to council."

Just how important place was to Darryl was illustrated dramatically during a trip we took together several years ago. It was after the devastating stroke that left one side of his body nearly paralyzed. Ray March, a newspaper editor who lives in the tiny town of Cedarville, located in the Surprise Valley in Modoc County in the northeast corner of California, had launched a literary conference, and he invited the poet Gary Snyder, the geologist Eldridge Moores, the scholar and cultural activist Jon Christensen, Darryl, and me, along with some local poets and writers, to lecture and teach.

Darryl was living in San Jose at the time, and I offered to drive him to the conference. I hadn't seen him in a while, and when one of his sons, now serving as his attendant, dropped him off at our

Berkeley office, I was shocked. My mind retained the image of Darryl as he was when I first met him: handsome, lively, and charming, a man of bullish physical strength tempered with athletic grace. The person I now saw was withered and frail, nearly deaf, scarcely able to walk, his once booming voice now hesitant and slurred. It was a warm day, and he was unable to get his jacket off without assistance, unable to take care of his basic needs.

With help, I got Darryl into my car and set off on what would be a seven-hour journey. The first leg of the trip, north through the Sacramento Valley to Redding, was excruciating. He had trouble hearing me, so I had to shout. His speech was so slurred I couldn't understand most of what he said, and getting him in and out of the car for the frequent rest stops he needed was a feat of engineering. For the first hundred miles or so, I was convinced that I'd made a dreadful mistake by offering to give Darryl a ride. Then, Akoo-Yet (Mount Shasta), the spiritual center of the Pit River world, came into view. Darryl struggled to sit straighter so that he could see it better, and he began to talk about the tiny but powerful spirit, Mis Misa, that lived within the mountain and was charged with balancing the world. As he spoke, he seemed to enter a trancelike state, as if taking dictation from the world beyond, his voice gaining force and clarity. Then, reaching Redding and heading east to Alturas, we entered Pit River Country, Darryl's homeland. With increasing excitement, force, and animation, Darryl began describing the sites we were passing. Up that road is where Craven Gibson lived, who used to tell us stories in the old language. Up that road is where Aunt Gladys and Uncle Rufus lived. That pile of rocks was dislodged by Coyote, who was chasing a woman up that hill. At that corner was a bar that served under-age kids. That waterfall has within it a Spirit Being with magical powers. That hillside was where women were collecting *apas* roots when a militia attacked and killed almost everyone; my great-great-grandmother was one of the few who escaped. In there is where I went hunting for deer with my father. Mile after mile the stories flowed. While I was exhausted from the seven-hour drive by the time we reached the conference site in Cedarville, Darryl walked out of the car with his body more alive, his voice now strong and clear, his being animated, looking youthful, confident, ready to take on the world.

"We were not created so fragile that our spirits can be broken with bullets," Darryl wrote in the opening paragraph of this book. Although referring broadly to his culture, this could very well be said of his life. As many times as the world dealt him a crushing blow, his spirit, nourished and sustained by the land of his birth, remained unbroken. As people gathered around him that day in Cedarville, Darryl seemed to glow with a power outside himself. I was reminded of the accounts of how the old-time Pit River shamans would summon spirit-helpers, the *dinihowis* and *damaagomes*, to assist them in their cures. Darryl had called upon the powers of Hamma'wi, his homeland, and they responded. Annikadel was by his side, as were Kwaw (Silver Fox), Jamol (Coyote), Wa-low-chah (Cloud Maiden). These and other Spirit Beings who worked within "The Great Mystery" to sing and dream the world into existence were there to welcome Darryl home. They came for the same reason we all came: to be in the presence of that rare and beautiful thing, an *It'jati'wa*, a real or genuine person. There are few enough of them in the world, and Darryl was clearly among them.

The Morning the Sun Went Down, Darryl Babe Wilson, Heyday, 1998, foreword to the 2016 edition

TRADITIONAL CALIFORNIA INDIAN CONSERVATION (1997)

It is often said that California Indians "lived lightly on the land." But before Europeans arrived in the Americas, California was the most densely populated area north of Mexico. Living lightly was not as simple as it might seem at first glance.

In their influential book *Before the Wilderness* (1993), Thomas Blackburn and Kat Anderson pull together some thought-provoking figures:

> A single cradleboard required 500 to 675 straight sour-berry sticks from six separate patches that had been burned or pruned prior to harvest, according to Lorrie Planas and Norma Turner.
>
> A medium-size cooking basket, notes Norma Turner, required about 3,750 deergrass stalks harvested from at least 75 healthy plants.
>
> A deer net forty feet long contained 7,000 feet of cordage, which demanded the harvesting of a staggering 35,000 plant stalks.

Multiplying these figures by the number of people and villages that crowded California's riverbanks and lakeshores, its broad valleys and coastal flats, one can see that the volume of plants, animals, minerals, water, firewood, and other resources that were necessary to feed, clothe, house, and otherwise outfit this large population was truly spectacular.

Yet despite such heavy demands on the land, California Indians did not deplete their bountiful resources or degrade their environments: early European visitors to California did not find polluted waterholes, diminished game, or impoverished vegetation. Far from it. California was a land of "inexpressible fertility," noted French sea captain Jean François de La Pérouse in 1786, a description repeated and elaborated upon by countless visitors to virtually every part of California.

It was no accident that such a dense population could sustain this abundance. It came about through conscious and highly evolved policies of what we now call conservation.

HUNTING

Because traditional conservation practices were so deeply embedded in the lives and habits of California's Native people, and because they do not always line up with the attitudes and practices of today's conservationists, such practices are not always easily perceived. Take, for example, the communal rabbit drive. These drives were common throughout most of California. Often, an entire community—men, women, and children—turned out for the event. Usually they would fan out over a broad area and—with much yelling and waving of arms—flush the rabbits out of the brush, driving them toward long nets or a row of waiting hunters, who would cripple the game by hurling rabbit sticks at their legs. Sometimes fire was used to flush the rabbits. Hundreds at a time might be slaughtered in this manner, the meat and skins later shared by everyone who partook. The entire event was said to have been festive, with laughter, feasting, and a general air of celebration.

This image of laughing men, women, and children engaged in the wholesale slaughter of rabbits would hardly gain the enthusiastic approval of most present-day environmentalists. Modern hunters might condemn these communal drives as unsportsmanlike. They would surely be illegal in today's world. Yet if we can put aside modern thoughts and values, at least for a moment, we may find a more productive way of understanding the social and ecological dynamics of the communal rabbit drive.

For one thing, the rabbit drive often had a purpose beyond the obvious one of obtaining meat and skins. It also served to check the numbers of a potentially ravenous animal, one known for its reproductive enthusiasm. As Lowell Bean points out in *Mukat's People* (1974), the Cahuilla often conducted rabbit drives "when fresh greens and seed-producing plants were growing lushly after winter rains. To allow these voracious browsing animals to eat their fill day by day would have reduced the potential food supply of the Cahuilla."

A similar dual purpose was at work in the hunting and gathering of squirrels, mice, gophers, and especially grasshoppers and moth larvae—all species that not only provide nutrition for people (grasshoppers taste like shrimp!) but, if let alone, have the capacity to damage plants upon which humans and other wildlife depend.

In cases where fire was used to help flush out the game, the fire itself, as has been increasingly understood in recent years, was beneficial in the management of land. By suppressing brush and coniferous trees, fire helped maintain a meadowland environment of healthy seed-bearing grasses, bulb-producing flowers, and other plants important to both humans and game.

Another aspect of the communal rabbit drive that is worth examining is the fact that the food and skins were shared by the entire community. The sharing of food, especially game, was common throughout California. In many places, for example, it was forbidden for a hunter (at least under certain circumstances) to eat what he had killed, lest it ruin his luck. He would have to give his kill to others, and he would receive sustenance from others as well. This economic system (quite different from modern systems based on competition and private consumption) had important social implications, knitting a community of people together. It also promotes what we are calling conservation. A system in which individuals hunt alone and compete against each other for a limited number of game animals leads to shortages and to insecurity for the hunter who fails to bring in game, while the successful hunter may tend toward overconsumption and hoarding. In an economy based on sharing, the peaks and troughs are leveled out somewhat, discouraging hoarding and over-hunting on one hand while hedging against famine and insecurity on the other.

Finally, an essential part of Indian conservation practice is the fact that, once killed, very little of the animal is wasted. Not only was the rabbit meat eaten or dried into jerky, the skins were used to weave warm blankets and cloaks, and (as with other small animals) the bones were sometimes crushed into a powder with a mortar and pestle and eaten along with the pounded meat and often much of the viscera.

In short, while the image of a festive people driving hordes of rabbits into nets might not fit the modern idea of conservation, when we examine the picture more closely we find that it is indeed ecologically responsible, serving not only to nourish people but to respect the needs of the land as well.

Communal drives were not, however, the only means of hunting. In contrast to this means of procuring common and voracious animals such as the rabbit, other manners and modes of hunting were used for rarer animals.

In his study of Sierra Mewuk life, *Miwok Cults* (1926), anthropologist Edward Gifford describes the huge number of rituals and restrictions that surrounded the hunting of condors, eagles, and prairie falcons. These birds were considered "chiefs," and their feathers were especially prized. But every step in the hunting process—from capturing the bird to killing it, handling its feathers, and disposing of its carcass—was surrounded by costly, elaborate, and time-consuming rituals. While such actions are certainly religious in nature, expressive of an understanding of the relationship between humans and the spirits of these chiefly beings, there is surely an ecological component as well. No wholesale or meaningless slaughter of these rare birds would be tolerated; a large number of human institutions had been put in place to limit the number of birds killed. As researcher Tom Reeves noted, it is interesting to recognize that these esteemed birds, whose populations were preserved through millennia of careful use by Native people, are the very ones that have been driven to the verge of extinction by modern practices.

A similar care was taken with the hunting of larger game, even economically significant game such a deer. While customs varied throughout California, in general a man was expected to have abstained from sex and to have sweated himself to cleanliness before hunting deer. He might not be allowed to hunt deer if his wife was "on her moon time," if there had been death or illness in his family, or during certain seasons. Among the Shasta, for example, the fall acorn gathering time marked an interruption in deer hunting; it was said that the deer were mating then and should not be disturbed. People gathered wood, shelled acorns, and generally prepared for winter, until the arrival of heavy rains would "clear the deer all up clean" and hunting could resume.

Rituals had to be performed and good manners observed during virtually every stage of hunting, butchering, and transporting meat, as well as cooking it and eating it. It was especially important for people to use as much of the deer as possible. Robert Lake in his book *Chílula: People from the Ancient Redwoods* (1982) writes:

> Almost every part of the elk and deer was used because it was considered a tribal violation against nature to waste food. As an example, all hides were skinned, scraped clean, and tanned with the animal's brains and a mixture of oak ashes. Hides with the hair on one side were used for winter cloaks and blankets, while the sacred Jump Dance and Deerskin Dance regalia were made exclusively from deer hides. Hides scraped clean and devoid of hair were tanned into buckskin and used to make women's dresses, blankets, winter moccasins, hair ties, knife sheaths, berry winnowing sorters, and various religious paraphernalia such as headdresses. All sinew from the deer was saved as thread for sewing of material, and used as domestic string during the making of personal materials. Elkhorns were converted into tools, money purses, and spoons for the men. Ankle and lower leg bone sections were used for Indian needles and awls. Thus, seldom any part of the deer or elk was ever wasted.

The reasons why people needed to treat deer and other important game animals with such dignity and care, both during the hunt and after as well, were generally phrased in terms of religious belief. In most modern cultures, hunting is seen as the conquest of an animal—the hunter, by skill or stealth, overcomes the natural defenses of the quarry and takes its life. But the traditional perception of hunting is different. To simplify a complex line of belief and feeling, one might say that the hunter does not take the life of the deer but rather the deer gives itself over to the hunter. It does so as a kind of exchange: the deer supplies the hunter with meat, skins, and other materials, while the hunter performs certain rituals and does certain acts that deer need to keep the herds healthy and the land productive. And, it is widely felt, the deer's spirit keeps watch over a hunter to make certain that he does indeed keep up his end of the bargain. If the hunter shows neglect or bad manners, if he mistreats the carcass or if food is wasted, such lapses of responsibility are observed and reported to other deer, who in the future will refuse to give themselves over to that hunter.

Among the Hupa it was believed that divinities called the "Tans" tended the deer. As Pliny Goddard explains in *Life and Culture of the Hupa* (1903):

> Every [Tan] has his definite abode; one lives near Mud Springs, eight miles east of the valley, another has his home on Bald Hill, and others on the principal ridges. They tend the deer on their special ranges. They are inclined to be stingy and hostile to strangers. When they wish they confine the deer inside the hills. When one of them sees a campfire on his territory he sends messengers to see who it may be and whether they are friends or strangers. A spider that comes down on a web and then goes back is thought to be the spy of a Tan. Small birds circling about are also his servants. To gain his favor, it is customary to spend the first night of a hunting expedition singing songs and making prayers to him. If he is pleased he will send out deer which will stand still to be shot. Should he take a dislike to a man, he will not only withhold the game, but

he will cause the hunter to become lost or even destroy him. He watches carefully to see that the deer he does permit to be killed are properly treated. It is believed that the deer's ghost tells his master that at such a house he was well treated and that he would like to go back again. This good treatment consists in the observance of all the many laws concerning the dressing, serving, and eating of the deer and also the disposal of the bones.

These beliefs that define the relationship between people and the animal world are basically religious, but it should be noted that they display a profound ecological wisdom. By demanding challenging practices such as partial fasting, sweating, and sexual abstinence before the hunt, by demanding time-consuming rituals and extra care in the butchering of meat and disposal of the carcass, and by insisting that the entire animal be used and that there be no waste, these beliefs discourage overhunting, "sport" hunting, or any other frivolous, casual, or wasteful practice. Religious belief and ecological principles are in deepest agreement that game is a precious resource and that restraint and care are demanded of humans who wish to benefit from that resource.

FISHING

When Europeans first arrived in California, the rivers and streams were clean, free-flowing, and crowded with fish. Throughout the fall, winter, and spring, millions of king salmon made their way through San Francisco Bay and the Carquinez Strait to spawn the further tributaries of the Sacramento and San Joaquin Rivers. Early visitors who stood at the banks of the Carquinez Strait commented that the salmon were so thick that it looked as if one could walk across the water on their backs. Coastal rivers too had great runs of salmon and steelhead, while inland lakes and streams were rich in trout, perch, sunfish, crappie, bullheads, and other native fish.

Wherever there were fish, there were people who were highly skilled at catching them. People fished with hook and line, with gigs, with a variety of nets and traps. In some areas people spread certain roots and herbs over the surface of the waters to "poison" a section of the stream, killing all the fish. Some created "drags" that were pulled up a river, sweeping fish along as if with a broom. In other places people built fish dams (weirs) that had the potential to block the migration of fish upstream to their spawning grounds. It was not because California's Native people lacked technology that the waterways were so full of life; rather, it was because potentially destructive technologies were applied with great restraint and intelligence.

Lucy Thompson, a Yurok woman who in 1916 published *To the American Indian* about her culture, describes the rules of the fish dams that were erected across the Klamath River:

> When the fish dam is put in, they have very strict laws governing it. There are nine traps which can be used: one belongs to Lock and his relatives, one to Lock-nee and his relatives, one to Nor-mer and her relatives, and so on down the line. [Lock is the person in charge of installing the fish dam; Lock-nee and Nor-mer, male and female, respectively, were his ritual assistants.] These families come in the morning, and each one takes from the trap that which belongs to them, as many salmon as they need, by dipping them out with a net that is made and used for this purpose; and they must not let a single one go to waste, but must care for all they take or suffer the penalty of the law, which was strictly enforced. After all these get their salmon, then

comes the poor class, which take what they can use, some of which they use fresh and the rest they cut up, smoke them lightly, then they are dried. When they are dried, they are taken down and packed in large baskets, with pepperwood leaves between each layer so as to keep the moths out of them, and then they are put away for the winter. The Indians from up the river, as far as they are able to come, can get salmon, and down the river the same.

In these traps there gets to be a mass of salmon, so full that they make the whole structure of the fish dam quiver and tremble with their weight, by holding the water from passing through the lattice-work freely. After all have taken what they want of the salmon, which must be done in the early part of the day, Lock or Lock-nee opens the upper gates of the traps and lets the salmon pass on up the river, and at the same time great numbers are passing through the open gap left on the south side of the river. This is done so that the Hupas on up the Trinity River have a chance at the salmon catching. But they keep a close watch to see that there are enough left to effect the spawning, by which the supply is kept up for the following year.

PLANTS

There is an aspect of European thinking that sees "wilderness" as fundamentally hostile. Nature is understood to be cruel; people must wrest their living out of a land that is less than forthcoming with its bounty. According to this way of thinking, we live in a dog-eat-dog world, one that rewards survival only to the fittest, a world in which humans are in constant competition with other life forms and with each other. This sense of scarcity and competition is built into all modern institutions—education, economics, government, etc.—and indeed into our daily habits and innermost thoughts.

While traditional Native people hardly felt that life was easy—it clearly wasn't—their attitudes toward the land and toward other creatures were nevertheless marked by a greater sense of comradery, respect, affection, and caring. These are the qualities that lend many Native conservation efforts a remarkable kindliness and quiet dignity. As Marie Potts, a Maidu elder, writes in *The Northern Maidu* (1977), "Our people were constantly aware of the need for conservation. In gathering roots some plants were left for seed and the disturbed ground was always leveled off . . . . A few berries were left on bushes for birds and squirrels and other animals."

The harvesting of seeds, berries, nuts, and roots was marked by consideration and gentleness. Seeds were collected from grasses and flowers with seed beaters—relatively flat, almost paddle-like baskets that harvesters swept through the plants to knock the seeds into collecting baskets. This method of harvesting seeds is less damaging than modern methods, and it is also less ruthlessly efficient: many seeds are left on the stalk, and some are scattered over the ground to feed other creatures or to sprout into new plants.

Roots, whether for food or for making baskets, were harvested with an apparently simple tool called a digging stick—a more or less straight stick with a fire-hardened point. The point was plunged into the ground and the root pried out. Compared to modern methods, this manner of harvesting dislodges a minimum amount of earth, while at the same time aerating and improving the soil.

California harvesting was marked by a moderate use of technology and by, as is well known, a deeply embedded conservation ethic that discouraged waste and encouraged people not to strip areas bare. Recent research, however, has been calling attention to other aspects of Native conservation. As is made clear in the path-finding work of Kat Anderson and others, as expressed in *Before the Wilderness* and in a number of subsequent journal articles, California Indians did not have a passive relationship to the land, collecting what the land "naturally" produced. By regularly burning the land, by pruning and coppicing certain shrubs, by carefully timing the digging of bulbs, and by other, often sophisticated practices, Native people consciously managed the land so as to preserve its wealth and increase its productivity. It is important to realize that California's bountiful harvests existed not despite a significant human presence but because of it.

To illustrate Native land management and conservation practices, let us examine a few of the techniques used to gather raw materials for baskets. Every household in California had dozens of baskets for cooking, eating, serving, and storage, for cradling babies, collecting seeds, carrying firewood, catching fish, trapping birds, and many other uses. To make these baskets, each community had to harvest—continually—tons of material: stalks, twigs, roots, dyes, and so on. Yet far from depleting supplies, Native weavers and their families gathered these valued resources in ways that protected them and in many cases increased their numbers. The following observations and quotes are taken from "Contemporary California Indian Basketweavers and the Environment," a paper by Beverly Ortiz originally presented at the seventh annual California Indian Conference in 1991, and later revised and expanded as a chapter in *Before the Wilderness*.

Pruning. Willow and redbud are among the plants that benefit from pruning; it can increase their vigor and productivity, and it stimulates the growth of the long, straight, flexible shoots preferred by weavers.

"We're always saying that when we gather, we prune at the same time. Then the shoots will grow again . . . and now and then when we do that, I sometimes clip more so that more will come up. And it does. It comes right back up." [Barbara Bill, Dunlap Mono, to Beverly Ortiz, 1991]

Digging roots. The rhizomes (underground stems) of sedge, bulrush, bracken fern, and woodwardia fern, and the roots of willow and spruce, were among the most favored basketweaving materials. Weavers often cultivated particular areas; especially favorable sites might be in the same family for generations. Loosening the soil, thinning the roots, weeding, and constant tending all conspired to increase the health and productivity of plants.

"One advantage of going back every second year—or at least every third year—to a good root-digging place is that you keep the roots from getting overabundant and tangled and thus hard to dig. When the roots are tangled— as they are in most long-untouched places—they are very hard to untangle, especially as you must try to keep them long, not allowing them to break into short pieces. When you run into roots of other plants, you should take them out so the sedge roots can grow without competition, much as you weed a garden. When there are many mixed roots, the Indian women must labor for hours to get out the long good roots." [Elsie Allen, *Pomo Basketmaking* (1972)]

"You make sure you cover the [spruce] roots back up. You peel up the moss. The ground beneath the spruce trees is soft. It's wonderful to walk on. You can take it and pull it back all the way. The roots lay right there on top. You hardly ever have to dig for them. Then you take a little bit from that root. Then you cover it back up and go to a different tree." [Elsie Griffin, Yurok, to Beverly Ortiz, 1991]

Alder bark dye. The bark of the alder tree provides a red dye used in basketry.

"With the alder dyes a lot of people say you cut the inner bark away, but you don't. You take a piece of the inner bark, not the whole tree. And then it won't scar the tree." [Elsie Griffin to Beverly Ortiz, 1991]

FIREWOOD

Native Californians used wood for cooking and for heating their homes and sweathouses. Where all that wood came from is an interesting and important consideration, for there was most likely much less deadwood in the old days than there is today. Old descriptions portray much of California that is now forested or thick with scrub as having been meadowland or open savannah. Even the oak forests were often depicted as resembling European parks, with large, fully matured, widely spaced oak trees and a clear, grassy understory. Very likely the frequent burnings by which Native people managed the land consumed much of the deadwood and suppressed brush and scrub wood that could have been easily gathered.

In parts of the world today, a large population combined with a diminished supply of firewood has been a formula for ecological disaster. The denuding of the Himalayan forests in Nepal and Tibet and the cataclysmic desertification of Africa are two of the most horrendous examples. Yet in California, despite an apparent scarcity of wood (at least in certain areas) and a significant population, no such environmental degradation occurred. In an unpublished manuscript ("The Achumawi," 1929), anthropologist and linguist Jaime de Angulo addresses the problem:

Two things are of prime importance in selecting a good [village] site. There must be a spring or a stream close by. There must be fuel nearby. The question of fuel is extremely important. The reader must not forget that these Indians had no axes. Firewood in Indian parlance means dead branches. It does not mean dead branches on the ground, either, for the supply of that would soon be exhausted around a village. It means dead branches still standing on the trees. The way to get those was to break them down by means of a long pole with a crotch tied to the end. It must be remembered that Indians did not need as much fuel as we do, for in the underground house packed with humanity, a very small fire was all that was needed to keep the house warm. But even so, the supply of dead branches in a locality must often have become exhausted. It must often have caused a village to change site.

As de Angulo suggests, the houses, by their structure, lent themselves to conservation of firewood. Semi-subterranean sweathouses and earth-covered communal dwellings were extremely well insulated, and could be heated by a relatively small fire. Other styles of dwelling—bark houses, brush houses, tule houses, etc.—were fairly compact and were oriented to wind and sun so as to maintain heat in winter while staying cool in the summer. The rectangular plank houses of the Klamath River area and Hoopa Valley often had river stones around their sills and elegant stone entryways. More than just decoration, the stones would absorb heat during the day and would transfer the heat to the interiors of the houses as the air cooled at night.

Cooking methods were also well adapted to using fuel efficiently. Pit ovens, stone-lined hearths, and stone boiling (cooking a basket of acorn soup, for example, by dropping heated stones into it) are all very frugal in their use of firewood.

The scarcity of firewood might also have contributed to social organization. Jaime de Angulo, again in "The Achumawi," discusses the manner in which food was divided:

> How the provisions . . . were apportioned I do not know. One might expect that since at the opening of spring all the occupants of a communal house went out "camping" and harvesting in separate families, that each family would keep its own store of food for the winter. But if families kept their own stores of food, it would mean separate cooking fires in the communal house. It would mean in fact more or less of a division of the communal house into apartments. This is not at all unthinkable, and in fact it is the practice among many peoples. But all the old Indians I have questioned deny this. They say there was only one fire, right under the smoke-hole.

The point here is not so much that the shortage of firewood led to a sharing of food; such socially complex behavior has origins and implications that go way beyond the conservation of firewood. Rather, it is that for Native people a sustainable and agreeable way of life was one that, among many other factors, worked with, rather than fought against, the limitations of the environment.

PROPERTY, TERRITORY, AND SOCIAL ORDER

Roland Dixon, in his study *The Northern Maidu* (1905), describes a remarkable Northern California quarry site:

Near Oroville was one of the best-known spots for getting flint, from a cave on or near Table Mountain. The opening to the cave was very small, but, once in, the size was such that a man could stand upright. A person going to get flint must crawl in, and then throw ahead of him beads or dried meat as offerings to the spirits for the flint he was about to take. A person was allowed to take only so much flint as he could break off at a single blow. The flint obtained, the person had to crawl out backwards. If the regulations were not complied with, the person would have bad luck; the flint would not chip well, or would fail to kill.

The religious nature of this approach to gathering flint has the effect of allocating a scarce resource in an ingenious way. By limiting access to the quarry site and further limiting the amount of flint that might be collected at any one time, the rituals and beliefs that governed this site helped protect the resource and make sure that no single family would gain a monopoly on its use.

Property rights and territorial rights might also be seen, at least in part, as ways of allocating and even protecting resources. It is a common misconception that California Indians had no property, that land and its resources were open to everyone. This was hardly the case. The ways in which property was defined varied widely from tribe to tribe, but it was always a well-articulated, well-understood body of law. Sometimes people owned plots of land, particular trees, or special fishing places outright; in other situations they owned "rights." One family, for example, might own salmon-fishing rights from a particular place along a river; another family might own the eel-fishing rights there; and a third family might own the rights to cross the river at the same place.

Samuel Barrett, in *Material Aspects of Pomo Culture* (1952), describes some of the ways in which the Pomo defined property and territory:

> According to my informants, property rights were every-where quite clearly defined. Certain areas and places were, as a rule, communally controlled. These were the hunting grounds of a village, and the spots where good fishing was to be had. Some of these were what might even be termed international, for they were open to all comers, regardless of tribal connections.
>
> Certain trees, however, were definitely individual, or at least family property. The same is true of certain open-ings where seeds were abundant or where "Indian pota-toes" grew. The practice varied somewhat from village to village, but in general the reserved spots, etc., were known to all and rights were respected.
>
> As for territorial limitations, informants stated that the head men met and agreed upon the boundaries of their respective territories. At meetings in the dance houses these boundaries were announced and discussed. Usually this was sufficient. However, if a boundary had to be marked, they simply tied a girdle of leaves (pep-perwood was frequently used) around the tree along the line, at intervals of about a mile. These girdles, which were renewed from time to time, were tied just as high as a man could conveniently reach. It is said that the primary pur-pose of such markers was to prevent the younger people from getting out of bounds.
>
> An oak tree, manzanita bush, or any other privately owned food source could be marked by tying to it a piece of brush or by setting up a stake. No one would then molest

it. Others used a system of blazing to mark their trees.

It is quite clear that any considerable disregard of boundaries, or of reserved spots or areas, and the consequent infringement upon individual or village property rights, might cause serious trouble. Instances of such difficulties which resulted, in some cases, in prolonged hostilities have been elsewhere recorded.

There was, however, relative freedom of intercourse among village units, and if the people of one village desired to secure some food from the territory of another village, it was usually only necessary to ask permission of the owners. Indeed, such a visit from the people of another village would very likely be made the occasion of feasting and dancing. There probably would be some exchanging as well, though this could hardly be considered real trade or commerce . . . . The people of the interior valleys, or even of the lake region, made one or two trips a year over to the coast to procure seaweed, salt, and other sea foods, and especially to procure the clam shells from which beads were made. They would probably take over to the coast magnesite, dried lake fish, and other items not common to the coastal region.

The modern world has given property ownership and territoriality a bad name. It may very well be that words describing property, ownership, and territory in terms of a Native relationship to land and resources do not have the same connotations that they do in English. At the heart of the Native concept of property, for example, was not just a bestowal of rights and privileges but an acceptance of responsibility. Anthropologist Robert Heizer had an interesting observation along these lines. He noted that the most common cause of warfare among traditional people was trespass, usually with the motive of acquiring plant or animal foods.

In this light, much of [tribal] warfare may be said to be motivated not by innate aggressive tendencies but as a conservation measure. Within group-owned territories there is commonly family ownership of food resources such as grass seed areas, patches of nut-bearing trees, fishing holes, hunting tracts, etc., which are inherited in either the male or female line. Private ownership of this sort is generally accompanied by requirements of regulated and limited gathering together with the physical protection of the resources. These concepts point up the awareness that future generations of users must be provided for.

There is an important suggestion here: traditional property rights and territoriality might be looked at afresh, not as examples of human greed but rather as systems to allocate resources and the responsibility for taking care of these resources in an equitable way.

CONCLUSION

In her article "Conservation as Formerly Practiced by the Indians of the Klamath River Region," written in 1932, Ruth K. Roberts says:

> The Indians, of necessity, avoided diminution of any natural resources upon which their life depended. Public opinion and community law disapproved of any waste. Trees were felled only for construction of canoes and houses, and dry brush and sticks were used for firewood . . . . To destroy wildlife for any other reason than to meet his need of food would have been as ridiculous a procedure to the Indian as if we entered our own gardens or went among our own herds and destroyed for the sheer

enjoyment of our prowess as destroyers . . . . In contrast to the white man's idea of sportsmanship, the Indian killed only what he needed for food, and he wasted no edible parts of the game taken by him. Even the entrails of animals were dried for winter food for the dogs. Anyone who caught more fish or killed more game than he and his family could use shared it with others who were less fortunate. To the Indian, hunting was not a sport; it was a means of obtaining his food supply, and the killing of wildlife was limited to his necessity for sustenance. To destroy this supply meant nothing short of self-destruction.

What we now call "conservation" was an everyday practice of the Native people of California, embedded in religious belief, social structures, good manners, and everyday habit. It was spread so widely over so many cultural practices that it is difficult to sum up, impossible to define. Yet surely there is a sentence in Ruth Roberts's article that bears deep thought: "To destroy wildlife for any other reason than to meet his need of food would have been as ridiculous a procedure to the Indian as if we entered our own gardens or went among our own herds and destroyed for the sheer enjoyment of our prowess as destroyers."

For the first Europeans who settled in California, the land was a "wilderness"; it belonged to no one, and its wealth was here for the taking. Certainly too much of that attitude remains today, worked into our laws, our institutions, and our daily habits. To Native people who have lived here for thousands of years, however, and whose actions shaped the landscape, it was indeed a garden—a garden that needed tending and care and that rewarded such efforts with bountiful food, a sustainable way of life, and an environment of almost unimaginable health, vigor, and beauty.

REFERENCES

Allen, Elsie. *Pomo Basketmaking: A Supreme Art for the Weaver.* Happy Camp, CA: Naturegraph, 1972.

Barrett, S. A. *Material Aspects of Pomo Culture.* Milwaukee: Bulletin of the Public Museum of the City of Milwaukee, vol. 20, pt. 2, 1952.

Bean, Lowell J. *Mukat's People: The Cahuilla Indians of Southern California.* Berkeley: University of California Press, 1974.

Blackburn, Thomas C., and Kat Anderson, eds. *Before the Wilderness: Environmental Management by Native Californians.* Ballena Press Anthropological Papers, No. 40. Menlo Park, CA: Ballena Press, 1993.

de Angulo, Jaime. "The Achumawi." Unpublished manuscript, 1929.

Dixon, Roland B. *The Northern Maidu.* Bulletin of the American Museum of Natural History, vol. 17, pt. 3. Originally published in 1905. New York: AMS Press, 1983.

Dozier, Deborah. *The Heart Is Fire.* Berkeley, CA: Heyday Books, 1998.

Gifford, Edward Winslow. *Miwok Cults.* University of California Publications in American Archaeology and Ethnology, vol. 18, no. 3. Berkeley: University of California Press, 1926.

Goddard, Pliny Earle. *Life and Culture of the Hupa.* University of California Publications in American Archaeology and Ethnology, vol. 1, no. 1. Berkeley: The University Press, 1903.

Heizer, Robert F., ed. "Primitive Man as an Ecological Factor." *The Kroeber Anthropological Society Papers*, vol. 13. Berkeley: University of California, Berkeley, 1955.

Lake, Robert G., Jr. *Chilula: People from the Ancient Redwoods.* Washington, DC: University Press of America, 1982.

Loeb, Edwin M. *Pomo Folkways.* University of California Publications in American Archaeology and Ethnology, vol. 19, no. 2. Berkeley: University of California Press, 1926.

Potts, Marie. *The Northern Maidu.* Happy Camp, CA: Naturegraph, 1977.

Roberts, Ruth K. "Conservation as Formerly Practiced by the Indians of the Klamath River Region." *California Fish and Game*, vol. 18, no. 4, October 1932.

Shepherd, Alice. *In My Own Words: Stories, Songs, and Memories of Grace McKibbin, Wintu.* Berkeley: Heyday Books, 1997.

Thompson, Lucy. *To the American Indian: Reminiscences of a Yurok Woman.* Berkeley: Heyday Books in conjunction with Peter E. Palmquist, 1991.

News from Native California, vol. 11, no. 2, 1997/8

WHAT THE TULE HOUSE HAS TO TEACH US
(1997)

One of the biggest challenges in teaching youngsters about California Indian life is to get them beyond the facts and fantasies, beyond the rote responses. It is easy enough, for example, to tell them that the Indians of the San Francisco Bay Area lived in dome-shaped houses made of tule (bulrush); getting them to imagine what life would have been like in a tule house is somewhat more difficult.

As a special favor to an old friend, I found myself in front of a group of fourth-graders one day describing a traditional tule house. I explained how the framework of willows was erected and how the tule was cut, aged, bundled, and tied onto the framework to form a watertight covering. I tried to evoke the texture of the tule and its distinctive smell—earthy and musty, a bit like Lipton tea. I asked them to envision what it would be like to crawl through the doorway into the cool, dark interior of the dwelling, to touch the earthen floor packed hard, almost to a polish, and strewn with sleeping mats and rabbit-skin blankets. I tried to get them to picture what it would be like to sleep in one of these houses shoulder-to-shoulder with brothers and sisters, uncles and aunts, parents and grandparents; what it would be like to wake up on a cold winter morning to hear the elders, who would have stayed awake all night to keep the fire lit, talking softly among themselves; or to look through the entrance on a bright spring morning to see the welcome sunshine.

"Now what do *you* think it would be like to live in a tule house?" I asked in my most ingratiating manner. A dozen hands shot up. I pointed to a little girl with dreamy eyes and a charming smile.

"Yucky!" she said, with unexpected clarity and force.

"Why?" I asked, shocked and completely taken aback.

"I like having my own room. I like how big my house is. I don't want to live on a dirt floor with tule walls and sleep with my whole family."

I was amazed and in truth delighted with the response—I realized that she had indeed been picturing life in a tule house. Her real, deeply felt answer, free of piety or politically correct platitudes, was a wonderful beginning for a discussion about tule houses. So without trying to "convert" her, I led the discussion along a different track.

Here are some of the topics we considered:

What would it mean if all the materials for building a house were free and readily available to everyone? It costs tens of thousands of dollars to buy the lumber, plumbing, wiring, tiles, and fixtures needed for a modern house. What if all the material you needed was growing all around you, free to anyone who wanted to gather it? The first thing that dawned on everyone was that under these conditions there would be no homelessness. (I was surprised at how deeply concerned these youngsters were with the problem of homelessness.) We also discussed how when you are an adult, you end up spending a quarter to a third of your waking hours earning enough for housing, not to mention the huge amount of time spent dusting, mopping, sweeping, painting, mowing the lawn, and fixing up. Living in a tule house might have its inconveniences, but it would free up a lot of time. "What would your parents do with the time?" we wondered. Would they, like Native people in traditional cultures, put more time into the arts, religion, ceremony, socializing, or even play?

We also touched upon the self-sufficiency of a society that has no need for the far-flung political and economic ties and massive transportation networks that ensure our access to housing materials, no need for our lumber and mining industries; tule and willow grow locally and in such abundance that they can be harvested without damaging the environment. Under such conditions, we would have a peculiar freedom—the freedom to develop our own languages, customs, set of beliefs and ways of doing things.

What would it be like if all the houses in your village were made of the same material and were more or less the same size? This question was loaded, and we edged gingerly around it, because what it kept leading to was a discussion of class—of how our dominant culture creates distinctions between people based on wealth, and it makes a difference whether you live in a mansion in the hills, in a rented apartment, or in a trailer park. We discussed, at least circumspectly, the implications of living in a society where the differences between being poor and being wealthy are not so dramatic as in our own.

What would it be like to live in a society where houses were not a major form of wealth? Owning a house in this culture gives people a huge piece of wealth, a way of providing for their old age, something to pass along to their children. What if you lived in a society where houses were not a form of wealth? How would your parents store wealth? In regalia? In baskets? Or would people redefine "wealth" more in terms of their relationships and connections to others?

Is privacy a good thing? Most of the youngsters either had their own room or shared one with only one sibling, and they liked it that way. In traditional times, it is true, there wasn't much privacy. Tule houses were used primarily for storing things and for sleeping. The rest of life—cooking, washing, entertainment, etc.—was carried on outdoors and in a more or less communal atmosphere. We considered the possibility that the privacy modern life affords us is a mixed blessing—does it bring an element of isolation, selfishness, and mistrust with it?

We discussed many other things as well, and in the end I asked the question again: "How many of you would like to give up your houses and live in an old-time tule house?" Still no takers. But we had accomplished something that afternoon—a recognition of the social and moral expenses of our way of life, and a recognition of the value of other peoples' choices. While no one in the class wanted to take up residence in a tule house, it was clear that at least some aspect of what it means to live in a tule house had taken up residence in us.

News from Native California, vol. 10, no. 3, 1997

INDIAN PEDAGOGY: A LOOK AT TRADITIONAL CALIFORNIA INDIAN TEACHING TECHNIQUES (2005)

To those who don't know much about Indian cultures, the phrase "Indian pedagogy" might seem like a stretch. Granted, Native cultures in California did not have what a modern resident would recognize as a formal educational system—designated teachers with specialized training, a defined curriculum, places and times set aside for instruction, clear standards for attainment, and so on. If we could have wandered into an Indian village a couple of hundred years ago, we might very well have concluded (as did other early visitors) that Native children learned simply by following their parents and other relatives around from one chore to the next, accumulating knowledge by absorption, imitation, and, at best, casual ad hoc instruction. Seeing no schools, courthouses, churches, or farms, we, like other early observers, might have concluded that these "simple" hunting-and-gathering cultures had little in the way of educational, governmental, religious, agricultural, or economic practice or philosophy, and what little they did have was "underdeveloped" and "primitive." In other words, they weren't like us.

It would be impossible in this brief essay to tackle all these ethnocentric assumptions—the arrogant belief, so deeply embedded in Western culture, that we occupy the pinnacle of human achievement and that others are to be ranked according to how close they come to us. Recent generations of anthropologists and other scholars have steadily underscored the fact that so-called primitive people led lives of considerable complexity that included highly evolved, sophisticated, self-aware systems of governance, religion, and landscape manipulation, as well as of education, even if these systems are not easily recognizable through the prism of modern Western culture.

Education, in short, was not something that incidentally and passively happened to Native children as they grew up. In fact, the need to properly educate children was striking, and considerable effort and skill was expended on it. Native California cultures had no writing; with no way to record knowledge—whether geographic, technical, artistic, social, or religious—transmitting and securing that knowledge deeply and accurately in the minds of a younger generation was of great concern. These cultures passed on knowledge with care, with strategy, with a self-conscious and articulated sense of educational theory. It is no exaggeration to say there was indeed a Native pedagogy.

Being neither Indian nor an educator, I don't claim the authority or the background to explore this subject in the depth it deserves. I am, however, able to draw on thirty years of research, writing, and publishing about California Indian communities. Here are a few observations that may be of value to educators (including parents) now. At the least, an open-minded consideration of these traditional techniques and the assumptions underlying them may prove thought-provoking and may point to places where our own methods and educational system are overly narrow or even dangerously ineffective.

REPAIRING FEATHERS

In 1987 I co-founded *News from Native California* with two friends: Vera Mae Fredrickson, an anthropologist living in Berkeley, and David Peri, a Coast Miwok Indian who taught at Sonoma State University. In our first issue we ran an article by Harry Roberts, who had long been associated with the San Francisco Zen Center.

Although non-Indian himself, Harry had grown up near the mouth of the Klamath River and had lived closely with the Yurok. Robert Spott of the village of Requa, a man Harry referred to as "Uncle," was a well-known Yurok political and cultural leader. One morning, Harry recalled, he was watching Uncle repair the feathers on the long headdress wands used for a healing ceremony called the Brush Dance. Uncle was working hard, meticulously smoothing old feathers and re-gluing new feathers in places where young Harry could scarcely discern any damage. Why all the finickiness? Harry asked. The damage was hardly visible in the daylight, and the Brush Dance would be held at night; no one, neither dancers nor audience, would ever notice all of Uncle's demanding, scrupulous work. For a long time Uncle Spott avoided answering the question. Instead he asked that young Harry work on the answer himself, while he gave Harry only occasional prods, hints, and stories. Only after Harry had been forced to think hard about his question did Spott discuss it at all, and even then not so much directly as by telling a story that would lead to understanding.

I remember my co-editor David Peri remarking at the time that this was an excellent example of how the older generation conveyed important information. Robert Spott could have answered the question easily and directly, David observed, but he hadn't. By refusing to answer the question and refusing even to have much to do with Harry until Harry was on the way to figuring it out himself, Robert first put pressure on the youngster so that he'd know that what he had asked was important. Then he let him work on it, and when young Harry seemed closer to figuring it out, Robert told a story that made it all come clear. Did I understand what was going on? David asked. Did I understand the difference between teaching and learning? In fact, David noted, there was a saying: When you teach someone something, you've robbed the person of the experience of learning it. You need to be cautious before you take that experience away from someone else.

This distinction between teaching and learning forms a basic element of what I am calling traditional California Indian pedagogy.

INITIATION

Among the most powerful memories of an older generation of Indians was that of their initiation. In many tribes a girl at her first menstruation would be sequestered, sometimes in a specially built shelter away from the family dwelling. Here she would eat special foods, perform certain rituals, and act in prescribed ways. Elders observed her closely, monitoring her gestures and her motions—there was only one approved way, for example, of scratching herself if her skin itched—and questioning her about her thoughts, even her dreams. Older women—her grandmother, her aunt, sometimes her mother, and others—would also lecture her, revealing secret knowledge that was kept from younger girls. After a period of time the initiate would be brought out in a public dance and celebration, transformed from a girl into a woman.

Boys often had a similarly dramatic and defined coming-of-age. In Southern California, boys reaching puberty would often be removed from their families and put under the care of spiritual leaders who would reveal secrets and transmit esoteric knowledge, often with the aid of powerful hallucinogens. Sometimes the initiate, in an altered state of consciousness, would be brought to a specially made sand painting, the patterns of which provided an explanation of how the powers of the world are aligned—nothing less than the blueprint of the universe. In Northern California a young man might be invited to join the men's society of the roundhouse. He might in fact spend an entire winter in a subterranean roundhouse where he would learn songs, sacred dances, rituals, and other arcane (as well as practical) knowledge before emerging in the spring as an adult.

Today we like to think that we live in a society marked by open access to knowledge, but even in this age of the World Wide Web, this is hardly the case. All kinds of information—nuclear secrets, military secrets, commercial secrets, private medical records, and so on—are kept out of reach of the uninitiated, often at considerable effort and expense. It is not unusual to visit a public archive to view someone's papers and discover that the files are under seal until fifty years after the person's death, because they contain "sensitive material." And we all know that once we discover that something is secret we are all the more eager to learn about it. Traditional societies used this universal human trait—our eagerness to reach out for withheld knowledge—in a very successful pedagogical practice.

Children learn differently from adults, the Indians felt, and therefore learning had to be paced. If exposed to adult knowledge while too young, people would misunderstand and devalue it. Children learn in a particular way, it was said, and you needed to respect that way. Once they reached the threshold of adulthood and were judged ready for the complex knowledge one needed to be a fully functioning adult, the knowledge was carefully prepared and presented to them—not thrown at them nor left around for them to pick at but handed to them in a highly ritualized setting that made the recipients feel that what they were being given was long sought, highly valued, and would consequently be cherished, remembered, and likewise passed on.

Paradoxically, making certain kinds of knowledge scarce helped ensure that it would be conveyed carefully from one generation to the next in a manner that reinforced its importance. For example, the creation myth is arguably the most important piece of knowledge in any culture, and transmitting it with total accuracy, with even the smallest details intact, is of major concern, especially for cultures that depend entirely on the spoken word and human memory. One would imagine that the best way of doing this would be to make sure that the creation story was told as often and in as many circumstances as possible, but this was not the case. Many tribes severely restricted the time and manner of telling. In some areas of California, for example, the creation story could be told only during the winter months, only at night, only in a sanctified space, only by a particularly trained and authorized person who had to fast for so many days or who had to sit in a particular posture, etc. Because the telling of the creation story was rare and difficult, its importance was emphasized, its recitation made keener, and the audience's listening more intense.

WHAT A SONG MEANS

In Southern California a few people still sing what are called "bird songs"—linked verses that used to be sung for four nights straight during the winter. They recount the wanderings of divinities over the world in the earliest moments of creation. My friend Ernest Siva, a Serrano and Cahuilla Indian from Banning, is one such singer.

Once after he had sung an especially lovely verse, I summoned up the courage to ask him what it meant. After some thought, he responded something like this: If I was asking what the words meant, he'd be glad to translate them for me. But that's not really what the song meant, at least to him. What gave the song its meaning was not just the words but who had taught it to him, when it could be sung, who could sing it, all the other times it had been sung, to whom he had taught or would be teaching it. When it was sung at a funeral, for example, that circumstance added to the memory and thus the meaning of the song.

Traditional societies personally transmit and personally use knowledge. It doesn't exist in books that can be shelved; songs are not recorded on CDs that can be played at will. Knowledge exists only because one person gives it to another, and it is kept alive only by repeated use and personal transmission. How one learns something and uses that knowledge are important in traditional societies. People in the dominant culture, on the other hand, seem to feel that whatever is to be learned exists independently from the way it is transmitted. If, for example, one person learns something from a parent, another from a teacher, a third from a computer, we like to assume that they all know the same thing. You simply know as a fact that the Earth revolves around the sun, whether you absorbed that fact in early childhood, learned it in adulthood, figured it out on your own, had to reject religious belief to get there, or learned it in English or in some other language. No matter how you learned it, it's a fact, and in our culture facts are seen as solid little building blocks, unchanged by how they are acquired or used.

In traditional cultures that does not seem to be the case. Knowledge, transmitted orally from generation to generation, comes with much more history, more personal interaction, more flavor, if you will, and perhaps is felt with greater depth and emotional complexity. I remember that in my grammar school a teacher I had a crush on would read us books such as *Heidi*. I still think of the Swiss Alps with a great yearning and great love that I can't help but think would not be there had I picked the book up from the local library and read it myself. Native pedagogy concerns itself not just with what is taught but with who teaches it and under what circumstances. Teaching is not, in other words, just a means of conveying knowledge and information; it is an integral part of that knowledge and information as well.

THE CENTER OF THE WORLD

Jaime de Angulo, a linguist and collector of folklore, was once working in the high, lonely country between Redding and Alturas in northeastern California, interviewing elders who still spoke the Achumawe and Atsugewi languages. When one old man began telling him the story of how Silver Fox created the world, Jaime interrupted. What do you mean Silver Fox created the world? I just heard from your neighbors that it was Coyote who created the world. The old man didn't pause. Well, he shrugged, over there they say it was Coyote, here we say it was Silver Fox, and he went on with the story.

I've witnessed the same thing many times. In northwestern California, for example, the Hupa have their world-renewal rituals at a place they consider the center of the world—the spot from which humans first emerged—Takimildin. A neighboring tribe, the Yurok, likewise have a center-of-the-world place, Kenek. And not far from them are the Karuk, with Katamin as their center of the world. And it is not unusual these days for a member of one tribe to visit another's rituals and even dance at their world center.

In Western cultures this level of tolerance would be almost

inconceivable. Were this Europe, we would likely have witnessed centuries of religious warfare, with lands laid waste and countless "heretics" massacred, until the location of the "real" center of the world was resolved. Western culture seems to crave certainty; we demand it from our religious beliefs and from our educational system alike. We seem to feel that questions have answers, and that these answers are exclusive—answering "yes" precludes answering "no." Things are true or they are false. Although we pay lip service to mystery, we construct educational systems around the assumption that things are knowable, and students are rewarded for knowing, for having the correct answer. If we don't know something it's because we're ignorant, rather than because some things—often the most important things—are simply not knowable.

Built into California Indians' traditional teaching methods, and indeed their overall philosophy, is, I feel, a marvelous acknowledgment that much in the world around us is fundamentally mysterious and cannot be known with certainty. In fact, an important aspect of Indian pedagogy is something that I find heartbreakingly beautiful: a sense of humility, a sense that the world is far bigger, more complex, and more mysterious than the human mind can ever encompass, and that to be a full human being you need to learn to live with ambiguity and a tolerance for the unknown. The alternative is to live with brittle delusions of certainty.

BUILDING A ROUNDHOUSE

Throughout much of north-central California—from Mendocino and Sonoma Counties east to the Sierra foothills—the roundhouse was (and in places still is) a major cultural and architectural attainment. In traditional times, this large communal building was mostly underground and served variously as a place of worship, a community center, and a university.

A few years ago I was at Chaw'se State Park [now Indian Grinding Rock State Historic Park], where the Sierra Mewuk community erected an especially graceful roundhouse in about 1970, then rebuilt it in the early 1990s. It is well used, especially at an annual September event called Big Time, when people come from all over California to celebrate the fall harvest, using the roundhouse for dancing, singing, praying, and otherwise honoring their cultures. Here, especially at dawn when dancers enter the roundhouse to greet the rising sun, one can feel the mystery, beauty, ongoing vitality, and truthfulness of California's oldest cultures.

One day I was talking with my friend Dwight Dutschke, whose family had taken part in the original construction and who himself has been actively engaged in the annual Big Time. Our conversation turned to how the roundhouse had been constructed, and I was questioning him about certain details: how the entranceway had been oriented, how the posts had been put in, how the rafters had been secured, and so on. Finally he said, I know what you are getting at. You're getting at the fact that we could have constructed it better. No, no, I protested, that's not at all what I was getting at. Well, he went on, we could indeed have constructed it better. A lot of the people who worked on it were into construction and we know how to build. We could have put creosote on the posts when they went into the ground. There's nothing in the old laws that says you can't do that. There's nothing in the old laws that says you have to tie the rafters with grape vine; we could have used wire and nails. We could have built it so that it would last a hundred years. But we didn't. We didn't because there was another law we had to follow. When you build a roundhouse, you construct it so that it falls apart every twenty years. That way every generation has the chance to rebuild it. Every generation has to learn the songs, the ceremonies, the techniques. If you want to make a building last you do it one way. But if you want to make the knowledge last, you do it another way.

Sometimes at these annual Big Times a group such as the Pomo dancers from Elem Colony near Clear Lake will perform a Big Head Dance. The Big Head is a mysterious figure, at least to me. Associated with a divinity called Kuksu, in some places it is whistled out of the forest where it dwells, entering the roundhouse with a grand halo of a feathered headdress, pounding the floor with bare feet in a rhythmic and repetitive dance, while the fire from the middle of the roundhouse casts great shadows on the ceiling. Powerful and awe-inspiring, the dance and the regalia associated with it are protected by ritual, rules, and cultural proscriptions. I once asked one of the Big Head dancers to explain it to me. His response was, I'm not sure what it means. All I know is that when I do the dance, it puts my head in the big way.

Both these phenomena—building the roundhouse and performing the Big Head Dance—point to yet another aspect of traditional pedagogy: a need not just to "know" but to experience. Knowledge is not just something to be stored and talked about; it's something to be lived. It's got to be "cooked into you," as they say. It's not enough to have a lot of information, to have the "right" ideas, to be able to answer the question correctly. Knowledge apart from experience cannot be trusted and won't last, certainly not in a culture without writing. A Western theologian might very well research and assemble facts about what the Big Head Dance means; the dancer, however, knows something more important and lasting: that it puts his head in the "big way."

Walk almost anywhere in the forested lands of northwestern California and you will hear the plaintive call of the mourning dove. On at least four separate occasions when I was with Indian friends, this call triggered the telling of the story of Mourning Dove, *o'row'e* in the Yurok language. It is perhaps the most popular and widely told of the old-time stories.

Like other such mythic tales, the story of *o'row'e* takes place in the distant past, shortly after the creation, when all the animals of the world were a kind of divine people (*woge* in Yurok). They seem to have lived and even looked much like people, and long ago their deeds established the world as we know it today.

In that old world, *o'row'e* was a gambler. Once he was deeply involved in a gambling game with others. He was on a great winning streak, piling up around himself great stores of Indian treasure: white deer skins, huge obsidian blades, red woodpecker scalps, long dentalia shells, in short all the wealth and beauty of the Indian world. He was interrupted by a messenger who had come to fetch him, to tell him that his grandfather was dying and that he needed to come immediately to the deathbed. Just a few more hands, just a few more hands, said *o'row'e*, and I'll be right there. He continued to play, continued to win, and his grandfather died.

When the time of metamorphosis occurred, when the *woge* of old took on the animal forms by which we now know them, *o'row'e* was transformed into the mourning dove. To this day you can see glistening around his neck the treasures he had won in that gambling game. And you can hear the call he will make through eternity as he mourns forever the grandfather he once ignored. Even today, every time someone hears *o'row'e* cry it calls to mind that ancient story and with it a constant reminder that one cannot let material gain get in the way of more essential human obligations. If you do, you will pay eternally for the lapse: just listen to *o'rowe*.

Stories like this were embedded everywhere in traditional culture: animals, plants, mountains, stars, even big rocks had a past, and wherever you went the sight of an animal, the call of a bird, the presence of a rock reminded you of an instructional story. You could not go anywhere without being informed, educated, lectured to by the world around you. This was not a soulless world that worked on principles of evolutionary biology, chemistry, and physics. It was a world alive with strands of consciousness. It had history, and it was profoundly moral.

We might, I suppose, view this simply as a pedagogical strategy. In cultures without writing, instruction can best be preserved by packaging it as a story and then attaching the story like a billboard to an animal, plant, or place so that people will constantly be reminded of it. That's valid, but I think there is something more: a sense that animals, plants, and everything else we see have something to teach us, that the important lessons in life are not just held by people but are part of the larger world. The world contains things that we need to know and that are too important to be left solely to human beings, and these essential lessons are embedded in the animals, plants, mountains, and rivers around us. Learning, in short, does not just take place only in deliberate teaching situations between people. The entire world is a teacher.

KNOWLEDGE COMES TO YOU

I'm not entirely certain, but I think I heard the following story a long time ago from a Hupa friend, Jack Norton. Jack told of a man, depressed and miserable, who sat by a creek. He had been sitting by the creek a long time when he was surprised to hear that the creek was singing him a song. He had never heard the song before, but when he went back home and sang it for an elder, the elder recognized it as a song that once belonged to someone who had died decades before. How did the creek get the song? asked the man. I don't know, answered the elder, but sometimes songs are like that. If they don't have anyone to sing them, they'll give themselves over to a creek for safekeeping.

I don't want to make too much of this—it's subtle, perhaps fragile, and I'm not sure how well I understand it—but many things such as songs, dances, stories, and prayers, which our culture sees as strictly human fabrications, seem to be viewed by some traditional cultures as entities that exist on their own. The song in the preceding story had a life outside the human race; if humans were to disappear, the song would still exist in the stream. To some degree, much of what people need to know is seen as residing in the world around them, with a mind and spirit of its own; in certain situations such knowledge gives itself over to people.

This is, I think, qualitatively and significantly different from the way the dominant culture views knowledge—as something we acquire and we own. In our society, where commodity and marketplace are the dominant metaphors, we see knowledge as something to be grabbed, possessed, controlled. This sense of going after knowledge wasn't foreign to Indian pedagogy. When, for example, a woman training to be a shaman wanted a certain power, she often went out to try to capture it. But perhaps more typically, the shaman-in-training would put herself out in the world, perhaps fasting or undergoing other deprivation, and the power might take pity on her, see that she was a good person, and voluntarily come to her. The world was alive, and the knowledge and teachings you needed were not necessarily yours because you wanted them or even worked directly for them. Knowledge often came as a gift, and the goal of Indian pedagogy was to teach people the respect and alertness necessary so that they could recognize, receive, and, in the end, use the gifts that the world had given them.

On the subject of gifts, let me conclude by gratefully acknowledging that my thirty-year involvement with the California Indian community has been an extraordinary gift. I hope these thoughts on traditional California Indian pedagogy are helpful to others. They certainly worked for generation after generation in traditional cultures, where they kept alive not only cultural information, technical know-how, artistic skills, and religious belief, but also an understanding of how to be a full human being in the natural world. Perhaps within this traditional pedagogy are hints as to how we too might devise a system of education that doesn't just produce people who can take tests but who have a chance of becoming "real persons."

Ecological Literacy: Educating Our Children for a Sustainable World, Michael K. Stone and Zenobia Barlow, eds. (San Francisco: Sierra Club Books, 2005); reprinted in *News from Native California*, vol. 19, no. 4, 2006

EXCERPT FROM THE INTRODUCTION TO
LIFE IN A CALIFORNIA MISSION (1989)

A *note from Malcolm: In 1785, King Louis XVI of France, concerned with the expanding empires of England and Spain, financed an expedition to explore the then unknown regions of the world. In charge of the expedition was a remarkable person, Jean François Galaup de La Pérouse. Two ships were generously outfitted with trade goods and scientific equipment, a library, and nautical charts. Members of the French Academy and other notable scientists, artists, cartographers, physicians, naturalists, and scholars were part of the expedition. It was a major enterprise, perhaps the equivalent of a moon launch today. For the next three years, this expedition would visit areas in the Pacific Ocean and prepare a comprehensive report on the lands that they visited, its vegetation and climate, the Native people that lived there, and the presence of other European powers in the region.*

The expedition went around Cape Horn and stopped in Chile, Easter Island, and Hawai'i and Alaska before arriving in Monterey on September 14, 1786. (Subsequent months would take them to China, the Philippines, the Sea of Japan, the Sea of Okhotsk, the Kamchatka Peninsula, Samoa, and Australia before the ships crashed on reefs near the Solomon Islands sometime in 1788.) Here they spent ten days at Mission Carmel.

It is difficult today to realize how utterly isolated California was in 1786, or to appreciate the excitement that the arrival of these two French vessels must have created. Monterey was then at the northernmost extension of the Spanish Empire, some two thousand miles from the colonial center of Mexico City, and unthinkably distant from the cathedrals and courts of Europe. The presidio at Monterey and the mission at Carmel a few miles away were at that time two tiny clusters of badly made mud huts. To the west lay the restless waters of the Pacific Ocean, its shores only partly known; for the soldiers and monks who gazed daily toward its horizons, its distances were enormous and daunting. The land to the east—the wide, swampy valley of the San Joaquin River, the peaks of the Sierra Nevada, and beyond—was still largely unexplored, its vast reaches inhabited by strange and likely hostile races. Only two fragile links connected the Monterey outpost to the known world: the thin, rough, north-south trail with the pretentious name, "El Camino Real," that went from Monterey to other distant, even more isolated and backward outposts, and the annual visit of the supply ship from San Blas, Mexico.

Mission Carmel had been founded in 1770. The first foreigners to visit this mission, La Pérouse and his party were able to see the condition of the Native people during the very first wave of colonization. So many of the forces that would play out in the next couple of centuries are visible at this moment; we're fortunate to have this eyewitness account of an outsider. La Pérouse's journals miraculously survived the expedition, found their way to France, and were published in 1797. In 1989, I published an English edition of the section of the journals pertaining to Monterey, annotated them thoroughly, and wrote a long introduction. What follows is an excerpt from that introduction.

A couple of days after his arrival at Monterey, La Pérouse paid a formal visit to Carmel Mission. In honor of his reception, the Indian neophytes were given an extra ration of food and were lined up to see him. La Pérouse's description of them is nightmarish: anonymous, lifeless, robbed of spirit, they seem to be a people traumatized, exhibiting what we would today characterize as psychotic levels of depression.

The mission records suggest that the people lined up to greet La Pérouse were those who had traditionally lived in the immediate area—the Rumsen (one of the main divisions of the Ohlone, or Costanoan, language group) who lived mostly along the coast, and another people who lived in the mountains to the south, the Esselen. The few descriptions of them from before the establishment of the mission suggest that they were a fairly handsome, dignified, gentle, lively people who lived in a land of great beauty and extraordinary abundance. Sebastian Vizcaino, who explored Monterey Bay in 1603, characterized them as a "gentle and peaceable people, docile, generous, and friendly, of good stature, fair complexion, and the women possessed of pleasing countenance." A year before the founding of the mission, Miguel Costansó, an engineer with the Portolá Expedition of 1769, described the people and their landscape in idyllic terms:

> The natives of Monterey live in the hills, the nearest about one and a half leagues from the beach. They come down sometimes and go fishing in little rafts of reeds. It seems, however, that fishing does not furnish their chief means of subsistence, and they have recourse to it only when hunting has yielded little. Game is very plentiful in the mountains, especially antelopes and deer. These mountaineers are very numerous, extremely gentle and tractable. They never came to visit the Spaniards without bringing them a substantial present of game, which as a rule consisted of two or three deer or antelopes, which they offered without demanding or asking for anything in return. Their good disposition has given the missionary fathers

well-founded hopes of speedily winning them over to the faith of Christ.

Modern scholarship suggests that for many thousands of years before the coming of Spaniards, successive waves of different people had entered the Monterey Bay area. Their varying histories of conquest and intermingling, followed by long periods of relative isolation, created a tribal and linguistic pattern of great complexity. No fewer than twelve autonomous political entities (often called "tribes" or "tribelets," for lack of a better word) lived within thirty miles of the site of Mission Carmel; five different languages (Esselen, Rumsen, Mutsun, Awaswas, and Chalon) were being spoken.

The Rumsen, to choose one example of many, were a group of about four hundred people who lived on the southern shore of Monterey Bay and in the Carmel Valley. The name Rumsen has also come to stand for the language spoken by these people and three neighboring independent tribal groups, although the southernmost Rumsen speakers of the Big Sur area had a dialect quite distinct from the northernmost. Altogether, perhaps eight hundred people spoke one or another dialect of Rumsen.

That so few as eight hundred people should speak a language and be further fragmented into tribal entities and dialect groups was impossible for the Spaniards to grasp. They were looking for Indian "nations" ruled by "kings"—or at least "tribes" ruled by "chiefs." And when the Native population failed to fit into the European vocabulary and conceptions, the Spaniards concluded that the Indians had no government.

The linguistic, cultural, and political situation of California Indians has proven difficult for the modern mind as well. It is logical to assume, for example, that the various groups must have been isolated from each other to allow the development of so many different languages and dialects. Yet at the same time there is strong evidence of intermarriage, trade relationships, gift exchanges, intertribal ritual observances, and a host of other practices that indicate a high degree of intercommunication. The people of the Monterey Bay area seem to have been isolated and bound together simultaneously—categories that, to our way of thinking, are mutually exclusive. But the simple fact is that our concepts of isolation and interconnection—along with other concepts of tribe, language, independence, etc.—which were developed to describe the realities of European people, are inadequate to describe the subtle, internalized, highly complex, and (to us) contradictory institutions and reciprocities that allowed diverse peoples to live in proximity for centuries without merger or conquest.

Not only did the people of the Monterey Bay area live together, but they seem to have prospered. Although in some years there may have been shortages of a particularly desirable food, there is little evidence in the mythology, the archaeological record, the reports of early visitors, or the handed-down memories of modern-day Indians that hunger was a problem before the coming of the Spaniards. On the contrary, the most common description of the Indians during the pre-conquest years shows them bringing gifts of deer, antelope, elk, and rabbit meat, plus fish, seed and nut cakes, and other foodstuffs to the Spaniards from their obviously abundant stores.

Virtually all early visitors were extravagant in their praise of the rich wildlife and resources of the Monterey Bay area. Each fall and winter steelhead trout and silver (or coho) salmon splashed up the larger streams to spawn in the clear, rocky riffles. Immense schools of smelt dashed themselves onto the beaches: Junípero Serra himself described one such school as running for twenty-three days, drawing Indians from the inland areas who camped along the beach and gathered the fish. Clams, mussels, abalone, and other shellfish were abundant along the shores. Great flocks of migrating geese and ducks—said, in those early days, to darken the sky with their numbers—settled each fall into the marshlands and estuaries of the bay. Deer were plentiful, as were elk, and herds of pronghorn antelope were said to run in herds of two and three hundred. Whales occasionally beached themselves on the shore and provided a winter's worth of meat and fat. Seals and even sea otters, more numerous and less fearful of people than they are today, would haul out on land where they could often be caught. There were also nuts—especially acorns and pine nuts, but others as well—plus wild roots and bulbs, the seeds of innumerable grasses and flowers, berries, and greens. In addition, the tastes of the Indians ran to foods generally avoided by Europeans—grasshoppers, ground squirrels, mice, and small birds—that were often plentiful and relatively easy to catch.

Yet while food was plentiful, it was also highly seasonal. The salmon, steelhead, runs of smelt, migrating waterfowl, and whales, as well as the nuts, bulbs, seeds, berries, and greens, each had relatively brief periods in which they would be available. Even animals such as antelope and elk tended to congregate in herds in certain places and at certain times of year, at other times being more spread out and isolated. To hunt or gather successfully meant that people had to be in close touch with the rhythms of nature. Timing was essential. Without it, people would not know when to prepare fishnets and head to the coast, when to travel to the upland meadows to gather seeds, when to store the nuts, burn the meadows, or gather the tule to make their boats. Without timing, which for the Indians was largely encoded in ritual practices and observances, the people of the Monterey Bay area would have gone hungry, even in this land of "inexpressible fertility," as La Pérouse described it.

An appreciation of the complexities of Indian culture is difficult, even for those studying it today. Many people still characterize traditional Indian life as "primitive," with those emotionally sympathetic to it often extolling its supposed "simplicity." The reasons for thinking this way are obvious. To raise a crop of wheat a European farmer has to plow, sow, weed, irrigate, control pests, and harvest, all with specialized tools and learned skills, and at great labor over an extended period of time. The Indian, on the other hand, is seen gathering acorns from an oak tree, taking what nature offers freely, all without apparent effort or advanced skill. Yet the use of acorns is anything but simple. It involves many hard-to-master and often elaborate technologies, such as making specialized baskets of varying shapes (some of them watertight), storing the acorns in specially constructed caches, drying, shelling, leaching, pounding, sifting, and cooking. To watch an Indian woman pound the kernels into a fine, silky flour, sift out the cruder particles with an elegant motion of the wrist, stir the rounded cooking rocks into the raw mix, and do the many other steps needed to make traditional acorn soup is to watch something of undeniable beauty and sophistication. In fact, if the entire process is measured carefully, it may take less work and certainly far less skill to create a loaf of wheat bread than a loaf of acorn bread.

Similarly, those who herd domesticated animals often envision hunting as a primitive activity, wherein the hunter goes into the woods, bags an animal, brings it home, throws it onto a fire, and eats it. What could be more "basic"? Yet the image of simplicity does not hold up under scrutiny. Deer hunting, to use one example, involved not only a high degree of skill, knowledge, and well-crafted tools, but it also entailed levels of religious and social complexity that we are only recently beginning to appreciate. The Indian hunter often underwent an extended period of preparation that included praying, sexual abstinence, dietary restrictions, dreaming, and other techniques to sharpen the mind, focus the body, and ready the spirit. And when the hunter was successful, he did not just throw the game onto a fire and gorge himself. In fact, in many cases the hunter would eat little, or even none, of the game he caught. A portion of the meat would generally be given to the headman of the village, who would put it aside for guests or others in need. Another portion would often be given to families and clans with whom the hunter had special ties. Hunting, in short, did not render a man "self-sufficient" but, like other aspects of Indian life, served to bind the hunter closer to others in strands of reciprocity. The continual, more-or-less ritualized sharing of food within a group gave everyone security; if the hunter died, was ill, or was down in his luck, he and his family would still eat. And beyond such practices among families and within the tribal group, there were complex trade relationships with those outside.

In short, individual Indians in the Monterey Bay area were not "self-sufficient." A man or woman left alone would probably die, not just from loneliness but from starvation. The people of the area were bound together in a highly evolved web of economic and spiritual relationships, developed over millennia, that, along with knowledge of plants, animals, and the rhythms of nature, had sustained them in relative prosperity and security for countless generations.

If the Spaniards, and indeed most Europeans, missed the subtlety of the Indians' material culture, failing to grasp the degree of skill and social complexity in their gathering of food and other resources, how much more did they miss of that part of the Indian experience for which there was little visual evidence—their political and religious life. The government of the Indians of the Monterey Bay area did not correspond even vaguely to the European forms, and neither did their religion.

Among tribal groups that consisted of a couple of hundred people, government did not entail the institutional structures or scale that the Spaniards had come to expect, not only from the European models but from what they had experienced with the Aztecs and the other nation-states of the Western Hemisphere. In the Monterey Bay area they found no palaces, courts, kings, constitutions, or standing armies with hierarchies of command. The "chief" (or "headman" or "captain," as he was variously called) was more like a banker, a negotiator, or an arbitrator than a king. Political power lay embedded not in a ruler but in the more prestigious families, and decisions were reached by an elaborate system of consultations, negotiations, and consensus. The chief did not give orders; he arranged and, in the end, articulated the consensus.

Further, there were no generals, war chiefs, or warrior class to whom the Spaniards could relate. Although the people of the Monterey Bay area were constantly embroiled in intertribal conflict and skirmishes, they were nevertheless unwarlike. They had no specialized tools for war and none of the value structure that glorified war.

The Native system of justice was also inscrutable to the Spaniards. Punishment was arranged by indirect and diplomatic discussions among people bound together by familial relationships and reciprocal economic and religious duties. In these small groups where no one was a stranger and where families felt responsible for crimes committed by their members, the judicial system bore no resemblance to the systems needed to regulate the larger nation-states of Europe and Mexico.

Because the Spaniards found all the Native forms of government unrecognizable, they assumed that the Indians of the Monterey Bay area had "no government" and lived in anarchy. Likewise, the Spaniards concluded that the Indians had "no religion." They found, after all, no churches, no temples, no visible or professional priesthood. There were shamans, to be sure, but in truth these were more healers (or poisoners) than priests. There was nothing that the Spaniards could, or cared to, identify as religion. The sense that animals, plants, rocks, and all other things of the world were alive, powerful, intelligent, and possessed of mythic history in the same way as people; that the energy from the time of creation still abided and could be sought; that Worldmaker (in the form of Eagle) had touched their land and bestowed power on the things around them; that dances and songs were to be performed at special times to put the world into harmony; that deer gave themselves over to hunters because of an ancient religious compact between people and animals; that dreams were real and provided pathways to the spirit world— these and countless other beliefs and practices, embedded in daily action and periodic ritual, the Spanish either failed to see or, if they did see them, they dismissed as superstitions or devil-worship. There was, in their eyes, only one true religion: the one the Spanish monks were bringing with them to the Monterey Bay area.

An obvious question presents itself: If traditional Indian life was so successful, if food was so plentiful, if people's skills were so advanced, if their knowledge was so profound, their political institutions so apt, and their religious practices so fulfilling, what was it that drew the Indians to a mission run by people so alien and unsympathetic to their ways? They were not, as is sometimes suggested, rounded up by soldiers and taken to the mission like prisoners of war. Initially, at least, the Indians seem to have come to the missions voluntarily, even eagerly.

Part of what drew them was, of course, the dazzle of Spanish goods. Guns, metal, cloth, exotic foods, horses that obeyed people and bore them effortlessly and majestically for great distances, cows that patiently gave them milk, carts pulled by stately and well-muscled draft oxen, boats in full sail that came from beyond the ocean—these were, for a people who had never conceived of such things, bewildering in their power and beauty.

Even everyday items seemed wonderful beyond belief. These strangers possessed items of vivid red, for example—a color that in the Indian world was of extraordinary rarity, found only on the scalps of woodpeckers and on fleeting spring wildflowers. Colored beads, to the Europeans baubles of little worth, to the Indians were money, and they responded much the way modern Americans would respond if an alien race were to arrive in Monterey today and begin handing out hundred-dollar bills. When the first Native person courageous enough to approach the missionaries returned to his village with beads that instantly made him the wealthiest man in the area, others overcame their terror and rushed to the mission to ingratiate themselves with the monks and receive the blessing of instant wealth.

The influx of new goods and technologies brought dramatic change to tribal life. How mundane and dull the old style of money—clamshell beads—now appeared next to the brightly colored trade beads of the visitors. The native stone axe looked shamefully inadequate next to a metal one; bows and arrows, no matter how skillfully crafted, seemed like children's toys next to the rifle. The prestigious families, whose prominence had perhaps always been secretly resented, now seemed laughably old-fashioned; how could their stores of feathered dance regalia, dried deer meat, and baskets of acorn even begin to compare with the bolts of colored cloth, paintings, metal items, and wonderful new foods of the strangers? Even the powers of the shaman over the animal world, once viewed as awesome, seemed paltry compared with the powers of people who could cultivate such an extraordinary alliance with the horse, cow, and ox.

As Indians began to look toward the strangers as the source of wealth, power, and prestige, the old balances, respect, and value systems within the Native communities broke down. Whereas life in traditional tribal society had been relatively closed—those not born to the better families had difficulty attaining prestige and wealth—the missionaries offered what seemed to be an open door. Join us, they were saying, and you too can be *gente de razon*, people of knowledge; you too can worship our gods, learn our skills, possess our powers, and enjoy all the benefits of our way of life. In short, what drew the Indians into the mission was not terribly different from the forces that even today cause people to flee tight-knit communities and self-sufficient rural areas to settle in horrendous city slums: the dazzle of technology, the hope to share in the powers and wealth that are laid before them, a desire to escape a social situation that (once comparison is offered) many see as restrictive—in a word, opportunity.

The opportunity, however, had a price, one that at first seemed modest enough. To enjoy membership in this new community, the Indians were invited to partake in the ritual of baptism, thus allowing them to communicate with the spirits and gods who had given the newcomers such great power and wealth. What the Indians could not have understood, however, was that the waters of baptism were, in the eyes of those administering it, taking away not only something called "sin" but freedom as well. After baptism, the monks felt that they had an obligation and responsibility not to the Indian's body but to the Indian's soul. The Indians had to be kept at the mission, by force if necessary, lest they revert to their old ways and stray into sin. To preserve the soul, the monks undertook to regulate the Indians' every activity, monitor their behavior, and teach them (by whatever means necessary) the correct mental and spiritual attitudes. The Indians became like students in a school, monks in a cloister, prisoners in a penitentiary; they were now wards of the church—their lives, their bodies, even their thoughts no longer their own.

Another question presents itself: Why didn't the Indians revolt? How was it possible for some eighteen ill-equipped soldiers and a pair of unarmed monks to keep hundreds of Indians in virtual slavery for decades?

There were a number of factors. For one thing, the Indians had no experience with organized warfare, nor did they have a tradition of war chiefs or strong leaders of any kind. Their nonauthoritarian form of government, in which decisions were reached by long and often indirect discussion, protracted negotiation, and ultimate consensus—so appropriate for small, stable societies—proved totally inadequate for mounting a successful insurrection, which would call for military discipline and decisive leadership. To make matters worse, the Indians at the mission spoke a number of languages and belonged to several different tribal groups, some of them traditional enemies, so that it became even more difficult to launch a concerted action.

Also, soldiers with rifles and swords—a troop of professionals, trained in military arts, obedient to command, without wives or families to protect—are an especially powerful force, even in small numbers, against a people armed only with hunting tools and incapable of large-scale organization.

The Spaniards also had an enormous psychological edge. They devalued the Indians' way of life—"despised" would probably not be too strong a word—while the Indians seemed to have been burdened by the incapacitating belief that the Spaniards were powerful magicians, deriving their powers not just from the bullets in their guns but directly from the gods. Proof of the alliance between the Spaniards and the gods was everywhere: the monks were seen constantly talking directly to their gods, and it seemed obvious that their gods were answering them. To rebel against the monks and soldiers meant to rebel against their gods as well.

More incapacitating than the Spaniards' military superiority or their perceived religious powers were the diseases the newcomers brought with them. Measles, mumps, smallpox, influenza, and syphilis—diseases against which the Indians had no immunity and for which they had no traditional cures—swept through the missions and spread in devastating epidemics to the still-independent villages. The death rate was horrendous, and everyone—Indians and missionaries alike—was powerless in the face of it.

Today we know that in the absence of medicines, the way of preventing the spread of such diseases would have been through quarantine. But the Indians, who did not have any experience with the idea of "contagion," and who in fact had a quite different concept of illness, did exactly the wrong thing. Shamans, trying to locate the disease within the body, bent over the patient to magically suck it out and get rid of it. Family and friends, assuming that the patients needed all the support they could get, gathered closely around the sick to sing songs and lend their strength. Diseases spread uncontrollably, and the dying and their families fled to the missions in hope that the newly arrived wizards had the magic necessary to cure the new and dreadful diseases.

As sickness took its toll, other factors came into play. As has been pointed out, the image of the self-sufficient Indian is a false one. Without the complex of familial, tribal, and trade relationships, people could not survive. Thus, as villages were depleted by disease or flight, it became impossible for those left behind to continue in their old ways of living with a weakened network of support and reciprocity.

As villages were deserted and remnants of broken families settled into the missions, desirable territories become temporarily vacant, and other Indians living miles away now expanded into them. After a relatively brief time, the Indians at the missions could no longer return to their homes to live. Their land had been usurped, their patterns of economic sustenance shattered. Even the ritual calendar—in which was encoded the cycle of dances and ceremonies, the timing of the salmon runs, the ripening of the acorns, and the arrival of the migrating waterfowl—had been replaced by a European liturgical calendar based on a seven-day week, with ceremonies keyed to events in the lives of European saints.

The severing of the Indians' linkage to the land was not just an accidental byproduct of missionary activity; it was consciously done, part of the missionary policy of "civilizing" the Indians. When Fermín Lasuén wrote about the difficulties of transforming "a savage race such as these into a society that is human, Christian, civil, and industrious," he concluded:

> This can be accomplished only by denaturalizing them. It is easy to see what an arduous task this is, for it requires them to act against nature. But it is being done successfully by means of patience and by unrelenting effort.

The unrelenting efforts of the missionaries produced virtually unrelenting misery for the Indians. Unable to rebel, their old way of life destroyed, they sank into the deepest gloom. The heavy depression that hung over Mission Carmel hung over other California missions as well, and La Pérouse was not alone in describing it. "I have never seen one laugh," wrote Louis Choris, an artist who visited the area in 1816 as part of a Russian expedition, about the Indians of Mission Dolores in San Francisco. "They look as though they were interested in nothing."

"A deep melancholy always clouds their faces, and their eyes are constantly fixed upon the ground," wrote Otto von Kotzebue, also of Mission Dolores. Captain Vancouver likewise noted that, "all operations and functions both of body and mind appeared to be carried out with a mechanical, lifeless, careless indifference."

The missions of California were places of defeat and death—not only physical death but cultural and spiritual death as well. This conclusion is unavoidable from reading what La Pérouse and others have said, and it is supported by what we can further deduce by reading carefully between the lines. La Pérouse mentions, for example, that the hair of the Indians was singed short. The cropping and singing of hair was not a customary fashion among the Indians but used only as a sign of mourning. The fact that La Pérouse presents it as a general style suggests the prevalence of death, the fact that he was seeing an entire culture in mourning.

La Pérouse also mentions that many children had hernias and were dying because of them. He points to this as an example of the low level of medical skill among the Spaniards, who were unable to treat simple hernias successfully. But for us there is the larger question of what kind of overwork or other mistreatment of children there must have been at the missions to have produced so many hernias, an ailment which seems to have been relatively uncommon before the coming of the Spaniards.

Then, too, La Pérouse provides us with a shocking description of how the Indians were butchering a cow, eating the meat raw, and croaking like ravens with pleasure when they found fat. La Pérouse assumes that this was a typical example of the Indians' uncivilized manners, but that was hardly the case. In fact, traditionally people were expected to show restraint in all things, especially eating, and good manners demanded that one express little interest in the food that was offered. The scene of people falling upon a butchered cow and eating it raw suggests something akin to—if not starvation—at least severe malnourishment. Indeed, from La Pérouse's description of their general diet we might assume that the Indians at Mission

Carmel were desperate for protein and fat.

The overwork, the hours of forced prayer (in Latin), the deadening of sensibilities and intelligence, the whippings, the remorseless tedium of daily routine, the utter hopelessness—all these things led La Pérouse, however reluctantly, to conclude that the mission resembled nothing so much as a slave plantation of Santo Domingo.

Mission life as it was described by La Pérouse did not take place in a distant country at a distant time among a people who no longer exist. It took place here, in California, and the people who partook in it were in many regards modern people. Two hundred years covers only three human lifetimes—not a very long period of time at all. And although technology has changed the world in many ways, it has not changed it as much as we would like to think. The events at Mission Carmel are not ancient history. They are, in fact, uncomfortably recent. And as we read the journals of La Pérouse, what we find unfolding before us is not a tale of a distant fantasy land but the far more gripping story of our place, of our times, the story of "us."

Life in a California Mission: Monterey in 1786, Jean François de La Pérouse, Heyday, 1989

INTRODUCTION TO *INDIAN SUMMER* (2006)

In the spring of 1850, a former military officer born in Kentucky, William Mayfield, led his wife and three sons eastward over the Pacheco Pass toward the San Joaquin Valley and the goldfields beyond. As Thomas Jefferson Mayfield, then six years old, would recount much later, they were making their way through the tall, waving grass when "suddenly my daddy pointed over the tops of the bare hills ahead of us and exclaimed, 'Look there!' And there in the distance, until then lost to us in the haze, was our valley. A shining thread of light marked the Rio San Joaquin, flowing, as my mother said, 'through a crazy quilt of color.'

"How excited we all were. Everyone wanted to talk at once. Then someone noticed that what we had at first taken for clouds still further to the east was a high range of snow-covered peaks, their bases lost in the purple haze." Ecstatic with joy, the family descended into the luxuriant meadowlands, where, wading through grasses as high as their stirrups, they stopped to bedeck themselves and their horses with wildflowers.

A tremendous awareness of beauty, itself like a "shining

thread," runs through the narrative: of the grand beauty of the "primeval" San Joaquin Valley; of the splendid herds of elk and antelope that roamed freely over its seemingly limitless breadth; of flocks of cranes, geese, and ducks that darkened the sky with their numbers; of the great expanse of Tulare Lake, once the second-largest lake west of the Mississippi; and especially of the Indian people whose long-established villages once rimmed the lakes and lined the rivers that flowed into the valley. It is a story of an extraordinary beauty now much diminished, almost (but not entirely) lost to the modern world.

It is something of a miracle that the story itself was not also lost. That it survived at all is due to the collaboration between two singular men. One was Thomas Jefferson Mayfield, a white man who had grown up among the Choinumne Yokuts during the 1850s and who, with a few months to live, broke a self-imposed silence of more than sixty years to tell the story. The other was Frank F. Latta, a self-defined historian and ethnographer of the San Joaquin Valley, who convinced Mayfield to recount his memories and who then went on to arrange, edit, and eventually publish them at his own expense.

After his mother had died, his father did not want to leave him in the gold mining towns because of the violence and depravity there. Mayfield, for a period of about ten years spanning childhood and adolescence, came to live among the Choinumne people of the Kings River area. He slept in their houses, joined them on their daily rounds, and followed them on their annual expeditions by tule boat to Tulare Lake. He spoke their language, wore their style of dress, ate their foods, absorbed many of their attitudes, and, in short, lived for some ten years almost entirely like an Indian. His remarkable narrative represents, as far as I know, the only account of an outsider who ever lived among a California Indian people while they were still following their traditional ways.

Although the original narrative created by Mayfield and Latta covers the whole of Mayfield's life, only the first part dealing with his experiences among the Choinumne is reprinted in this edition. As the subsequent parts of the narrative explain, after he left the Choinumne in the early 1860s, Mayfield tried his hand at herding sheep and prospecting, making trips to Utah, Oregon, the high Sierra, and the deserts of California in search of gold and other rare minerals. When not tramping the hills and deserts of the West with his burro, he would return to a small mining town in the southern San Joaquin Valley called Tailholt (later renamed White River), where he did odd jobs. Finally too old to prospect, he retired there to become something of a local legend, a grizzled old bachelor known to everyone as "Uncle Jeff."

Early settlers of the region often characterized the local Indians as thieves and murderers. Yet, paradoxically, life in the early mining communities of the San Joaquin Valley and the foothill region was, at least as Mayfield remembered it, one of overwhelming lawlessness and violence. In the latter part of the Mayfield narrative (not reprinted here) we find described in some detail robberies, gangs, rustling of livestock, rumors of buried treasure, and, most noticeably, one murder after another—deaths involving not only strangers but members of Mayfield's own family.

It was into this harsh, Indian-hating frontier world that Mayfield emerged after having spent most of his childhood among the Choinumne. Faced with hostility and prejudice whenever his association with the Indians was suspected, he fell silent about his childhood experiences. From the early 1860s until shortly before his death in 1928, he did not, as he said, spend as much as a total of one half hour talking to others about his life among the Choinumne. Ironically, this silence is undoubtedly what helped preserve the story. To have brought out his memories in an atmosphere of brutality and contempt would have surely altered them, perhaps giving them a defensive tone, perhaps eroding them until they became closer to what others wanted to hear. Instead, when at the very end of his life he found a receptive ear into which to pour his memories, they came bursting forth out of sixty years of protective silence with freshness, clarity of detail, and startling vivacity.

The person to whom Mayfield entrusted his memories was Frank F. Latta, a man many years his junior. Latta was born in 1892 in Stanislaus County, California. His mother was a teacher, his father a Presbyterian minister. When he was fourteen, a schoolteacher encouraged him to record the history of the school district by interviewing the original settlers of the area. From that early age almost until his death, Latta never stopped interviewing, ultimately collecting several thousand accounts from the Indians and pioneers of the San Joaquin Valley.

The early decades of the twentieth century were an especially fertile time for historical and ethnographic research. The gold rush of 1849 was still a living memory, close to the hearts of the "old-timers" who hung around the grocery stores and gas stations of the small valley towns, eager to reminisce about how they had crossed the prairie in wagon trains, how they had staked out their first claims, how they had found (or more likely failed to find) gold, and how they eventually had moved into herding, farming, logging, or other rural occupations.

If the memories of the old-time settlers reached back to the gold rush era, the memories of many of the elderly Indians of the area went back much further. Still alive in the early decades of that century were many who remembered the traditional ways of life before they were disrupted—who remembered a world deeply rooted in the soil, rivers, and lakes of the San Joaquin Valley, a world that, having evolved and flourished for untold centuries, was now fading with a terrible and tragic rapidity.

The California Indian world was not one that an outsider could easily understand. At the time of the gold rush, an estimated eighty thousand Indians were living in the San Joaquin Valley, a people generally referred to as Yokuts. While the Yokuts spoke a more or less common language, it was broken up into several quite distinct dialects. Nor were the Yokuts anything like a political or cultural unit. There was no Yokuts tribe, for example, but rather dozens of small nations, each with its territory, its leaders, and with customs and beliefs that were widely divergent. Adding to the complexity, yet other peoples lived in the foothills and mountains that rimmed the San Joaquin Valley, each of them speaking different languages and following different customs.

Latta threw himself into this rich complexity with the greatest of zeal. In a succession of vehicles, Latta—in later years often accompanied by his wife, Jean, and their four children—set out along dirt roads to the most remote corners of the San Joaquin Valley to record and photograph the Indian people. While supporting himself and his family mostly by teaching high school, he tirelessly did very basic, pioneering ethnographic research, sorting out the names and territories of the various Yokuts groups, using lists of words that he elicited from various Native speakers to identify the dialects, collecting volumes of information on place names and on the customs and technological skills of the people he encountered. At reservations, Indian settlements, and in private homes throughout the valley, Latta became a familiar sight, a tall, slender man nicknamed *Wee-chet-e*, man with "little sticks," so called because of the bundles of pencils he always carried with him for taking his voluminous notes.

It is clear from reading through the boxes of Latta's papers, now stored at the Yosemite National Park Research Library, that of the many thousands of interviews that Latta conducted among early pioneers and Indians, he valued the Mayfield material most highly.

Indian people, of course, knew their own culture with much greater intimacy and detail than Mayfield could ever have known it. But Indians of that generation often did not speak English well—many, in fact, did not speak English at all—and being so immersed in their own culture, they did not quite know how to interpret it for others: what to emphasize, what to describe. In Mayfield, Latta found a man who had not only lived within Indian culture but who, as a member of the dominant society, had the perspective to sum it up and describe it in a way that corresponded with the thinking and categories of the Anglo mind.

Latta lost no time in publishing the Mayfield narratives as a series of newspaper articles. Then, within a year of Mayfield's death in 1928, a slender volume appeared published by the *Tulare Times Press* in an edition of five hundred. The book was titled *San Joaquin Primeval: Uncle Jeff's Story, A Tale of a San Joaquin Valley Pioneer and His Life with the Yokuts Indians*. It was a hastily done and unattractive hardcover book, fewer than one hundred pages in length, with the type jammed onto each page in double columns, badly printed, and without photos, maps, or other graphics. Latta himself was dissatisfied, and when donating a copy to the New York Public Library in 1931 he wrote: "Accept my apologies . . . , as we are disappointed in the booklet. It was printed from type used in a newspaper set-up and is quite crude in composition. Stanford University Press is now preparing to publish the same in a nice edition which will be upon the market as soon as business conditions warrant."

Stanford University Press had indeed expressed an interest in publishing another edition of *Uncle Jeff's Story*, and the Latta Archive at the Yosemite National Park Research Library has a thick folder devoted to the correspondence between Latta and William Hawley

Davis, editor. For a period of four years, while Davis kept trying to reach a decision about whether to publish the book, Latta continued to send him more and more Mayfield-related material. He sent additions, corrections, and amplifications to the original manuscript, apparently from his interview notes with Mayfield. As he interviewed other valley pioneers, he also sent in their comments whenever they corroborated something that Mayfield had said. He also began to collect photos: photos of Mayfield, of the places Mayfield mentioned, of life in the San Joaquin Valley.

For several years Latta kept sending new material, and Davis kept promising to reach a decision. When the decision finally came, however, it was negative. America was in the midst of an economic depression, money was scarce, and "Californiana" was not selling.

While the correspondence with Davis came to an end in 1934, the compiling of additions to the Mayfield book did not, and for years afterward Latta continued to assemble corrections, additions, corroborations, and photographs.

It was not until 1976 that Latta was finally able to republish the Mayfield narratives. Retitling the book *Tailholt Tales*, he brought it out under the imprint of Bear State Books, a publishing company that he and his family formed specifically to publish the results of their historical and ethnographic research.

Forty-seven years had elapsed between the publication of *Uncle Jeff's Story* and *Tailholt Tales*, nearly a half century of frustration coupled with steady accumulation of new material. While *Uncle Jeff's Story* was 88 pages long, *Tailholt Tales* came to 320 pages, largely due to these additions.

At the core of *Tailholt Tales* is the simple story that Mayfield had told years before, corrected and amplified, apparently from the original interview notes. This narrative is then interspersed with comments by Latta in his own voice, and further glossed with the inclusion of interviews with other early settlers who substantiated what Mayfield had said. The new edition also includes a foreword by the linguist and anthropologist John P. Harrington, a reminiscence by Latta about the life and personality of Harrington, notes on the history of Bear State Books and other Latta family projects, plus scores of photographs. Some of these photos are of Mayfield; some show places mentioned in the narrative, often much changed by the time the photos were taken; some are stills from a film that Latta helped produce, showing modern-day Yokuts dressed in animal skins and posed in reconstructed villages; and some show Latta and his family pursuing their ethnographic research, vacationing in Mexico, and forming Bear State Books.

Tailholt Tales, in short, is not only *Uncle Jeff's Story* corrected and expanded but a commentary on and concordance to *Uncle Jeff's Story* as well. The inclusion of family photos and tangential text were clearly intended to provide a full context for the Mayfield material—a multidimensional presentation of not only the Mayfield narrative but of the people who produced it. So many voices, however, along with the eclectic photos, give the second edition a scrapbook quality. Indicative of the changes between the two volumes is the fact that in *Uncle Jeff's Story*, Latta lists himself simply as editor—"Arranged by Frank F. Latta," to use his exact phrase. In *Tailholt Tales*, he lists himself as author, and with just cause. *Tailholt Tales* is largely a book of Latta's creation, in which the Mayfield narrative is a major but no longer exclusive part.

Anyone interested in the totality of San Joaquin Valley history, in its early pioneers, or in the life of its premier historian, Frank Latta, might do well to search out a copy of *Tailholt Tales* in a library or used book store. My own interests, however, lie with Mayfield's description of life among the Choinumne, and it is my hope that, cut back to the simplicity of the core story, this extraordinary narrative will reach a wider readership than the more thoroughly annotated version of 1976 might. Consequently, I have included only the material from the original *Uncle Jeff's Story*, adding from *Tailholt Tales* those amplifications and corrections that Latta presented as being in Mayfield's own voice, presumably from the original interview notes. I have also taken the liberty of rearranging the sequence of incidents to form a more coherent narrative.

The account before us is clearly one of the most remarkable and valuable documents in the entire range of California Indian material. As John P. Harrington wrote in his foreword to *Tailholt Tales*: "Few readers will realize that this information which Mr. Latta has preserved lies on the very outskirts of human knowledge and that he has rescued practically all of these facts from oblivion." Indeed, the work before us has not only major ethnographic facts about how people hunted, fished, cooked, and built their houses but also insights into the manners of everyday life—intimate glimpses into how people washed their hands and faces, for example, or how they salted their fresh greens.

More than a compendium of valuable facts, the Mayfield narrative also manages to catch something of a flavor, a tone, a way of being, that is generally absent from more conventional anthropological works. In places, we can almost hear the voices of the old people staying awake most of a cold winter night to keep the house fires going, of dozens of young boys playing Indian football, of mothers teaching their children to swim, of men excitedly commenting upon an immense flock of geese rising up from Tulare Lake.

For those who are hungry to know more about the old ways of life in California, the Mayfield narrative offers tremendous riches; and in the face of such a gift, it seems petty to criticize. It would be as if a starving person, after having been given an immense banquet, were to complain that a few of the dishes were not cooked to perfection. Yet it should be acknowledged that for all its undeniable virtues, the narrative before us does have some important shortcomings.

To begin, we must recognize that these reminiscences were dictated some sixty-five years ago by a man with almost no schooling who had spent much of his adult life prospecting for gold and doing odd jobs around the small towns of the San Joaquin Valley. Despite his extraordinary childhood experiences, he was in many ways a man of his times, and these were hardly the most sensitive of times. The modern reader cannot help but wince at certain of Mayfield's attitudes and expressions. In particular, his referring to Indian women as "mokees" or "squaws," likely done with affection, is jarring to the modern ear and insulting to Native people today. The editor of this volume therefore took it upon himself to change such expressions to "woman" or "women."

Other biases were, however, more embedded in the text, and these were not altered. Most troublesome are the disparaging references to the Monache. Now generally called the "Mono," "Western Mono," or "Sierra Mono," these people were in the 1850s relative newcomers to the area, having slowly migrated across the Sierra from the Mono Lake and Great Basin areas into the more hospitable lands long used by Yokuts groups. The Yokuts viewed these people with considerable alarm and hostility, and this is how Mayfield presents them—as murderous, thieving, untrustworthy people. Yet anyone who is acquainted with Mono traditional life or who knows personally members of today's Mono community will surely recognize that such sentiments reflect the biases of the Yokuts and the fears of the white settlers more than any truth about the Mono people.

It is also necessary to remember that Mayfield was a six-year-old boy when he first took up residence with the Choinumne, and still a teenager when their traditional way of life came to an end. His experiences and his memories reflect all the enthusiasms and limitations of his age and gender. Thus we find wondrously detailed descriptions of how to play field games, how to build pigeon traps, and how to construct a fish gig, while other important aspects of Yokuts culture—religious philosophy, the gathering of basketry material, the making of baskets, girls' coming-of-age ceremonies, etc.—are almost entirely absent from this narrative.

Finally, there is the inescapable fact that Mayfield was not an Indian. As the last chapters of this book poignantly demonstrate, he was, in the end, very much a white man, clearly and perhaps tragically a product of his time.

In short, the volume before us is not a full and well-balanced depiction of Choinumne life. Rather, it is an eyewitness account by a particular person who lived among the Choinumne at a particular time, and who told the story of that time with verve, passion, and (despite his limitations) great fidelity. The story that he told, while less than perfect, is nonetheless amazing, providing us with a unique description of the Choinumne world, a world into which it is hoped the reader will move with a sense of awe and wonderment, and per-haps with appreciation for Latta and Mayfield, the two unusual men who worked so hard to keep the memory of that world alive.

Indian Summer portrays a world which is now tragically faded. The herds of pronghorn antelope, the flocks of geese, the grand stretches of oak forest, and the luxuriant, flowery meadows have all been dread-fully reduced. Even Tulare Lake, once measuring hundreds of square miles, has been rendered insignificant. As an elderly Yokuts woman named Yoimut, born on the shores of Tulare Lake, complained some seventy years ago, where there had once been natural beauty there was now only "cotton, cotton, cotton."

Likewise, the Choinumne people and their culture have been severely reduced. They have been driven from their lands, while their customs and beliefs have been mocked and sometimes even outlawed for most of the last hundred and fifty years. In the face of such assault, many Choinumne people have lost most of their traditional ways. Others have found that they can continue to be Indian only on the fringes of the dominant society, as if being Indian were a crime, something that can be done only in secret.

Yet, while greatly diminished, neither the beauty of the land nor the greatness of its Native people has been entirely destroyed. In the remnants of an oak forest, in the honking of geese settling into a patch of wetland, in the soaring of a hawk, or in the fragrance of a spring breeze, one can now and then still catch a glimpse of the ancient grandeur.

So too with the people. The open-hearted hospitality and generosity with which the Indian people greeted the first white settlers—carrying their goods (and often their persons) across rivers and supplying them with food from their own surplus—is, despite everything that has happened, still very much a part of Indian culture today. The Choinumne dialect, cherished by Mayfield as he recalled the vocabulary of his childhood, is still a living language, spoken by a handful of elders. Likewise, many of the old customs, attitudes, and beliefs described by Mayfield can even yet be found among the Choinumne and other Yokuts people today.

Like the natural beauty of the area, Indian life has been pushed to the edge. Forced to struggle and adapt, admittedly fragile and threatened, it nevertheless, miraculously, continues to exist.

Today, at least at more optimistic moments, one feels that there is a new attitude developing among many people. The old frontier mentality that gave the dominant culture the unquestionable right to exploit other people and abuse the land seems on the wane. Environmental groups have arisen in recent years and are struggling to keep the land from further degradation, and perhaps even restore some of it to a state of greater natural beauty. Likewise there are those within the Indian community who, even at this late date, are working hard to assure the continuation of their cultures and restoration of Indian rights. Native languages are being studied by a younger generation, elders are being listened to with respect, songs are being relearned, rituals long dormant are again being performed, and Indian children are being taught pride rather than shame in their heritage. It is in hopeful times such as these that we offer this exceptional narrative. May the vision of a magnificent past inspire and nourish those who are working toward a better future.

Indian Summer, Thomas Jefferson Mayfield, Heyday, 1993, introduction to the 2006 edition

INTRODUCTION TO
LIFE AMONGST THE MODOCS (1997)

On August 17, 1870, Joaquin Miller stepped off the ferry from New Jersey onto the wharves of New York City, thus ending his long-anticipated cross-country journey. The Transcontinental Railroad had been completed the previous year, and although he complained that the trip had been "incessant," in truth it had taken only two weeks—easy and even luxurious compared to the bone-rattling crossing of some eighteen years earlier, when at the age of fifteen he had traveled with his parents by covered wagon from Indiana to Oregon.

After a brief stay in New York, Miller boarded a ship for Europe, reaching the British Isles in fourteen days. The voyage among "cold seas and cold seamen" was undoubtedly disagreeable, as Miller depicted it in his journals; but by then steamship travel had long been established on the transatlantic routes, largely freeing tourists and merchants from the inconvenience of contrary winds, rendering the once fearsome voyage relatively safe and predictably on schedule. In 1870 the world was shrinking fast. The voyages of Cook to the South

Pacific, which had so startled Europe with depictions of scantily clad women and fiercely tattooed cannibal warriors, were now a century old. Two decades had elapsed since Sir Richard Burton's penetration into the strongholds of Mecca and Medina. Within months of Miller's arrival in London, Sir Henry Stanley would be setting forth to find Dr. David Livingstone and virtually complete the exploration of the "dark" continent.

An era was drawing to a close so suddenly that few people realized it, and even fewer understood its significance. As colonial administrators, engineers, representatives of mercantile houses, and churchmen spread out from the capitals of Europe on missions of political, economic, and cultural domination, the great world—once of infinite mystery and terror—was shrinking with alarming rapidity to the dimensions of a Victorian parlor, its wondrous variety of humanity reduced to figurines on knickknack shelves.

This conquest of the globe by Europe created an appetite for the exotic—a romantic, yearning, sometimes almost pornographic curiosity about the lives of non-European people. It also produced in some a fear that the deep beauty and wealth of the Earth were being plundered, and that the black coats, top hats, and constricted morality of the Fleet Street bankers would be the uniform of the future.

Perhaps there was something in the tone of the times that might help explain the conspicuous attire of the man who arrived from America in 1870. Joaquin Miller, then thirty-three years old, took to the London streets wearing a wide-brimmed sombrero, a flaming red flannel shirt, a blue polka-dot bandana, and—in case the rest wasn't enough—a gaudy sash tied around his waist. On some days he chose to wear cowboy pants with chaps; other days he donned more conventional trousers, which he tucked into high-heeled boots upon which he affixed a set of spurs. He was much inclined to wear a pistol on his hip, but newfound friends advised him that this would be "going too far." He nevertheless did cultivate a swagger and cock-sure attitude. Christened Cincinnatus Hiner Miller by his Quaker father and hymn-singing mother, he had even shed his given name for the swashbuckling "Joaquin."

Obviously, Miller wanted to be noticed, and he was. By 1871 he had published, at his own expense, a volume of poetry, *Songs of the Sierras*, which was received with great enthusiasm and gained him access to many of England's most illustrious poets, such as Robert Browning and Dante Gabriel Rossetti. His reputation was greatly enhanced when a couple of years later his *Life Amongst the Modocs* was published to huge critical acclaim from his English audience. Subtitled *Unwritten History*, it purports to tell of his experiences among the Indians and miners of northernmost California.

From a character such as Miller, one would hardly expect a conventional book—safe, factual, and footnoted. Indeed, despite Miller's declaration that he had made the book "true in every particular," the work before us, while based on real incidents and actual experiences, is clearly as much a novel as it is a work of history. It is of utmost importance to recognize this fact when reading *Life Amongst the Modocs*. Those approaching it as a work of history—demanding that it be trustworthy in its details and sound in its conclusions—will find it wanting. Those who, however, understand it as, at least in part, a work of fiction, will find themselves hugely rewarded. The literary imagination has tremendous powers. It can leap with surety through a thousand details to the heart of a complex situation; it embraces contradiction and ambiguity without the encumbrance of interpretation; it can engage our emotions as can no mere assemblage of carefully footnoted facts. *Life Amongst the Modocs*, with its unique mixture of fact and fiction, is indeed such a work, presenting us with a daring view of this difficult era. It has such scope and, in its odd way, such profound truthfulness that its equal cannot be found anywhere else in the literature of the West.

Separating fact from fiction in *Life Amongst the Modocs* is no easy task. We know with certainty that Miller had indeed lived in the mining camps and among the Indians of Northern California. He had married an Indian woman who taught him the Wintu language, and he had taken part in some of the skirmishes, battles, and even massacres of the 1850s. Characters and incidents in the book can be matched with people who actually lived and events that actually took place—a task which historian Alan Rosenus tackles in his valuable afterword to this volume.

Yet despite the factual core, Miller cannot seem to resist swaggering through the pages of the book, dressed in outlandish attitudes, any more than he could resist swaggering through the streets of London wearing colorful outfits. He struts, he lies, he boasts. On one page he presents himself as abjectly weak and passive, a few pages later he bursts forth as a decisive military leader. He wallows in his defects, parades his strengths, and in short pushes himself into the face of the reader every chance he can get.

Miller's vanity and self-obsession are great, sometimes ludicrous. As we read him, we sometimes see someone posing before a mirror, trying on different costumes, adopting different postures, admiring himself endlessly, exulting in his considerable powers as a poet and the freedom it allows—at liberty to blurt out the most outrageous and startling truths and fantasies. He is, at worst, an impossible egotist, self-absorbed and self-deluded. But it is not for his worst aspects that we still read Miller with fascination, even hunger. It is for his best aspects, and in these he is extraordinary.

The time and place covered by this book, the 1850s in Northern California, was an era of upheaval, contradiction, and great complexity. Take, for example, the people whom Miller generally calls "Indians." Far from comprising a single culture or "tribe," the

Indians of this part of California spoke four mutually incomprehensible languages: Wintu, Shasta, Modoc, and Pit River. Each of these languages had dialects, and within a dialect group were often many politically and culturally distinct peoples. Some of these people lived along salmon-rich rivers, some alongside lakes and marshes, some in pine forests, and some in high deserts. Their ways of living differed greatly, and they were variously at war or at peace with one or another of their neighbors.

Likewise, the white settlers were far from uniform. Only half the residents of the area, for example, listed their occupation as "miner" during the 1850s. Others were shopkeepers, farmers, blacksmiths, carpenters, soldiers, etc. While overwhelmingly white, the towns and mines of the Mount Shasta area also had black and Chinese people, as well as a large foreign-born population from places such as Ireland, Scotland, France, Norway, Portugal, Mexico, and the various German principalities. Among the American-born were well-educated young men from the eastern seaboard, pious and sober young men from small New York and Pennsylvania farming communities, and the roughest of frontiersmen from the mountains of Tennessee and Kentucky.

The clash between the Indians and the white settlers was gruesome and soul-sickening. In later years the description of this confrontation would take on a brutal simplicity: the whites came, took over the land, and nearly annihilated the Indians. But to those who lived during this tumultuous era, the conflict, while brutal, was anything but simple. Whites, for example, did not just fight against the Indians; the two groups battled each other in endless duels, robberies, ambushes, and vigilante actions. Likewise, the Indians warred fiercely against each other, as they had done for millennia. Neither side was innocent of mutilation, torture, or the murder of women and children. And when whites did fight against the Indians, they were often joined by "friendly" Indians who served as scouts or as soldiers.

In later years other writers would struggle to characterize the Indians of California and describe the horrors of their conflict with the white world. Borrowing concepts from anthropology, ethnohistory, linguistics, and other disciplines, drawing upon the accumulated writings of previous historians and literary people, they would over time develop a body of ideas, of frameworks, of language—in short, they would work out the highly evolved and largely acceptable way of describing Indians and the history of Western settlement to which modern writers are heir and now largely take for granted. But this would come later. Miller was a literary pioneer. There was for him no established school or scholarly tradition, no path to follow, no adequate language for describing what he had lived through. Embroiled in the chaotic events of the time; living partly within the white world of the mining camps, partly in Indian villages; a blond youth married to an Indian woman; an insider (at least by marriage) to regional Indian culture; and with ambition to make a name for himself in the world, Miller found himself without anything in the body of existing literature or conventional ways of thinking that could be used to describe his experiences.

He might, I suppose, have taken a different route—that of a journalist or historian, sticking to the facts with scrupulous attentiveness, weaving together strands of contradictory stories to get at some approximation of a complex truth. But this would have been for another personality. *Life Amongst the Modocs* is not a book of small, trustworthy, literal truths—of detailed ethnographic information about the Indian people of the area or strictly reliable accounts of conflicts and battles. These can be found elsewhere. What *Life Amongst the Modocs* offers is something more ambitious.

For the first readers of *Life Amongst the Modocs*, one of the big truths that jumped off the pages was one with which modern readers have become more familiar: namely, the horrifying accounts of the massacres of Indian people by whites. While such knowledge was not entirely absent in the 1870s—reports of massacres had been a staple of frontier newspapers for nearly two decades—previous accounts were brief and transitory, and in them Indians were presented largely as nameless and pitiful victims. Bodies of men, women, and children might be counted, but virtually nothing was said or known about who these people were. Not only did *Life Amongst the Modocs* provide a book-length treatment of this hideous period of American history, but for the first time in Western literature the Indians who were being massacred were portrayed not just as Indians but as people—people with whom Miller had lived, people whom he knew and admired.

Also new to his early readers were the huge, sweeping, poetic depictions of nature. In this period before John Muir, exultant descriptions of Western wilderness were rare, and even rarer was a sense of what we now call ecology—a recognition that the environmental degradation caused by mining had affected the herds of elk and the spawning of salmon, and in doing so had reduced to starvation the Indians who depended upon them. As modern people we are all too familiar with this line of thought. But for most of the original readers, "progress" and economic development were still unmitigated virtues, wilderness was something to be tamed, and Indians clearly needed to be conquered. For them Miller's way of thinking was something of an eye-opener.

Also startling for readers of the 1870s, and perhaps even more so for readers of today, is Miller's literary rather than scientific approach to history. Ordinarily we read history to give a sense of order to the past. That is what historians tend to do: they bring order, define themes, show that the chaos of the past is only apparent and that beneath it are larger purposes, causes, inevitabilities. Miller, however, does not set out to tame the chaos, to fit it into theories, to explain it and deaden it with the language of the dispassionate historian.

Rather, Miller embraces the chaos. We feel in *Life Amongst the Modocs* the raw crosscurrents of violence and love, of divided people and split loyalties, of delicacy and brutality, all presented to us full face. In quick and astoundingly energetic strokes, piling incident upon incident, image upon image, he captures the movement and the emotion of the times. Reading other accounts from more conventional historians we get the feeling that we are standing at a safe distance looking back upon stormy times. *Life Amongst the Modocs*, however, gives us the feeling of having entered the storm itself.

In a review of *Life Amongst the Modocs*, critic Hamlin Garland once commented: "Such pictures as these were unknown to our literature when they were written, and they stand unsurpassed today in their largeness of movement and their mass of light and shade." Like others, Garland borrows the language of art criticism to describe *Life Amongst the Modocs*. And for good reason. In the early 1870s, Impressionism was taking hold of the European imagination, and in 1870 Monet and Pissarro, fleeing the Franco-Prussian War, took up residence in England. Their paintings were shown in London in 1871. Whether or not Miller was directly influenced by this school of painting is not clear, but he certainly shared its goals. Just as the Impressionist painter might avoid a "realistic" portrayal of solid objects in order to capture the fleeting qualities of light and motion, Miller in his writing seems to avoid fidelity to historical detail in order to explore other aspects of experience. *Life Amongst the Modocs*, rather than providing us with reliable reportage, gives us instead a rendering of elusive states of mind. Miller was the first of the Western writers to attempt to portray the emotional landscape of early California, to deal with themes such as loneliness and defeat, melancholy and rage, weakness and strength, joy and loyalty—the insubstantial but all-important parts of life that modern writers who cover this era have all but forgotten to ask about, let alone describe.

Central to *Life Amongst the Modocs* is Miller's fascination with what he calls "the real Indian." What he means by this is something quite specific—not the Indian "willing to mix with us on the border" but rather the Indian who "retreats from the white man when he can." Miller had indeed caught a glimpse of this real Indian. He had lived among a people whose personalities had been formed before the coming of whites and who were still leading a largely traditional life. The quest to describe the real Indian haunted him, just as it was to haunt other writers for the better part of a century—not only white writers but Indian writers as well.

Perhaps it was the shrinking world in which Miller was writing that gave this need a certain urgency. It seemed inevitable to Miller and his contemporaries that Indians would soon disappear, and even the memory of them would become yet another trophy of European culture, to survive only within the constructs of the conqueror. Miller, however, knew that he had seen another kind of being, and in the pages before us one senses him as almost desperate to find a language with which he can describe the people he knew, throwing himself at the task again and again in his attempts to convey something of what he had witnessed.

The real Indian, Miller tells us, was "a druid and a dreamer—the mildest and tamest of beings. I saw him as no man can see him now . . . the worst and the best of men, the tamest and the fiercest of beings. The world cannot understand the combination of these two qualities."

We read such descriptions with a sense of great surprise. This is not the language to which our ears have become accustomed. Instead of delineating kinship systems and analyzing material culture, he talks of things like mildness and fierceness, melancholy and joy. We sense that there is something new coming off the page here, and we almost hold our breath to see if Miller, with all his outlandishness, can bring it off.

He does bring it off to an amazing degree, and indeed one cannot help but feel that he succeeds in the larger task to which he applied himself—to present the unwritten history of his era. He succeeds because of his powers as a poet, his courage as a writer, and yet something else. The reason *Life Amongst the Modocs* still holds our attention and, despite its flaws, holds our great respect is that it is pervaded by something that might be called (if we are not too embarrassed to give it its proper name) love. A strange and wonderful love seems to fill the book, and it is, I feel, this quality that makes the vanities, the foolish posturings, even the outright lies bearable. He was, as Ambrose Bierce would later say, "the greatest-hearted man I ever knew," and it is this greatheartedness that helps carry the reader, transfixed, through the book.

There is for the modern reader brought up on more cautious and conventional scholarly works something wonderfully liberating about reading *Life Amongst the Modocs*—as if for too long our thoughts and feelings were moving in narrow channels and we can only now see the possibilities of plunging into deeper, perhaps more dangerous, but infinitely more exciting waters. Among the grand sweeps of the book, the dashing forays into truths, the startling asides and odd, uncensored thoughts, the mind feels enlarged, refreshed, and enlivened.

Miller clearly recognized a certain roughness within himself. In the work before us he writes:

I think what I most needed in order to understand, get on and not be misunderstood, was a long time at school, where my rough points could be ground down. The schoolmaster should have taken me between his thumb and forefinger and rubbed me about till I was as smooth and as round as the others. Then I should have been put out in the society of other smooth pebbles, and rubbed and ground against them till I got as smooth and pointless as they. You must not have points or anything about you singular or noticeable if you would get on. You must be a pebble, a smooth, quiet pebble. Be a big pebble if you can, a small pebble if you must. But be a pebble, just like the rest, cold, and hard, and sleek, and smooth, and you are all right. But I was as rough as the lava rocks I roamed over, as broken as the mountains I inhabited.

Life Amongst the Modocs, like its remarkable author, is not a smooth pebble, ground and polished, sleek, hard, and cold. The book before us has not been smoothed out, edited for good taste, correct thoughts, or even factual accuracy. It is rough and jagged, and even after so many years it still has the power to catch us and move us as no other work of this era can.

Life Amongst the Modocs, Joaquin Miller, Heyday, 1997

WAHHOGA VILLAGE: A PLACE TO MEET (2013)

The Southern Sierra Miwuk Nation has been trying to build a roundhouse on the site of Wahhoga Village in Yosemite Valley since the 1970s. The reason is as simple and solid as the bedrock mortars scattered over the Valley floor. "We needed a place to meet," explained Jay Johnson, as we sat around the table at the Miwu Mati Healing Center in Mariposa. Jay, who traces his ancestry to Yosemite Valley, chairs the Wahhoga Committee—an intertribal group comprising members of the Southern Sierra Miwuk Nation, the Tuolumne Band of Me-Wuk Indians, the North Fork Rancheria of Mono Indians, the Picayune Rancheria of Chukchansi Indians, the Bishop Paiute Tribe, and the Mono Lake Kutzadika-a Tribe. Lindsie Bear, editor of *News from Native California*, and I had driven in from Berkeley, invited guests at their monthly meeting, honored and pleased to be there.

After some hesitation, Jay edged into a description of what felt to him like a fated visitation that had brought the need for a roundhouse to everyone's attention. "There was a carload of . . . well, spiritual people traveling around. I didn't want to say this at first, but I'll just say they came up and visited us in the Valley. And their job was to help the Indian tribes that don't have nothing or not much, like us. They told us that we should start something, ceremonies and cultural activities or whatever it might be that would bring our people together. So that's the word they gave us, gave me. I said, No, that's impossible. There is no place for ceremonies. You get two million people coming in the Valley."

Indeed, with Yosemite Valley as crowded as a shopping mall, holding ceremonies presents a special challenge. After the "spiritual people" left, a roundhouse was built near the visitor center in 1974, and while over the years it has been used, it is too small and too public. Early on, a desire arose among the Indian community for a larger roundhouse at the site of Wahhoga Village.

The building of a roundhouse, any roundhouse, is and always has been a major undertaking and a serious commitment. Serving as cathedral, university, theater, and town hall, roundhouses are architectural marvels. Semi-subterranean, they are warm in the winter, cool in the summer. The enclosed space with its earthy smells feels as safe and intimate as a womb, yet also timeless and infinite. Here in a space both comfortable and sanctified, stories are told, the sick are healed, weddings and first-fruit festivals are performed. Babies are named and the dead are mourned, and in the great cycle of annual ceremonies the Creator is thanked for the gift of life. Roundhouses, now as in ancient times, "give life to the community," in the words of Wintu artist, educator, and ceremonial leader Frank LaPena. The roundhouse binds members of the community to each other and connects them to the spirit world.

For the people of Yosemite, the desire for a roundhouse is especially keen, a deep craving rooted in painful history. Expelled repeatedly from their homeland, they have watched as, over the decades, their beloved Valley has been transformed from a place where people gathered acorns, hunted deer, made baskets, and raised children to an international icon and major tourist destination. To John Muir, it was a cathedral; to the National Park Service (NPS), the birth of "America's Best Idea"; to the United Nations, a World Heritage Site. Artists, writers, photographers, and millions of tourists overrun the Valley in their eagerness to wrest inspiration from its cliffs and waterfalls.

The grandeur and beauty of Yosemite is undeniable, but it's a grandeur and beauty stolen from the original inhabitants and given to others. It is the paradise from which the people native to the area, at least as a living culture, have been repeatedly expelled. They were not only evicted physically but have in many ways been expunged from the very idea of Yosemite. They were removed from the Valley to help keep that landscape "pure," to save it from human "disturbance." Indeed, their very existence has been denied, as, despite heroic efforts, they have been refused federal recognition as a tribe. True, many have been hired by the National Park Service, some as cultural interpreters and demonstrators, employed to carry on the basketry traditions and other arts of the past. This is commendable, yet it points to a contradiction: while Indian culture can be demonstrated in the Valley, it cannot be lived there.

There are many ways of destroying a culture, but surely one of the most effective and insidious is to turn living people into nostalgic symbols of the past while denying them existence in the present. This practice has deep roots in Yosemite, going back to the first encounters between Indians and whites. In his account of how the white settlers "discovered" Yosemite, Lafayette Houghton Bunnell tells how, in the midst of driving the Indians out of Yosemite, the conquerors came upon a lake and decided to name it after Chief Ten-ie-ya:

I called him up to us, and told him that we had given his name to the lake and the river. At first, he seemed unable to comprehend our purpose, and pointing to the group of glistening peaks, near the head of the lake, said: "It already has a name; we call it Py-we-ack." Upon my telling him that we had named it Ten-ie-ya, because it was upon the shores of the lake that we had found his people, who would never return to it to live, his countenance fell and he at once left our group and joined his own family circle. His countenance as he left us indicated that he thought the naming of the lake no equivalent for the loss of his territory.

It might be useful at this time to coin a phrase—the Tenaya (modern spelling) Phenomenon—to describe the honoring of the image of a people while robbing them of land and power. The Tenaya Phenomenon is widespread, but it is particularly flagrant in Yosemite, where a museum, a reconstructed village, and an active program of interpretation all thrive side by side with a history of expulsions, betrayals, and contempt.

Take, for example, the story of Wahhoga Village. Wahhoga, near the base of Yosemite Falls, seems to have been one of the nine original villages recorded in Yosemite Valley. In a paper delivered at the Society of California Archaeology meeting in 2009, tribal members working with the Southern Sierra Miwuk Nation gave an overview of the rich social complexity of the Valley in traditional times: "Who lived here? There are eighteen lineages from eleven cultural groups, and eleven cultural routes circling resource harvest and chains of villages. There were forty to forty-five captains, chiefs, appointed chiefs, and dance captains which have been identified."

After decades of expulsions, by 1920 most families who

returned to live in the Valley were clustered at the village of Yawok-achi, on the site of what is now the Yosemite Clinic. This is the site referred to even today as the Old Village. By the early 1930s the Old Village was deserted, and the Indians living in Yosemite took up residence in fifteen cabin homes built at Wahhoga.

As Lindsie and I sat around the table at the Miwu Mati Healing Center, some of the elders shared pleasant memories of their childhoods there. Lois Martin recalls, "We were able as children to run around all over there in that Valley. Our parents were working, so the grandparents were the ones that took care of us. They couldn't chase us all over. But the older kids like Jay's brother and Bill Tucker and that age group, they were a little bit older than I was, so they watched after the younger children up there. We were always with the older kids, down at the river or playing in the meadow. You know, I always felt safe. Surely my grandmother thought we were safe, because we'd all come back when we were supposed to. That was just the atmosphere there. It was a family of families living there. We had some good times. There were some dinners, people getting together for community dinners and a lot of joy and music. It was a good time. I have a lot of good memories. I'm sure a lot of hard times too, especially when people had to move. Back then if you didn't have someone working for the Park Service or for Curry Company, people had to move out of there. That was hard, because where were you going to move to? You never had any place. Those were difficult times."

Beginning, it seems, in the 1940s, the National Park Service made it an official policy to once again remove Indians from the Valley, and, as Lois Martin alludes to in her reminiscences, the next decades saw a steady eviction of people and razing of buildings. One elder told me how the Park Service sent her husband out on a work assignment to the backcountry, and while the man was out of the way, park employees came to evict the woman and her children.

❖ ❖ ❖

Expelled and unrecognized as a tribe, the people of Yosemite came to view the building of a roundhouse as a long-sought affirmation of their rights, a return as a living culture to their homeland. Discussions between Miwuk elders and the National Park Service about the roundhouse have been going on since the 1970s. In 1980, Secretary of the Interior Cecil Andrus approved the building of a roundhouse as part of an Indian Cultural Center. No one can accuse NPS of moving precipitously, and indeed it took another seventeen years, until 1997, to reach a formal agreement between the Southern Sierra Miwuk Nation (also known as the American Indian Council of Mariposa County) and Yosemite National Park for "conducting traditional activities." For the next decade, this proposal for a roundhouse moved through the various legal requirements, with reports and consultation to comply with acts such as the National Environmental Policy Act (NEPA) and the National Historic Preservation Act. Issues of safety were discussed with the park's safety officer, superintendent, and deputy superintendent. The Yosemite Conservancy put in some funds, and in June 2009 ground was broken. Present and officiating was the then-acting superintendent of the park J. F. Hammet, who not only sanctioned the groundbreaking but supplied the machinery that started the digging and blessed the enterprise by telling the Indians present, "This place was yours." Officially sanctioned, with a solid background of compliance and written agreements, with the full cooperation of everyone, and with money allocated, it seemed that nothing could stop the building of the Wahhoga Roundhouse.

Construction was well under way in the spring of 2011 when a new park superintendent, Don Neubacher, arrived at Yosemite. Citing a Park Service requirement that all buildings in the national parks be built to newly adopted building codes, he halted construction of the roundhouse, intending to iron out a few difficulties. He had no doubt that, with compromise and adaptation, the construction of the roundhouse could be finished. He felt and still feels that he had no choice but to have the roundhouse conform to code, and he seems genuinely concerned that without structural modifications it might collapse under the weight of snow or during an earthquake, injuring or even killing scores of people inside.

But Jay Johnson, Les James, and the other members of the Southern Sierra Miwuk Nation found themselves insulted, betrayed, and angry. They had an agreement, and now the rules had been changed. It was in effect another broken treaty. In a series of meetings, NPS personnel laid out their demands. At first they put forth requirements that were almost comic in their inappropriateness—an electrically lit exit sign, for example. Some of these demands were dropped, but the NPS officials kept bringing in structural engineers and experts, none of whom had any experience with or knowledge of traditional California roundhouses or their history and construction.

I talked with Don Neubacher and some of the NPS people, and they view themselves as responsible citizens standing up for safety, and they are puzzled at the unwillingness of the Wahhoga Committee to compromise and "listen to reason." In their view, the codes were developed to protect life and limb.

But there is an older code that the Wahhoga Committee is obliged to follow. A roundhouse is a sacred space, and the rules for its construction do not come from bureaucrats in Washington but from the spirit world. "We can't change something that's been going on for years and years and years," said Jay Johnson. "It's not right for us. And we know that and we feel that. So we said we can't add anything. Anything we add to it, it takes away the medicine that we put into this setting up the four poles and the crossbeams."

"My grandchildren live in Castro Valley," said Sis Calhoun,

another member of the Wahhoga Committee at the table with us. "And in their classroom they were told that all the Indians are dead. The roundhouse gives them the opportunity to connect with the spirits of the land, where our people came from. That's where our roots are; that's who we are. And it's an opportunity to see those ceremonies done in a sacred way as our ancestors did it. The roundhouse to me is so important. What upsets me most about Don Neubacher and his staff is that they're dictating to us about what our culture is. They're tearing apart our culture."

A fierce irony is that Wahhoga Village is not far from Camp Four, the camp frequented by rock climbers. Why, one wonders, is this clearly dangerous activity not only condoned by the Park Service but encouraged? Why don't they focus some of their rules and safety concerns on these climbers rather than on the Indians? "I don't get it," commented Lois Martin. "They're so worried about liability, but there is nothing that anybody can find in research that ever shows a roundhouse collapsing or anybody ever being injured by one. Yet that's his [Neubacher's] big issue. The rock climbers can climb up there and not even think about not making it or freezing to death hanging there on a cliff. But all that stuff is okay. We're safe; we're concerned about our people and our grandchildren, and there's no history of anything happening to the Indian people in the roundhouse."

The battle against what the committee feels is interference with their cultural and religious rights is more than just a local battle. Commenting on the situation, the National Congress of American Indians issued a resolution that reads in part:

> Building a traditional ceremonial structure according to building code would destroy the spiritual context. Allowing onerous and unnecessary building codes to restrict

traditional ceremonial structures will set a precedent locally, regionally, and nationally, negatively affecting all efforts to construct traditional ceremonial structures in the United States, repressing spiritual, traditional, and cultural customs of all American Indians, impacting their ability to properly conduct spiritual ceremonies.

In meeting after meeting, the Wahhoga Committee has tried mightily to get their point across to the staff at Yosemite. They have approached the Department of Interior in Washington. And they have continued to urge Don Neubacher and his staff to keep the discussion going. Every month now for the last two years they have announced monthly meetings and invited NPS personnel to come. Every month Jay Johnson calls the meetings to order, and all eyes turn to the chairs put out for the Park Service representatives. For well over a year now the chairs have been empty.

The negotiations seem frozen, the talks at a standstill, and it seems possible that the Southern Sierra Miwuk Nation may lose the battle to get the roundhouse it so deeply yearns for. This would be tragic. But to the people sitting around the table, there's something worse than losing the roundhouse, because, in truth, the struggle to build a roundhouse is only one part of a bigger struggle: the struggle to keep the culture alive. As important as the roundhouse may be, I came to realize, the center of the culture is not so much a physical building but perhaps more essentially the idea of what the building means, of how it connects people to the spirit world, to the past, to each other. To accept the demands of the Park Service may result in a physical structure that might look like a roundhouse. But as I cast my gaze over the stubborn, brave people sitting around the table, it becomes clear to me that there's something more at stake. A round-house built to specifications handed down from a government agency in Washington will, in the end, be at best an imitation of the real thing—a false image, perhaps even a fraud. The real roundhouse is rooted in tradition, in the soul of Native people, in the power of the medicine and the purity of heart with which it is built. By refusing to give in, I realize, the Wahhoga Committee is keeping the roundhouse alive.

News from Native California, vol. 27, no. 1, 2013

HAWAIIAN CONNECTIONS (1992)

The Tongva lived for centuries in the soft air and sweet valleys of Southern California, undisturbed until 1771, when San Gabriel Mission was established. In succeeding decades they watched as the pueblo of Los Angeles grew and grew, slowly at first, then ferociously, beyond all bounds and beyond all sense. Its homes, office buildings, freeways, malls, airports, and factories spread over the landscape, swallowing the ancient village sites, the sacred places, the valleys where seeds once were gathered and deer were stalked.

Life is not easy for an Indian, but for the Tongva, rendered strangers in their own homeland, it has been particularly hard. The federal government has never given them recognition or acknowledgment as a sovereign Indian nation. Most people still call them Gabrielinos or Fernandeños after the missions into which they were once drawn. Anthropologists generally ignore the living descendants, having declared the culture all but extinguished. Linguists have long listed the language as dead. Often one hears it said—behind their backs, of course—that after more than two centuries of acculturation and intermarriage, they're hardly Indians at all, but maybe "some kind of Mexicans."

Yet in the face of such ruthless and constant denial, the Tongva continue on, struggling to preserve what they know of their culture, struggling to recapture what has slipped away, struggling to achieve validity and recognition in their own eyes if not in the eyes of others. And so do their neighbors to the south, the Ajachmem (often called Juaneños) and those to the north, the Chumash.

Perhaps the struggle for recognition in a world that insists on negating them accounts for the intensity, generosity, and ceremony with which the Indians of Southern California greeted a delegation that had been sent from the Native people of Hawai'i to establish diplomatic ties with other Native communities and to sign treaties of recognition and mutual aid. The event was arranged at UC Irvine in early April by Carolyn Kuali'i, herself part Hawaiian, part Native American.

Assembling in a hall in the campus student union were the Ambassador Plenipotentiary and the Secretary of State for the Native people of Hawai'i, and greeting them were the tribal chairs, spiritual leaders, and elders of the Southern California tribes, joined later by representatives of the Ione Band of Miwok.

In the midst of general camaraderie and good food, the provisions of the treaties were discussed and negotiated. An outdoor fair was held on campus, with Hawaiians from the Los Angeles area and Native people displaying beautiful objects and sharing traditions. The Hawaiians treated everyone to a genuine hula dance—a sensuous, stately, spellbinding dance far removed from what has become a degraded tourist attraction elsewhere. At a magnificent ceremony held on a beach, a sacred Hawaiian drink was shared, and the Acachme people performed a deeply moving ritual and dance. At the end, an impressive feast was prepared as Indians gathered from everywhere to witness the massive exchange of gifts and the signing of the treaties.

Like all such state events, the signing of the treaties had its share of pomp and circumstance, an element of theatricality and formality. It was also an event with profound practical consequences. The treaties of mutual aid point toward a more cooperative effort in which each group, in dealing with the federal government, will also watch out for the interests of its treaty allies. Also, the signing of such treaties affirms the principles of sovereignty, which the federal government would like to reduce to little more than a legal fiction that grants a few carefully defined and relatively minor privileges. Sovereignty is much more than that, of course, and brings with it the possibilities of tribal laws, tribal courts, the sanctity of tribal territory, even the ability to issue passports (as does the Iroquois federation) that are recognized worldwide. By signing these treaties the Native people of Southern California went beyond resisting a government that tries to erode tribal rights, and took it upon themselves to expand those rights as befits nations that are independent not only in name but in spirit as well.

While this was primarily a political gathering, the spiritual significance was never far from anyone's mind. As the ceremony on the beach was being held, suddenly and gloriously a humpback whale emerged from the ocean and spouted. This whale, native to both the coast of California and the coast of Hawai'i, seemed by its presence to become part of the treaties as well. "All my relations . . . ," a voice muttered as the whale paid its regards and slipped back into the sea.

While the whale paid tribute to the ceremonial aspects of the event, what sticks in my mind are two private moments. The conference was held on the UC Irvine campus, one of the most recent and modern of the UC campuses. The contrast to the Indian world was dramatic. Manicured green lawns covered the ground, clean and efficient spaces defined the interior, and bureaucratic regulations covered everything. For the first several hours of the gathering, everyone's focus was on the parking guidelines. All participants had been issued parking permits, but the rules were so complex and so badly phrased and the penalties for parking in the wrong places were so Draconian that, for the first day, all anyone could talk about was whether or not they would get towed. Finally, L. Frank burst in with this wonderful comment: "Let's talk about something else. Extinct people can park anywhere." I've long cherished that remark, and I suggested to her that it would make a great title for her autobiography.

The second memorable moment came toward the end of the event when, after the business was taken care of, treaties signed and sovereignty acknowledged, the participants celebrated with a cultural sharing. The Tongva people sang songs, displayed traditional artwork, and told stories. The Hawaiians responded with a traditional hula. The hula dancers were gorgeous, and their moves were sensual, but it was unlike the hulas done for tourists. At various times, the hula master gave interpretations of what the dancers meant, and at one point she said, "In the next dance, you'll notice the smile sneaking over the girl's face. It's a dance that we do for our genitalia." I was standing next to Jimi Castillo. A solidly built man in his fifties or sixties, Jimi was then working in prisons, serving as a Native American chaplain. He had seen a lot of hardship and violence in his life, and he had the look of someone you'd like to have on your side if you were in a barroom brawl. I was struck by the comedy of this Jewish guy from Boston and an urban Indian from Los Angeles watching young women dance for their genitalia. We watched slack-jawed with amazement. I looked up and suddenly noticed big tears coming out of Jimi's eyes. Finally he sobbed, "How could anybody hurt people like this?" He was weeping for the Hawaiians but especially for his own people. More than just political and economic sovereignty, the events of the last several days had provided a vision of what might happen to the human spirit when it was liberated from colonization and oppression.

News from Native California, vol. 6, no. 3, 1992

LEADERSHIP TRADITIONS IN NATIVE CALIFORNIA: AN IMPERFECT ART FOR AN IMPERFECT WORLD (2012)

In 1930, William Raganal Benson, a Pomo basketweaver, story-teller, and tribal scholar from Clear Lake, told linguist Jaime de Angulo how the first "chief" came into being. The story is embedded in Benson's wonderful account of creation:

> He lived in the north, the Old Man, his name was Marumbda.
> He lived in a cloud-house, a house that looked like snow, like ice.
> And he thought of making the world.
> "I will ask my older brother who lives in the south," thus he said, the Old Man Marumbda.
> "Wah! What shall I do?" thus he said.
> "Eh!" thus he said.

No wonder Marumbda was puzzled. The world had never existed before, and it was hard work figuring out how to make it happen. Marumbda and his elder brother, Kuksu, had to create and then destroy four different worlds before they got it right. Humans were especially troublesome. Marumbda fashioned them as best he could, setting them up to lead good lives, but they quickly descended into wickedness and incest. Marumbda kept trying, giving them the knowledge of how to do things right, but they always forgot, they always threw the knowledge away. We can picture him saying, "Wah! What shall I do?" Then the solution burst upon him. He approached a village where the people were gathered at the entrance to the dance house. He singled out one man from among the crowd.

"Stand here," he said to him.
"Let me teach you!
"You will be the head-chief of these people.
"You will teach them.
"You will make plans for them.
"You will harangue them.
"You will take care of them.
"This is your village.
"And they in turn will take care of you."
Thus he spoke.

And so the chief's duties were set in primordial time, their roots long and deep. Encoded in Benson's account are chiefly obligations that would have been familiar not only to traditional Pomo leaders but to chiefs all across Native California: taking care of a tribe's food distribution, event planning, feast hosting, and speech making. Of course, specific leadership functions varied across the rich array and incredible diversity of societies in California. But as the story of Marumbda demonstrates, the chiefly duties and powers were all rooted in an ancient past.

It is hardly unusual for rulers to derive legitimacy and power from divinities. Throughout the world and throughout history, kings, pharaohs, and emperors have claimed divine authority, sometimes even divine lineage. The kinship of rulers and gods is so pervasive that often "God" or "Creator" is described as a sort of mega-chief, "King of the Universe," as it were. But perhaps it would be helpful to reflect a bit on the nature of California worldsmakers. In the Judeo-Christian tradition, and many other traditions as well, the world was made by an omniscient, omnipotent God who commanded a world into being and with consummate authority endowed it with its powers and traditions. The creation of the world according to Native California accounts was entirely different.

Whether the world was made by Coyote, Silver Fox, twins born of an egg, beings in cloud houses, or entities known as "Earth Initiates," there seems built into the very fabric of the world a tentativeness, a mystery, a confusion. The divine creators of the California Indian world were not decisive chief executives who said, "Let there be light," and with a snap of the divine finger light appeared. Rather, like Marumbda, they seemed a bit at a loss. Faced with the momentous task laid before him, Marumbda said it best: "Wah! What shall I do?" To the extent that the chief of a tribe reflects this root of his authority, it might be helpful to realize that perfect knowledge and unlimited power are not part of the package.

With perfection off the table, what then was expected of a traditional leader? As with everything else in Native California, there was astonishing diversity. Smaller villages and communities were often simply extended families, and leadership was invested in the family patriarch, or in many cases the family matriarch. Clusters of smaller villages might look to a larger village, which served as a ceremonial and trading center, and the leader of the larger village might be seen as the "big chief" of the region. Other groups had a more complex and formalized political structure. For example, the Pomo village of Pdahau, perched along the foam-carved coastline of Northern California at the mouth of the Garcia River, had three chiefs and two sub-chiefs.

In general, but not always, it seems that leadership ran in certain families. The Coast Miwok chief, or *hoipu*, was advised by four elderly women, and was himself "bossed," in the words of elder and dreamer Tom Smith, by a female chief called the *maien*. She was technically head of the women's ceremonial dance house, but her advice, orders, and guidance were looked to above everyone else's. An early visitor to California, Stephen Powers, claimed that the authority of a Karuk or Yurok chief was quite limited. He could "state the law or the custom and the facts, and he could give his opinion, but he could hardly pronounce judgment. The office was not hereditary: the headman or captain was generally one of the oldest, and always one of the astutest, men of the village."

As with everything else in traditional Native California, the closer one looks, the more varied and complex things get, and the more difficult to make any generalizations. Yet this brief introduction is being put together in a year of an American presidential election [2012], and even the most cursory survey of leadership in Native California points to some interesting and thought-provoking comparisons.

CHANGE AND STABILITY

In modern societies, those vying to be leaders generally promise change, something new. Someone running for president or governor must present himself or herself as dynamic and forward-looking. But this was hardly the case in traditional California communities. An early phonograph recording from the 1920s or 1930s captures a speech given by a man named Molestu (Tom Williams) at the Mewuk community of Chakamichino. In translation, the speech reads:

> The young chief is going to do the same as his father used to do.
> Now all of you men get ready. Put those poles up for him.
> All of you men get ready.
> Have the ceremonial house ready just the same as for his father.
> The young chief is going to do just the same as his father did. He is going the same way as his father did.
> It is just the same, just the same.

CHARACTER AND SECRECY

Another interesting point of comparison is the matter of "character." In modern society, we generally choose leaders whom we do not know personally, especially for national or statewide offices, but often for local offices as well. These leaders are presented to us through the media, their images often manufactured by political consultants. This leads to a deep suspicion that the candidate who is being presented as a paragon of good sense and virtue is really a monster with secrets, and a good part of a modern campaign is to dig up dirt on your opponent and expose his or her history for what it "really is."

In the small tribal communities of traditional times, though, everyone was well known. There was no hiding; the chief did not live in a palace or a gated community, his or her past hidden, his or her image manufactured and presented carefully to the public. The chief lived with others, his dwelling not much different from those around him, his character and behavior well known to all.

POWER AND PERSUASION

In modern Western societies, politicians make laws and have at their disposal courts, a police force, and if necessary an army that can be used to enforce the laws they pass. In traditional California societies, there were no sheriffs, no prisons, no institutionalized means by which the leader could enforce his pronouncements. There did not seem to be any dictators or autocrats among California Indians. The power of a chief was largely the power of persuasion, which made oratory such an essential art.

The ability to make a good speech was valued highly from one end of the state to another. Typically, in much of California, a leader would get up before dawn, climb to the roof of the communal roundhouse, and deliver a morning sermon, urging people to be industrious and fair, to avoid fights, and so on. A Modoc leader, in the words of anthropologist Verne Ray, "spoke in a loud voice so he might be widely heard, and expressed himself in carefully chosen phrases. Listeners were admonished not to gossip or quarrel, to work assiduously at the food quest so that none might starve in the spring, and to arise early to such purpose." As Patrick Miguel (Quechan) phrased it, "It was by [a chief's] speeches that people knew he had great power and was *kwoxot* [a leader]." In a world without a police force or prisons, in small communities where one saw the same people day in and day out, persuasive speech was a powerful and in fact irreplaceable tool.

STATUS AND RESPONSIBILITY

As is true of leaders everywhere, the chief in traditional California enjoyed elevated status. He had special privileges and honors. Kinsmen would often bring enough food to relieve him of the need to hunt, he and his family would often have exceptionally valuable and beautifully made dance regalia, and he might have a prominent place to sit in the roundhouse or a prominent role to play in the ceremonies. Many chiefs were polygamous, keeping several wives while other men generally only had one, in part to make the chiefly lineage robust, but also to secure diplomatic relationships with a range of families across a tribal region. For the Chumash, in order to accommodate the chief's polygamous lifestyle, a chief's wives moved from their birth villages to live with their husband in his, upending the traditional pattern of men relocating to live in the villages of their wives.

But it often seemed that the benefits of leadership were balanced by the responsibilities. This amassing of wealth in the form of food and also precious items such as feathers and shell money was not seen as greedy or self-serving; it was expected that the chief would host visitors, sponsor festivals, and provide food and resources for the ceremonies that he scheduled and presided over. In a sense, the chief functioned as a community banker, and the wealth he accumulated was not really his own but in some respects was a public trust. Anyone who went hungry or homeless in a village would cause the chief utter shame and disgrace, so all those in need were tended to with donated stores of food and wealth. Sometimes, it was hard to persuade the next in line to take on the role of chief because, as Edwin Loeb writes of the Eastern Pomo, the chief, though wealthier than everyone else, had to cover war debts, had to put up the most money when a new ceremonial house needed to be built—in short, was responsible. And this responsibility was not to an abstract constituency. In these small societies, the responsibility was to the people you knew and saw every day, the people you ate with and sang with, the people you were linked to by a thousand emotional, familial, and economic ties.

It wasn't always a desirable job. Perhaps the saving grace was that no one expected you to be perfect; you were too well known for that.

Note: This article was written with the assistance and collaboration of Sylvia Linsteadt, who worked with Malcolm for several glorious months in early 2012.

News from Native California, vol. 26, no. 1, 2012

DREAMING US HOME AGAIN: GREG SARRIS (2012)

Greg Sarris, muscular and intense, seems to be leading several lives in the space ordinarily allotted for one. He's chairman of the Federated Indians of Graton Rancheria (Coast Miwok and Southern Pomo), with about thirteen hundred enrolled members. He's a professor at Sonoma State University, he has a PhD in modern thought and literature from Stanford, and he's written several books and co-produced the HBO movie *Grand Avenue* with Robert Redford. A short story, "Bluebelly," was anthologized in Heyday's *New California Writing 2012*, and Greg agreed to read at a reception for the book at the California Historical Society in San Francisco on May 16, 2012. We both showed up an hour early and had a rollicking, funny, and lively conversation, from which the following has been drawn.

MM: You've done a lot, Greg. What are you most proud of?

GS: If I've accomplished anything in my life—the books, the movies, the PhD from Stanford—I think that my greatest accomplishment is that for twenty years I've kept thirteen hundred people—we're a large tribe for California—from factionalizing. We even amended our tribal constitution so that no current members or their offspring can ever be disenrolled. We just got approval of this from the BIA [Bureau of Indian Affairs]. And to make sure that this policy stays in place, I put in a monetary incentive not to disenroll in the gaming compact just negotiated with the State of California. If [when we open the casino] we revise the constitution and disenroll people, more money goes to the state.

MM: That's radical and far-reaching, and it suggests a thoughtful process. What's the tribal government structure like? What powers do you have? How do you interact with the tribal council?

GS: I'm chairman, and we have a constitution that we're always amending, changing, trying to make better—a fluid constitution. We have elections every year, and terms are for two years.

There are seven people on the tribal council, and we have staggered elections so that one year four seats are up, the next year three seats are up. I've served as chairman for twenty years, ever since Kathleen [Smith] and Bev [Ortiz] sent me an article when I was down at UCLA saying that another tribe wanted to open a casino in our territory. But I'm up for reelection every two years.

MM: A constitution that is always being changed and elections every two years . . . I couldn't think of a better recipe for chaos.

GS: I'm happy to say that we have had a consistent council ever since we got restored [as a federally recognized tribe] in December of 2000. The same council. Everybody's up every two years, [but] the same people get put in. So that shows you, I would say, an incredible satisfaction among the tribal members with what we are doing. Joanne Campbell, Gene Buvelot . . . I have sat there and looked at the same people for twenty years.

MM: Is there ever opposition?

GS: No one's ever run against me. I've never been challenged in twenty years.

MM: Why?

GS: Maybe because I'm a weirdo. I speak two languages. I speak the language of the Indian world and that of the government and of the controlling class. I can speak both languages. And I love my tribe and fight madly for them and have given a lot.

MM: So what does the council do? What do you do?

GS: There's the vice chair, Lorelle [Ross]; the secretary, Jeannette Anglin; and our treasurer, Gene Buvelot. Then our members at large, and they all have their duties as described in the constitution. For me, I oversee the daily operations of the entire tribe. That means our TANF program—Tribal Aid to Needy Families program—our housing programs, all reports come to me. I've also been the sole person on the development board. I negotiated a contract with Station Casinos that is unprecedented, giving the tribe 100 percent control of the development board. It's been very strange working with the casino business. As you know, Malcolm, I'm a nerd. I have a PhD in modern thought and literature. What in hell ever prepared me to do this?

The other thing I do as leader is not just the administrative stuff, overseeing the development and that kind of thing, but I fancy myself a kind of preacher or a leader because I do a monthly column and in that column I talk about everything in tribal terms, especially about internalized oppression. Why is it that we tear one another down? I try to make people conscious of the homelessness that seeps into the pores of my people. Why do we turn against one another? Why do we destroy one another? That's what we know from colonization. You just see it again and again and again. So what I'm trying to do is make everyone conscious of those disruptive patterns, all the while preparing us for the casino.

MM: A preacher, eh? That's what the traditional people used to say: the prerequisite for a good leader was skill at speaking.

GS: And that's true. Look at my great example, Essie Parrish.

MM: Would you say that Essie was your role model?

GS: Her and Mabel [McKay], too. When you saw Essie—even seeing her in a film like *Sucking Doctor*, where she's standing there and she's speaking Pomo—the richness of her language and metaphors and how she talked to her people and how she knew her people, that's a great model.

So I write every month, and I preach. Every two months, six times a year, we have a general membership meeting where we'll have two or three hundred people all come together. Also, every two weeks we have the council meetings; they're open to all members and we serve dinner. So we encourage them to come and listen to what's going on, and we feed them a wonderful meal. We always have twenty or thirty guests or tribal members there. They can bring their kids. I keep the books open, so nothing's hidden. But at those big meetings, and even at those council meetings, I will start on a riff—I don't necessarily call it "critical thinking," but I talk about what makes something you've heard true or not true.

MM: Could you say more about what you learned from Mabel and Essie?

GS: You know, I was a bad kid, really a kind of angry kid. And knowing Mabel and then knowing Essie, I realized there was something bigger than me, something that I couldn't explain. And they were also kind. Mabel always made you aware. "You're an Indian doctor," someone would say. "What do you do for poison oak?" "Calamine lotion," she'd answer.

"Do you talk to plants?" someone asked.

"Well, yeah, I sing when I have to use them."

"Do plants talk to one another?"

"Well, I suppose they do."

"What do they say?"

"I don't know. Why would I be listening?"

MM: Great story. That generation was so real, not at all puffed out.

GS: That's what made them saints. They surrendered the ego to something bigger. There was no ego there. I remember the Pope wanted to meet Mabel, and she just couldn't be bothered. She said, Bring him by and we'll take him to Happy Steak. Needless to say, it never happened.

MM: Do you have people you are mentoring for roles of future leadership?

GS: Lorelle is there, and there are others, but I'm hoping education will create new leaders. You know, Malcolm, the other thing I do—and it's a bit brutal—all our housing programs and our TANF programs, we call it a "hand up," not a "hand out." So if you are getting any of the benefits that the tribe offers its members—housing, for example—you have to take a biweekly class that we offer at night on how to manage your money and rent. If you're getting assistance through our tribal TANF program, you have to take a family practice and parenting class. All that kind of stuff.

MM: How do you handle disruptors and malcontents?

GS: We've had them, and one of the things we do is make sure there's no swearing in our meetings. You can't use the F-word; that's forbidden. The minute somebody uses it, you get one warning. If somebody is hostile to somebody else, you get one warning and then you are asked to leave. We don't tolerate any of that kind of stuff. The membership is in general agreement. And also when people use certain tones . . . some people are very hostile. And often they're not even conscious of their hostility, their anger. And I say, "Listen to how you said that. You're asking me a question that's really an accusation; you're asking the question as if you presume an answer, aren't you? You're asking the question as if you're assuming that I did this wrong, aren't you?" And I say, "That's offensive to me. That hurts me. What you should do is let me show you how to ask that question so that I'm not offended and other people aren't offended."

So, you know, Malcolm, I keep talking to folks and reminding them of the incredible opportunity we now have. One of the things I'm saying is, People! You have to realize that, for the first time since European contact, we are not only going to have control of our lives but control of the community in which we live. We're going to make more money. We're going to have the biggest operation around. Think of that!

MM: What do you think brings dysfunction to other communities?

GS: It's internalized oppression. We have to constantly make people aware of it and how ubiquitous it is in our lives. And I always give a simple example: a girl who had an abusive father. She says, "I'm never going to marry a guy like that. Never!" She goes to a party and there are a hundred guys, and the one she picks is just like her father. And I say, Why? Why? Because at a deep level, below language and intelligence, is emotion. And down there is home. She sees in him what is familiar, what is home, and we seek—even if it's pathological— what is home. So we have to get to a place in ourselves where we stop that, because that home is not beautiful.

The other thing is that we're victims, victims in this culture of homelessness. You get trapped into an us/them dichotomy. How do we get a "we" instead of an "us/them"? Indian people always had a "we." But as soon as you get dislocated—and we are dislocated, we're strangers in our homeland—how do we come home again, all of us? That's one of the big things that maybe this casino and the other things we're doing can [help us] come to terms with. I have a big dream that it can somehow bring us all—Indian and non-Indian—home again. And the big question for today is, How do you stop this us/them dichotomy that is a cancer that will kill us?

MM: You know, Greg, maybe your awareness of the harm that the us/them dichotomy brings is because you yourself are mixed race.

GS: I'm glad you raised that. That's the hardest thing for me, because I don't fit in anywhere. I'm constantly reminded of this everywhere I go. It's been really hard, and it's been really lonely, and it's been thrown in my face. I try to get back to what Mabel told me when I was nineteen years old. She said I had a lot of anger in me. She said, "You're going to let holes grow in your heart, hatred and poison will go there, and you're going to poison yourself and you're going to poison other people." She said, You don't have to do that. She said, You have another choice. All the things that have happened to you, she said, could become medicine. She said, This is an opportunity to doctor.

MM: Do you figure that leading a tribe is different from being a leader in the dominant culture? Do you think you could do Jerry Brown's job and govern California? Although, come to think of it, I wonder if Jerry can do Jerry Brown's job.

GS: Or could Jerry do my job? I like Jerry very, very much. The problem is that politicians are so compromised. Whatever ideals they have, they're so compromised by money and all that. The joy I have, so far—knock on wood—my ideals of creating huge organic farms, which we're in the process of doing, of getting people to school, of getting the old people housing—all of those things are not compromised. I'm making them happen. I have nobody in the tribe telling me no. I'm not having to rob Peter to pay Paul. So far, I haven't had to do that. If I were to do Jerry's job, I'd have to do a lot of it. But you know, the big test will come when the casino opens and the money comes. But I'm preparing.

MM: Thanks, Greg. Anything you want to say to sum this up?

GS: I think it's especially important for a modern Indian leader to be able to work well in both the Indian world and the non-Indian world, so that he or she can translate both sides. In my case, having this ability to translate enables me to be visionary, to see a future for my people as empowered and engaged individuals who can work together as a tribe to recreate for all members of our community, Indian and non-Indian alike, those ancient ethics and aesthetics of place that make for all a safe, sustainable, and cherished home. This kind of vision and leadership is particularly necessary where tribes have economic power and can influence and shape a sustainable future with that power. Power should not rest in one individual, or a few, but in a community that is happy and safe and sustained by a healthy, equitable relationship between all peoples and their larger natural world.

News from Native California, vol. 26, no. 1, 2012

CEREMONIAL ENCLOSURE AT YA-KA-AMA (1991)

George Somersal drove up the dirt road from the administration building, past the greenhouses and native plant nursery, until he reached a large open meadow. Here he stopped his car and looked out at the couple of hundred people who had assembled. The occasion was a conference of Native California basketweavers, and people had come from as far north as the Klamath River, as far south as the Colorado River, from the Central Valley, the foothills, indeed from all over California to gather on the grounds of Ya-Ka-Ama, just west of Santa Rosa. Cars, pick-ups, campers, and vans were parked everywhere on the grass. Tents were set up at the edge of the meadow, under the shade of an oak-bay forest. A group of youngsters was playing with a frisbee.

"Look!" said George. "All these people and no alcohol. Not a single can of beer!" With that thought, George drove off on yet another errand.

The 1991 basketweavers' conference lasted two days, June 29 and 30. Within an open-air ceremonial enclosure—a large circle of stakes with a net-roofed arcade around the perimeter—people gathered, talked, complained, laughed, ate, and shared their concerns and their skills. Panel discussions and demonstrations were interspersed with prayers, formal announcements, and traditional dance performances.

There was, to be sure, a poignancy to the gathering. Although no one spoke of it, I think that everyone was aware of how many great basketweavers had passed away or had become disabled in the last couple of years: Laura Somersal (George Somersal's mother), Elsie Allen, Frances McDaniel, and Dorothy Stanley were among those who had so recently died, while Mabel McKay was in a convalescent hospital. More than that, perhaps, was the sad realization that this complex and highly evolved art form that was once the common property of tens of thousands of "ordinary" California women was now entrusted to so few. The fragility of it was shocking. But against the fragility was the beauty, the strength, the joy of that day at Ya-Ka-Ama. One could not help but be astounded, even worshipful, of those elders present who had kept alive their traditions through so many difficult decades. And one could not help but be encouraged by the number of younger people who had been drawn to the art.

"Are you a basketweaver?" one would ask.

"I'm still learning," was the response from virtually everyone under the age of fifty.

George Somersal returned from his errand and parked his car. Instead of heading toward the ceremonial enclosure where basketweavers and representatives from the U.S. Forest Service, the National Park Service, and the State Department of Parks and Recreation were discussing access to basketry materials on public lands, he walked over to the cooking shelter to check on the food preparation. As chairman of the Board of Ya-Ka-Ama, which hosted the conference, and as the son of one of California's most renowned basketweavers, one might have expected that George would have taken a central role in the conference—that he would have made speeches, given blessings, and otherwise made his presence felt. Yet I suspect that most of those who attended the conference never really got to meet George, and in fact I doubt if there were many who were aware of who he was.

Instead of placing himself in the center, George seemed always to be on the periphery of things, taking care of the thousand details that made this such a smoothly run, successful event. Food appeared, always on time, delicious, and in ample quantities. In the afternoon heat, chilled cans of soda and pitchers of lemonade and iced tea magically materialized. From the moment the first people arrived on Saturday morning, enough chairs and tables were in place, and the loudspeakers and recording equipment were set up.

There were even enough outhouses, and the dirt roads and parking areas had been dampened to keep down the dust. All these things happened so quietly that the workings of the conference were by and large invisible to those who attended—as if hundreds of chairs, dozens of tables, electronic equipment, and so much wonderful food had somehow grown out of the meadows of Ya-Ka-Ama.

It would embarrass George, and be factually incorrect as well, to single him out as the main reason why the conference worked so well. A conference of such scale takes the efforts of many—hundreds of hours of work by coordinator Sara Greensfelder, by the staff and volunteers associated with Ya-Ka-Ama, and by others. Yet as I watched George move about the perimeter of the group, now doing this, now doing that, I had the odd sense that he was like a sewing needle, not part of the fabric, but in his darting in and out, repairing and making whole, he was the instrument that was keeping everything together. In the end, perhaps, no one would remember the needle; yet without it the entire fabric would have become frayed and perhaps even unraveled.

If George Somersal was largely invisible to those who attended the basketweavers' conference, his presence was nevertheless hugely felt—not just in terms of the mechanics of keeping the conference functioning but especially in terms of the open-air ceremonial structure in which people assembled. This structure is of George's creation, born to a large extent out of his imagination and vision. Something like a brush house, it is nevertheless unique, of its own design. On one hand it feels very traditional, very "Indian," yet on the other hand I have never seen anything quite like it. It consists of stakes set in a huge circle to define an inner space. (A center post, such as might be found in a roundhouse, had been erected in the center of the circle by the late spiritual leader Genny Maruffo, but when she died recently the post was removed.) Around the circle of stakes, about six feet away, an outer rim of stakes was erected, and these two concentric circles of stakes formed a kind of arcade. The arcade was covered with netting to create a slightly dappled shade.

When Ya-Ka-Ama was first founded, this meadow had been the site of a ceremonial arbor. "Essie Parrish and all the elders who came here put it up as a spiritual place," said George. "It was blessed by many shamans. They used material from the land. They used bay laurel branches, pepperwood. They held dances here for eight years. Then the elders passed on." In more recent years another brush enclosure was erected for special occasions at the entrance to Ya-Ka-Ama, near the administration building. Other times people danced in the open. But until George built the current ceremonial circle, the site of the old brush arbor had remained deserted.

Perhaps the idea for it grew out of another plan that George has had—to build a roundhouse at his reservation, the Dry Creek Rancheria. After his mother's death, however, that dream has been put "on the back burner." As George became more and more involved with Ya Ka-Ama, at first just spending time there and helping out, then later becoming president of the board of directors, the idea of an open-air enclosure developed.

"The circle means a lot to Indian people," explained George. "To some it's a church, to some a place to gather. It has good vibes. The circle can bring people together. It stops bickering among tribes. This is a circle for world peace. A circle for everyone. Look at the entranceway. In our tribe, it's always on the west. But this isn't just for our tribe. For other tribes it's on the south or north or east. Here we have four entrances, one in each direction. It includes everyone.

"We have a twenty-year celebration for Ya-Ka-Ama coming up. I want to invite everyone to dance here. Dancers from all over. Aztec dancers. Fancy-footwork dancers. Our own dancers. I want to include all tribes, work together with all Indians. The arbor means unity. I want to bring unity and peace to people everywhere."

George pauses as we look over the crowd of basketweavers assembled within the circle. "I feel good about this," he smiles. "People from all over California. All the Ka-rocks, all the Yu-rocks, all the other 'rocks.' Everyone sitting down and discussing baskets and everything else. If we can do that, we can do everything. We can get things done."

It is indeed a beautiful sight, all these "rocks," all these people, from the Klamath to the Colorado River, talking together, sharing knowledge and concerns, moving within the ceremonial enclosure. George remains outside it, however. He looks toward it with satisfaction and pleasure, and perhaps, one feels, with a slight longing. But only for a moment. Someone comes up to him. The people serving soft drinks need more ice. George turns the keys in the ignition and heads back to the administration building.

News from Native California, vol. 5, no. 4, 1991

STILL HERE (2019)

I settled into Berkeley in the late 1960s. An intense surge of interest in Native American history and culture characterized those years. The occupation of Alcatraz began on November 20, 1969, and came to an end on June 11, 1971. Daily broadcasts from the island by the Berkeley radical radio station KPFA brought Indian voices into kitchens, workshops, and automobiles, providing the entire Bay Area with a nineteen-month immersion in Native history and resistance. The charismatic leaders of the American Indian Movement (AIM) were treated like rock stars. Vine Deloria Jr.'s *Custer Died for Your Sins* (1969), Dee Brown's *Bury My Heart at Wounded Knee* (1970), and other bestselling books flowed out of Berkeley's many independent bookstores, bursting upon public consciousness with a compelling revision of how the West was really won. Universities and colleges throughout the Bay Area created Native American studies departments; their standing proudly alongside French literature, ancient Greek history, and nuclear physics suggested that Native culture, long dismissed as "primitive," had substance, sophistication, and nuance that would reward careful study by accomplished scholars and intellectuals. Edward Curtis photos, masterworks of sepia courtliness and nostalgia for a lost world, competed successfully with Escher prints and psychedelic posters for wall space in homes, schools, and offices. And the words of Chief Seattle, Black Elk, and others inspired everyone—at least of my generation—with a sense of nobility and courage. Indians and their ways moved from the cultural backwaters to take a place of prominence alongside other ideas and actions that we hoped would reshape our culture: exciting new (at least to us) ideas such as sustainability, ecological responsibility, social justice, community, governance by consensus, a life of the spirit, and so on.

Although a few Native Californians were producing commendable artwork earlier, the vibrant California Indian art scene that is the subject of this book came into being during the 1960s and 1970s, and worked deeply into it are many values, attitudes, and assumptions of this period. Allowing for variation and exception, it seems to me that many Native Californian artists who emerged at this highly politicized time tended to see art as a tool, maybe even a weapon, in the fight against racism and oppression and were less involved with the ins and outs of the museum and gallery worlds.

In addition to fighting the racism and remorseless oppression that had been inflicted on their communities since the first contact, the Native people of California had yet another challenge, a challenge of special concern to artists: invisibility. While Indian presence, values, and ideas spread rapidly throughout Berkeley and the rest of California during the 1960s and 1970s, they were almost entirely imported from elsewhere. And many of those that did develop locally arose out of Indian communities brought to the Bay Area by the American Indian relocation programs of the 1950s, whose tribal origins were out of state. Indigenous local Indian culture was eclipsed, and to many people from Native Californian tribal groups, the newfound popularity of Indian values—the ascendancy of new leadership, the spread of powwows, the drumming circles, turquoise jewelry, peyote, and a host of other symbols and practices—represented yet another conquest from the outside, another incident in a long chain that served to drive Native California culture underground, rendering it all but invisible.

How does one fight against invisibility? Clarence Lobo (1912–1985) was chief of the Juaneño Band of Mission Indians (now called Ajachmem), a major political figure, and a courageous leader of the Southern California tribes. When he went out in public, he generally wore a feathered headdress or war bonnet, a dramatic symbol of American Indians from the Plains. Whenever he was criticized, he explained that he was proud to be an Indian, and he wanted everyone to know it. The people of the area knew so little about the local Native people that if he had dressed in more authentic garb no one would have recognized his Indian heritage.

Along with invisibility, the 1960s were marked by a deep and fatalistic sense of cultural loss. At the time of European contact, as many as one hundred different languages were spoken in California, each a unique treasure-house of musicality and meaning. By 1970 many of these languages no longer had living speakers; those that did could count only a handful of them; and nowhere in California was a Native language being passed down to a younger generation. Ceremonies, skills, and a wide range of Native practices were likewise being abandoned. Roundhouses collapsed and were left unrepaired. Songs, dances, and rituals—gifts of luminosity and power that the divinities had given humankind in ages past to guide us through the world—were slipping away. As each elder passed away, a unique body of knowledge—indeed, a never-to-be-seen-again way of being human—passed with them. It was as if a terrible black hole had appeared, swallowing languages, ways of being, and some of the best people this world has ever seen. Carobeth Laird, widow of the linguist and anthropologist John P. Harrington, summed it up with a haunting image: "The vessel of the old culture had broken, and its precious contents were spilling out and evaporating before our very eyes." The light of the old world was flickering, and it seemed fated and inevitable that it would soon be extinguished.

Writing about the future, Frank LaPena laid bare the bleakness of the prospects ahead: "When there are no more Indians then will we end. When the songs and dances are forgotten, and when our language is forgotten, and when we do not honor the earth because we have forgotten that all living things on earth are sacred and important: then the world will end. But just before that time we will know the time of emptiness." The depth of despair in these lines sums up a sadness and a deep sense of defeat that ran through the entire Indian community. Later in the same article, after reviewing an exhibition of paintings by Judith Lowry, LaPena concluded: "I believe that art is one answer to preventing the emptiness that the loss of culture or the indifference of society will impose. We are still alive."[1]

"We are still alive!" "We are still here!" After decades of genocide, loss, displacement, and erasure, what began as a tentative statement of hope became a battle cry. "We are still here!" The message was repeated endlessly in interviews with artists, in notes to exhibitions, and in artwork itself. The need to assert the reality of one's very existence, to prove what other artists take for granted, characterizes much of Native California Indian art, giving it an elemental urgency and power, and setting it apart from mainstream traditions and the traditions of other Indian artists as well.

One manifestation of this is apparent in the predominance of representational and narrative art in California. Artists from other traditions had a huge inventory of readily available images they could draw from, images that not only triggered waves of emotion in the artist but carried meaning for others as well. These images provided the shared visual language through which artists could tap into their deepest feelings and communicate with others. But to communicate with the world at large, artists from one or another of the shattered little nations of California teetering on the brink of oblivion first had to create this storehouse of images. In this way, many artists became researchers, chroniclers, and historians of their own cultures.

Take, for example, Frank Day, whose work—and indeed life— would serve as a model and inspiration for so many other artists in this book. Day was born in 1902 in Berry Creek, Butte County, California. The elders of this Konkow Maidu community had come of age before the gold rush, and many elements of traditional culture were still intact when Day was alive, not only the major and readily identifiable aspects of culture—such as language, ceremony, and traditional arts, skills, and beliefs—but the more fleeting and fragile everyday ambience of that old lost world.

Day never attended art school, which may explain his attitude toward art. "I'm not a doctor," he once said. "I'm not a soothsayer, I'm not a shaman, I'm not a spiritual man, I'm not a medicine man. I'm just an ordinary man. My business was to be around older folks, to listen, to learn. Once in a while I take up color and paint a little bit, because if I do not do this all things will be forgotten."[2]

Day used his paintbrush as a key to open the door to the past. Commenting on his painting of the Berry Creek Roundhouse as it was in 1907, I once noted: "A group of men are in front of it, kneeling and facing each other in the familiar position of men playing grass game. Billy Day, Frank's father, is there, as are other 'old-timers' Frank remembered. The summer air shimmers with light; the roundhouse, a tree, and the little whiteman-style house in the background all pulsate with life. It is an ordinary day at Berry Creek many years ago, painted by a man who described himself likewise as ordinary."[3]

Day was, in the words of fellow artist Judith Lowry, "the first

Maidu artist to record the myths and rituals of his tribe with paint and brush on canvas. Day's visual record of ancient stories and ceremonies constitutes a vital historical document and a valuable tool with which to begin to understand the ways of our ancestors . . . . In raw, vigorous brushwork, scenes of dances, ceremonies, sorcery, illness and healing, animal spirits and plants, along with scenes of everyday life, poured from Day's prolific and spirited imagination."[4]

Harry Fonseca, another artist much influenced by Day, recalled his presence as "just magic." Writing in 1997, he said:

> His paintings have a visual wonder about them, and those (especially anthropologists!) who have looked at them trying to determine whether or not they are "true" have had a problem with that [artistic] freedom . . . . His work has a base in Maidu traditions, yet it also has a sense of transcendence, a quality similar to the work of other outsider artists, though in a way I think he runs rings around most other self-taught painters.
>
> More than just being a painter, Day was an incredible storyteller. His stories embraced and riveted you. Listening to him tell a story would take me right out of the room and into his world. Frank's storytelling was inseparable from his art, and those stories are conveyed in his paintings by his imagination and the freedom he allowed himself in terms of drama and subject matter. [5]

There was perhaps no artist more central to the concerns and direction of modern California Indian art than Frank Day. He exhibited and sold his art at Pacific Western Traders, a trading post and art gallery in Folsom that, under the ownership of Herb Puffer, functioned as a museum and cultural center for the California Indian world. Puffer provided Day with space at Pacific Western Traders where Day formed a group called the Maidu Dancers and Traditionalists. Gathering younger artists and tribal scholars, Day transmitted what he knew about doing the dances, singing the songs, making the regalia, and performing the ceremonies. Over the years, other elders added knowledge. This group, founded in 1973, is not a piece of theater or a museum replica of something that once existed; rather, it is fully alive in the present. Through his paintings, Day brought back the memories and images of traditional Maidu culture; by launching the Maidu Dancers and Traditionalists, he did more than bring back images: he brought back the thing itself. Songs, dances, and the beliefs that fuel them are now a living part of California Indian culture.

Among those who gathered to learn from Frank Day was a young Wintu artist, Frank LaPena, who would eventually take over the leadership of the Maidu Dancers and Traditionalists. In a *News from Native California* column from 1988, LaPena wrote: "The Native American Artist is important in helping keep tradition alive."[6] This simple statement is, when you stop to think about it, unusual and provocative. In contemporary American culture, the role of the artist is rarely seen as keeping tradition alive. Rather, contemporary artists generally seem to be in a constant state of rebellion, often with a license to lead outrageous lives, to produce works that shock cultural norms, and to get us to see things in a new way.

The major artists of modern times, if they are politically motivated, seldom espouse traditional values but, rather, place themselves at the forefront of various liberation movements. Performance artists seem generally to take great delight in flouting community values, producing work that the society finds irreligious and reprehensible. In contemporary America, the artist is generally an outsider, often deliberately so, exiled or at least kept on the margins. When a young person in the dominant culture announces that he or she wants to become a poet, a sculptor, or a violist, the family reacts with horror. The modern artist is seen as someone who is shaking off community ties and family responsibilities in order to lead a life of self-indulgence.

This is generally not the case with Native California artists. So many of them are community leaders, active in tribal affairs, and participants in ceremonies. Although there are exceptions, most often their work reflects, rather than contradicts, the deepest values of their culture. There are probably many reasons for this. One may be the fact that the arts were always integrated into Native culture to a much greater extent than they were into mainstream culture. Every woman was a basketweaver, and indeed baskets—everyday cooking and eating utensils—were among the most sophisticated and stunning pieces of art that the world has ever seen. Similarly, almost every man was a singer, a dancer, a maker of dance regalia. Writer and frontiersman Joaquin Miller characterized the old-time Indian as "a druid and a dreamer"—fertile ground for the growth of art. As has often been pointed out, traditional culture did not have a word for "art." It was simply part of life. Basketweaving, dancing, singing, and a number of other arts were not only not marginalized, they were widely practiced, and the most skilled and proficient practitioners were honored.

That said, I think there's another and perhaps more significant reason that can help explain the Native artists' embrace of tradition. What leads many people into the artistic life is a love of beauty, a yearning for meaning, a demand for truth. Beauty, meaning, and truth, while not entirely absent, are not words that readily come to mind when describing contemporary American culture. We live in a world marked by greed, aggression, and alienation from nature. Artists in today's mainstream American culture seeking beauty, meaning, and truth have to leave a good part of their value system behind and look elsewhere. By contrast, the Indian world, while far from perfect, is built on a foundation of beauty, balance, and magic that still glows beneath the surface of everyday life. Native artists did not have to go elsewhere to find a world that spoke to them of beauty, truth, and meaning. In their quest for inspiration, earlier generations of European painters went back to biblical times or to ancient Greece to find stories and images that would transport them out of the pain and pettiness of the workaday world. To many Native artists, stories and images from their own tradition were sufficient—and then some.

I offer these thoughts and observations not as an artist or even a participant in California Indian culture but as a writer, a book publisher, and especially in my role as publisher of the quarterly magazine *News from Native California*. I founded it in 1987 with David Peri (Coast Miwok), who taught at Sonoma State University, and Vera Mae Fredrickson, who had just lost her job at the Museum of Anthropology at the University of California, Berkeley.

From the very first issue, *News from Native California* covered the modern Indian art scene. Frank LaPena began his hugely influential art column in that inaugural issue, and he would continue his coverage and promotion of California Indian art for three decades. His steady presence and passionate advocacy furthered the careers of dozens of Native artists and taught the rest of us to open our eyes to the art that was flowing with increasing power, sophistication, and surety from Native artists in places like Susanville, Hoopa, Auburn, and Eureka.

The calendar of events for that first issue announced an exhibition of recent works by Rick Bartow at American Indian Contemporary Arts in San Francisco. Pacific Western Traders in Folsom held a posthumous exhibition of paintings by Frank Day. A ten-year retrospective of Harry Fonseca's Coyote art was being given a place of honor at the Natural History Museum of Los Angeles. An exhibition of contemporary artists at the Vacaville Museum, reviewed by LaPena in his column, included paintings and other artworks by Fonseca, LaPena, George Blake, Dalbert Castro, Vivien Hailstone, Jean LaMarr, Josephine Peters, Brian Tripp, and Karen Noble.

Because it came into being at a time when a cultural revival seemed to be erupting everywhere in California Indian country, the magazine is sometimes given more credit than it deserves. As is obvious from the listings in the very first issue, we didn't create the cultural revival; we reported on it and, in reporting, spread information about it from one community to another. I'm proud of what we did. In that age before the Internet, many areas of California—especially rural areas—were isolated from one another; spreading the news of how, in various communities, members of a younger generation were, by and large on their own, reviving language, dance, song, traditional arts, and skills, as well as spiritual practice, was a laudable service. It is worth noting that many of those reviving traditional skills, language, and practice were modern artists: LaPena, Tripp, Julian Lang, L. Frank, and Linda Yamane come immediately to mind. Taking tradition beyond the canvas, breathing life into it, and putting it back into the community, they did the great work of their time. As publisher of *News from Native California*, it was my pleasure and honor to witness this miracle and report on it. I'm grateful for the opportunity.

NOTES

1. Frank LaPena, "A Time of Emptiness," *News from Native California*, vol. 13, no. 1 (Fall 1999): 56.

2. Rebecca J. Dobkins, *Memory and Imagination: The Legacy of Maidu Indian Artist Frank Day* (Oakland: Oakland Museum of Cali-

fornia; Seattle: University of Washington Press, 1997), 76.

3. Malcolm Margolin, "Editor's Notes," *News from Native California*, vol. 10, no. 4 (Summer 1997): 2.

4. Judith Lowry, "The Burning," *News from Native California*, vol. 14, no. 1 (Fall 2000): 4.

5. Dobkins, *Memory and Imagination*, 88.

6. Frank LaPena, "Keeping the Tradition Alive in Art and Practice," *News from Native California*, vol. 1, no. 6 (January/February 1988): 18.

When I Remember I See Red: American Indian Art and Activism in California, edited by Frank LaPena, Mark Dean Johnson, and Kristina Perea Gilmore, University of California Press and Crocker Art Museum, 2019

INDIAN MARKET (2012)

Early on the morning of Saturday, May 19, 2012, California Indian artists in a variety of pick-up trucks, vans, sedans, and station wagons straggled into the parking area of the Black Oak Casino, followed the directions of strategically placed guards, and pulled up to the curb alongside the shady oak knoll known as Heritage Park. It was the tenth annual Indian Market sponsored by the Tuolumne Band of Me-Wuk Indians and the Black Oak Casino. There was the usual sense of anticipation and excitement that one always feels when setting up for a fair—the hope of big crowds and strong sales; the greetings and warm embraces of longtime friends; the jockeying for position as one tries to get a place in the shade and next to people one wants to spend the day with; the unpacking of boxes and spreading out of table coverings; the magical unfolding of displays of basketry, stonework, jewelry, featherwork, paintings, and other examples of California Indian art and skill; the creation of a temporary community that, like some fragile wildflower, would blossom for only one day. It was a joy to be there, and I couldn't help but observe how it had grown from the first Indian Market, in 2002, with its fifteen vendors. This year there were fifty-two—a full deck, I think, as I look past the knoll toward the casino.

From the moment one receives an invitation to be part of the Indian Market, it's clear that this is not an ordinary fair. Elsewhere, artists are typically treated as vendors: they pay for their table space and cover all their own lodging and other expenses, hoping to recoup their costs from the sale of their work. This is the commercial model—artist as shopkeeper—and it's a good one when it works. But those receiving an invitation to be part of the Indian Market are blessed with a different experience. There's no fee for display space. On the contrary, the promoters of the Indian Market not only don't ask for money but they offer artists free lodging at a local motel and provide free meals. Although this is still a fair where people sell their goods, one feels that it is curated carefully, that you are being honored and even cherished. In some ways it is more like being invited to be part of a museum show than a trade fair. The arts and the artists are esteemed. Jennifer Bates, who organizes the event, greets everyone as if they were long-lost and very distinguished relatives. As the vehicles pull up to the curb and begin to unload, crews of polite and muscular casino employees materialize to carry boxes and help set up displays. In so many ways you feel more like a guest than a vendor. As the glorious day unfurls, fifty-two artists will forget their unpaid bills, their lack of retirement plans, their sense of being underappreciated and marginalized. For one glorious day we will sit under the oaks, the air will be warm and fragrant, and the food will be delicious. Old and dear friends will come by for a visit, and we will have all the time in the world to talk and reminisce. Stories and gossip will flow, the laughter will be easy, and once in a while that rarest of being, a customer, will show up and money will change hands. It will be a day to remember, and we will walk away feeling that a lifetime of devotion to the arts has been amply rewarded.

❖ ❖ ❖

There are so many centers in the California Indian world. Every tribe seems to have its own—for some a roundhouse or a dance ground, for others a spring, a mountain, or perhaps a sacred rock. Such a big state, so many centers! But I know the true center. It's Jennifer Bates.

I've known and admired Jennifer for many years—decades, in fact. I knew her first as the daughter of the formidable Dorothy Stanley, still remembered as Momma Bear. I knew her as Craig Bates's wife and Carson's mother. I knew her as board chair of the California Indian Basketweavers Association, from its founding in 1991 until she left the board thirteen years later. Before that came the astounding interlude in her life when she opened the Bear and Coyote Gallery in Jamestown, showing the best of California Indian art and creating a convivial clubhouse and drop-in center for everyone passing through the Sierra. Then onto her role coordinating the annual Acorn Festival at Tuolumne Rancheria, and today being the founder, inspiration, and coordinator of the annual Indian Market. I've watched her over the years, observing how she'll work hard all day at creating and administering the institutions that have furthered California Indian artists. Then at night it's dinner at Jennifer's house—a feast and a party. A great party, actually. And when the party's over, she'll thank everyone for coming and eventually do the dishes.

Jennifer has always been especially dedicated to supporting California Indian artists and culture. Powwow culture is fine, she allows, but she feels a special draw and responsibility to California. When she went to work for the Black Oak Casino—she is now the personnel development manager, responsible for succession planning and career coaching—she found herself thinking, "Wouldn't it be nice to have a market that was just for California people? The public could learn things and understand and see the differences." When she discussed the idea with members of the community, she felt she had hit a responsive chord.

Two important members of the Tuolumne community in particular offered to support the idea at the tribal council level: Lorraine Forde and Rhonda Standage. Lorraine, then tribal treasurer, now describes herself as "tribal elder" and is the employee relations advisor to the tribe. Rhonda was then vice president of the tribal council and is now president of the Tuolumne Economic Development Authority. They would work together for the next ten years, Jennifer dealing with the artists and administering the program, Lorraine and Rhonda running the Indian taco booth and maintaining tribal support and assuring allocation of tribal resources and funds.

On Friday, June 1, a couple of weeks after the Indian Market, I drove from Berkeley to Tuolumne with my assistant, Sylvia Linsteadt, to interview Jennifer, Lorraine, and Rhonda. Ron Patel, general manager of the Black Oak Casino, joined us for part of the interview. We sat on the outside veranda of the casino. The warmth of the afternoon had scented the air with the slight piney foothill perfume, and our conversation was punctuated by noises from the construction work on the casino hotel.

One thing that stands out at the Indian Market is the high quality of the work. How are such high standards maintained, I wondered. Both Lorraine and Rhonda credit Jennifer with this—her long history in the Indian community and especially her connections. "That's pretty much what started it," said Rhonda. "She had those connections and brought those people here. She'll screen them very carefully and will make sure that they are true artists. She pretty much knows who has high integrity as artists and respect, because there are some people out there that have asked to come and we have to say no. Things have gone on in that artist world, and not all people are what they pretend to be."

The Indian Market is clearly a source of great pride to everyone involved. "We get a lot of compliments from the vendors on how well they're treated and how generously," said Lorraine. "They ask why we do it. We do it for traditional values. A lot of the vendors here keep coming back year after year after year because they like the environment and like the way they are treated."

"I wasn't aware until we started having the Indian Market how close-knit the California Indian community is, because I'm not an artist," said Rhonda. "So I don't socialize in that circle. But I was never aware of how they do all know each other and look forward to certain events where they can go socialize. Which keeps with what we always believe is a traditional value: socialization, when all the people come together and share stories or share everything about their lives, whether you have a loved one who is no longer here or you've got new babies in the family or kids are growing up and having families. So you know, to somebody from the general public it would look like, Oh, what a nice arts and crafts fair. But for us and the circle that we've come to be part of it's much more than that."

The social aspects of the Indian Market remind Rhonda of an older and slower time. "People used to visit. People used to talk. You'd go sit on somebody's front porch. Everybody had front porches. So in weather like this, you're all out on your front porch. On a weeknight or whatever, my dad would come home and we'd all sit on the front porch and watch everybody else sit on the front porch. That's what everybody did. So you know, it is kind of . . . almost like time stops. If you allow it, you just stop. That was part of what everyone was doing. As a kid, when you got tired of playing in the dirt or you got tired of playing with your sisters or whatever, you'd go sit down. And you would listen to somebody tell a story or gossip or whatever. But it was just that time when you sat there and you didn't realize how much you were relaxing or kicking back. Now people rarely take the time to sit down and do that—connect with each other or just kind of think about what you did during the day."

Along with nostalgia for the old days, though, is the memory of hardship and poverty. Lorraine recalls a childhood in which "there was no electricity. Water we got from a PG&E ditch that used to run behind my aunt's house. There were no paved roads. You had no plumbing, only an outhouse." There were no opportunities on the rancheria, and when Lorraine graduated from high school in 1965, she was one of three youths who were relocated to San Francisco through the Bureau of Indian Affairs's relocation program.

Those were dirt poor and often despairing times, and for Lorraine, sponsorship of the Indian Market is part of an overall and somewhat miraculous enlargement of Tuolumne's place in the world. "Say fifteen years ago, nobody even knew how to say Tuolumne, much less knew where it was. Now it's all over the place. You see the word Tuolumne everywhere. When I watch TV or go down to the Bay Area and see commercials, it's like everybody now knows how to say Tuolumne. And I thought, Wow, that's something. That is so much. You would never have thought in a million years that you would see the word Tuolumne outside of the community."

It is clear to everyone that the Black Oak Casino has brought tremendous benefit to the community. It is controlled by the tribal council, and in certain key ways it respects tribal values and sustains tribal culture. The very name, Black Oak, derives from the tree that bore the most delicious of acorns and nurtured people for millennia. Among the slot machines and craps tables are vitrines with old baskets and older memories. The Seven Sisters restaurant is named after Lorraine's mother and her sisters, with an odd concession to modern marketing: "My mom had nine sisters, but when it came to signage they felt that seven sounded better than nine." Adaption, I think; how often the cost of keeping memory and tradition is to allow it to change and adapt.

The budget for running the Indian Market, now around $10,000 a year in out-of-pocket costs, plus considerable logistic support from the tribe and the casino, comes out of the casino's marketing budget. But I can't help but feel that what is being "marketed" is something bigger than the attraction of card tables and slot machines. Perhaps it's identity and pride.

"We're not just a casino," explains Ron Patel. Ron is a consummate gentleman, an affable visionary who, while running an enterprise that is economically productive, has instituted policies that nourish the best in those who work at the casino. Born in England and of mixed-race background, he is paradoxically utterly at home being an outsider. "Many tribes have casinos. I think from the conception here, it wasn't just going to be a casino, this building itself, but a beautiful restaurant. On the first floor we've got a family floor that has nothing to do with casino gaming. So I think when Rhonda and Jennifer and Lorraine first started to talk about the Indian Market ten years ago, it wasn't at all strange. It fit in with everything we are doing."

I go to many events around California, Indian and non-Indian, and the Indian Market is among my favorite. A table and a couple of chairs were set up for me under the shade of an oak. My name badge identified me as being from the Berkeley Rancheria. On the table, I laid out the books we publish and issues of *News from Native California*. Amora Stevenot, Jennifer's niece, was handling the logistics with her aunt, and she made sure I had coffee and food and was well taken care of. All day people wandered by, sat down in the extra chair, and we talked and talked and talked. We talked about people we know, about the old days, about kids and grandkids. The day was long and full and I wish it could have lasted forever. As the sun set, I packed up the unsold books and drove to a nearby stadium. There, as a guest of the Black Oak Casino, I witnessed my first roller derby. Side by side with the great artists, grand culture bearers, and treasured elders of the California Indian world, I cheered Amora on as she sped around the rink on roller skates, bumping and swerving, speeding and maneuvering. Go, Amora, go! It was a perfect day.

News from Native California, vol. 26, no. 2, 2012/3

ACKNOWLEDGMENTS

After nearly fifty years of deep hanging out, I have accumulated debts of gratitude that I can never repay. They range from the people, Native and non-Native, who have instructed me and shared their thoughts and their lives with me to the staff of Heyday and *News from Native California*, who read and edited my work, put it into print, and sent it out into the world, as well as to the foundations and individuals who supported us financially and to my family. I am humbled and honored by their acceptance of me, by their patience, and by their love. There are too many people to mention, and I'm afraid if I single people out I'll omit others who have been essential. I have often said of myself that I'm the stone of stone soup, and I thank everybody for having made such a delicious meal of it.

For this book in particular, I want to thank Steve Wasserman, my successor at Heyday, who suggested this work, gave it its title, and has so generously seen it through. Thank you, Steve. I also want to thank Gayle Wattawa, Heyday's general manager and editorial director, who capped almost twenty years of our collaboration by working with me to pull the material together, select it, and word-for-word help me write the introduction. To Mark Johnson, Sonia Tamez,

Peter Nabokov, and David Nawi, all friends of long standing, who gave me feedback on the manuscript and advice on how to strengthen it; to the Heyday staff, including Ashley Ingram for her design, Diane Lee for overseeing production, Lisa K. Marietta for copyediting, Julie Coryell and Christopher Miya for sales and marketing strategies, Emmerich Anklam for scanning the articles, and Terria Smith for her advice and support; to the staff of California Institute for Community, Art, and Nature, including Claire Greensfelder, Pamela Michael, Erika Veidis, Lydia Lapporte, Zev Marx-Kahn, and Julene Freitas; to Lou Fancher for last-minute assistance; and more than anyone, to my wife, Rina, whose constant presence over the years can be felt throughout this book and whose practical help and skilled editing have filtered out the worst in me and have added insights and language beyond anything I could have done myself: thank you.

ABOUT THE AUTHOR

Malcolm Margolin is an author, publisher, and cultural advocate who has been living in Berkeley, California, since the late 1960s. He is the founder and for over forty years was the executive director and publisher of Heyday Books. Through Heyday, he published hundreds of books and launched numerous museum shows, conferences, and large-scale collaborations with many of California's most prestigious museums and cultural and environmental organizations. He cofounded two magazines, *News from Native California* (1987–present) and *Bay Nature* (2001–present), and several other institutions, including the Alliance for California Traditional Arts and the Inlandia Institute. He was also instrumental in the creation of the Advocates for Indigenous California Language Survival, the California Indian Basketweavers Association, and various other groups active in the cultural, environmental, and literary life of California. After retirement from Heyday in 2015, he founded the California Institute for Community, Art, and Nature (California I CAN, californiaican.org), drawing on his wide connections and longstanding friendships to create an organization both visionary and personal at the same time.

He has written several books on California natural history, cultural history, and Native life, including *The Ohlone Way: Indian Life in the San Francisco–Monterey Bay Area* (1978), which was designated by the *San Francisco Chronicle* as one of the one hundred most important non-fiction books of the twentieth century by a western writer, and *The Way We Lived: California Indian Stories, Songs, and Reminiscences* (1981). His books have been translated into Japanese, German, and Turkish, among other languages.

He has received many prestigious awards, including an American Book Award for publishing/editing from the Before Columbus Foundation, a community service award from the San Francisco Foundation, Lifetime Achievement Awards from the Bay Area Book Reviews Association and the California Studies Association, a Cultural Freedom Award from the Lannan Foundation, the Chairman's Commendation from the National Endowment for the Humanities (the second such recipient in the United States), and PubWest's 2020 Jack D. Rittenhouse Award to honor his important contributions to the Western community of the book.

For more information about Heyday, Margolin, and *News from Native California*, please see *The Heyday of Malcolm Margolin* by Kim Bancroft (2014).